INTERNATIONAL COMPARISONS

INTERNATIONAL COMPARISONS

OF

MONEY VELOCITY

AND

WAGE MARK-UPS

BY

JOHN H. HOTSON

AUGUSTUS M. KELLEY · PUBLISHERS

NEW YORK 1968

First Published 1968 by

AUGUSTUS M. KELLEY · PUBLISHERS

NEW YORK NEW YORK 10010

LIBRARY OF CONGRESS CATALOGUE CARD NUMBER

68-56840

PRINTED IN THE UNITED STATES OF AMERICA

by SENTRY PRESS, NEW YORK, N. Y. 10019

To Irving Fisher, then

and

Sidney Weintraub, now

PREFACE

This book grows out of my doctoral thesis and my continuing concern regarding the cause and "cures" of the "creeping inflation" loose in the land once more. If the Board of Govenors of the Federal Reserve System and the Eisenhower administration succeeded in slowing the "creep" to a "crawl" in the late 1950s, it was only at vast cost in idle men, productive capacity, and recurring recession. Now with growing military expenditures added to a seven year expansion the crawl has become a renewed creep.

Other than the fiscal policy tools of higher taxes and lower expenditures, which I shall not discuss, two anti-inflationary weapons come to hand: incomes policies such as the Kennedy-Johnson "guideposts" or monetary measures of the Fed's "tight money" policy. Neither is wholly satisfactory. Enforcement of the guideposts has been left to presidential "open mouth operations" to induce noninflationary wage and price moves. Other than expressions of official displeasure there has been no sanction for noncompliance. Furthermore, only those whose wage and price boosts are highly "visible" have been urged to moderate them. The steel and auto workers have been much exhorted while construction workers and college professors obtain over guidepost boosts without criticism. The primary metals industries have been much bullied to forego price increases while the automobile industry's failure to cut prices to pass on its extraordinary productivity gains to consumers goes unremarked. Lately even the weak and uneven incomes restraints formerly used have been put in abeyance and many have concluded that the voluntary guideposts are now dead.

We are warned of the dangers to the smooth workings of our economy and to our precious freedoms if we escalate the anti-inflation effort by making the guideposts mandatory. One does indeed shrink back from the prospect of the government having the final work regarding cutting the price of Chevys or allowing "catch up" gains to the profs. With mandatory guideposts, every "special case", and every case is special to the parties concerned, becomes a matter for administrative decision, or lack of decision while necessary adjustments are thwarted.

Would it not be better, then, to rely on monetary restraint? This is a general restraint which does not involve complex decisions as to whom is to be denied credit, but simply makes it more expensive and less available, thus cutting aggregate demand and, presumably, preventing price rises. The effect of "tight money" on the economy is all pervasive and yet almost invisible, consequently it does not ordinarily lead to confrontations between interest groups and the authorities. Most of the unemployed never heard of the Federal Reserve Board who "unemployed" them and the fact that the august Board does not have to listen to the complaints of the people it hurts is a great advantage; to the Board.

How many people did the Fed "fire" in 1966 with its boost of the discount rate? Was it 5,000, or 50,000, or 500,000? Does the Board know? Does it care to know? Let us not smooth over this matter with polite words. The Federal Reserve Board achieves what ever success it has in slowing inflation by hurting people, lots of people, enough people so that demand slackens. Those hurt are not those whose decisions to strike busy plants, or to raise prices, or to save the national face in far countries, have caused the inflation. Those hurt are the marginal workers who fail to obtain employment, or lose their employment, as the club descends. What a system of social ethics this is! To punish the innocent weak for the misdeeds of the strong! What a travesty, what a perversion, that the sophisticated measures and concepts of "post-Keynesian" economics should be employed to cause unemployment rather than cure the curse of joblessness! Shades of Marx' reserve army of the unemployed!

There is, of course, less unemployment per annum now, with Fed and administration guidance of the economy, than in the bad old days of boom and bust. But this is no defense of the policy the Fed has followed since the Korean War. What would we think of M.D.s if, having learned to curb certain epidemic diseases, they started to use their knowledge to kill instead of cure? Would we accept their bland assurance that they know best concerning life and death and that, anyway, the public has no complaint because the doctors kill far fewer people than disease used to?

To repeat then, monetary restraint operates by keeping several million administratively unemployed as vicarious atonement for others sins in raising prices. Not only is this grossly unjust, it is not even effective in appeasing the inflationary gods to whom we offer up these human sacrifices. What must be sacrificed if we are to have truly full employment and stable prices is the freedom of large unions and firms to sin against the economy by agreeing to pay out incomes which can only be financed by price boosts.

The guidepost policy is a sword which, if properly used, can slay the demon. This weapon will work without cutting up, or clubbing down, innocent bystanders. Let us have the courage and responsible attitudes to use this weapon while relegating monetary policy to the house keeping function of keeping the supply of money growing at about the same pace as full employment output.

This book does not attempt to deal with guidepost administration. Its aim is the more modest one of showing that the structural underpinnings for guideposts are sound and that the underpinnings of monetary policy are shaky. The underpinnings are the fact that the price level changes with changes in Unit Wage Costs, or ratio of the average wage to output per man. The price level does not vary as does the ratio of money to goods, as Quantity theorists would have us believe. This is because the mark-up over Unit Wage Costs is all but constant, in the U. S. it hasn't moved a half an index point for 10 years, while money velocity has been wildly variable.

One *caveat* to the reader. While the book was in page proofs I spot checked the frequency distribution calculations in Chapter Four, which years ago I ground out on a desk calculator, on a computer. To err is human! I am satisfied that these errors do not change the findings, however, (by causing a "t" test to miss a significant difference, for instance) and so I have let the tables stand.

I wish to thank Dr. Sidney Weintraub for his unfailing kindness and encouragement during the writing of this study. I only wish, as I am sure he does, that I did not take so long. He, of course is not responsible for any of the book's shortcomings. My wife, Elisabeth Siegrist Hotson, is likewise pleased to see it completed. Without her wifely encouragement and help with the typing it would still be but a pile of notebooks. I also owe a debt of gratitude to Dr. Kenneth J. Curran, Dean of the Colorado College, Dr. Edward N. Chapman, and the trustees of the Chapman Fund for valued financial aid. Finally, I want to thank Miss Linda Bjelland for her long hours of calculator punching and Eleanor, Howard, and David for their help in reading galley proof. Anna and Rachel can help on the next one.

Colorado Springs, Colo. John H. Hotson
September 1967

CONTENTS

Chapter 1

INTRODUCTION: THE CASE OF THE UNITED STATES

A high degree of stability has been observed in the wage share of gross product produced by business in the United States over the past half century or longer. Upon this near fixity of labor's share of gross product Dr. Sidney Weintraub has erected a theory of the price level which, in simplest terms, states that since the wage share is so close to constant the general price level moves only in response to changes in the ratio between the average wage and output per man.[1]

This "Law of the Price Level" is then a heavily cost oriented explanation of price level changes, Weintraub holding that factors causing "demand pull" such as too rapid increase in the money supply, do not lead directly to inflation as quantity theory thinking has lead us to believe. Demand factors have their impact mainly on the level of employment and output and affect the price level only to the extent that they induce changes in the ratio of the average wage to average output.

It is the purpose of this study to discover whether this stability of the wage share, or its reciprocal which Weintraub dubs $\underline{k}$, is to be observed in the national accounts of other nations, at aggregated and disaggregated levels, and, to the extent possible to set forth the reasons for the presence or absence of the wage share stability which is observed.

Dr. Weintraub proposes to replace the familiar Equation of Exchange - MV = PQ - and its alternatives with a similarly simple identity which he derives as follows.

[1]For a full statement of Weintraub's views see: S. Weintraub, *A General Theory of the Price Level, Output, Income Determination, and Economic Growth*, (Philadelphia: Chilton 1959); *Some Aspects of Wage Theory and Policy*, (Philadelphia: Chilton 1963); or *Growth Without Inflation*, Nat. Council of Applied Economic Research (New Delhi 1965). The best short statement of his, "A Keynesian Model of the Price Level and the Constant Wage Share," *Kyklos*, Vol. XV - 1962 - Fasc. 4.

"sales proceeds ($Z = PQ$) are equal to some multiple ($\underline{k}$) of the wage bill, that is, of the money wage ($\underline{w}$) times the volume of employment (N). The symbol Q will denote physical output while A will signify the average product per worer, so that $A = Q/N$. Thus the following definitional equations can be developed:

$$Z = \underline{kw}N$$
$$PQ = \underline{kw}N$$
$$P = \underline{kw}N/Q = \underline{kw}/A = \underline{k}R$$"[2]

The letter R stands for the ratio $\underline{w}/A$, thus unit wage cost. The final formulation states that the price level is a function $\underline{k}$ of unit wage costs.

The advantages claimed for this Wage Cost Mark-Up (WCM) truism over the Equation of Exchange (EOE) are:

1. Unlike the V of EOE, $\underline{k}$ is highly stable, so much so that Weintraub calls it the "magic constant."
2. Unlike V, $\underline{k}$ is readily ascertainable from available statistical data.
3. The EOE is not a useful predictive tool because a change in M can be offset by changes in V or Q as well as impinging directly on P. However, $\underline{k}$ is fixed and we can generalize that the price level will rise only if R rises. When tested empirically this generalization will be borne out.
4. The EOE affords no way of "'determining' the source of inflation, for the determining characteristics must come from behavioral or structural relationships; the EOE can only indicate the movement in components, and not the causal factors."[3] With the WCM truism we can determine the source of inflation; "a rise in R will raise the level of prices,"[4] (with only slight reservations because of slight fluctuations in $\underline{k}$ or A).
5. The EOE mis-leads us into believing that by controlling M the Federal Reserve Board can control the price level. The impact of changes in M, Weintraub argues, are on Q and only indirectly on P. The Board can achieve price stability in our unionized economy only at the cost of un-

[2]Weintraub, *A General Theory*, p. 5.

[3]Weintraub, *General Theory*, p. 5.

[4]*Ibid.* p. 54.

> employment sufficiently great to brake wage demands, and a lower than necessary rate of growth. In a continuous production economy cost of production, not total money supply, determines prices. "The wage level, not the money supply, governs the price level."[5]

Let us develop the component series of both the Wage Cost Mark-Up Equation and the Equation of Exchange in the United States and see how well the facts bear out Weintraub's contentions.

THE WAGE COST MARK-UP EQUATION

As the empirical measure of Z, or gross product, Weintraub used the Department of Commerce series, "Business Gross Product," (BGP). BGP differs from Gross National Product in excluding General Government, Households and Institutions, and the Rest of the World. For the wage bill he used "Compensation of Business Employees," (W_b). The Mark-Up Factor $\underline{k}$ is defined as: $\underline{k} = Z/W_b$ =Business Gross Product/Compensation of Business Employees.

In the U. S. from 1929 through 1964 this ratio has fluctuated between 2.16 (wage share 46.2 per cent of gross product) and 1.86 (53.8 per cent), a change of about 15 per cent. The largest one year change of .09, or 4.5 per cent, occurred between 1929 and 1930. See Table 1.1. for the values of Z, W_b, and $\underline{k}$ from 1929 to 1964.

Dr. Arthur Grant has carried the measurement of the WCM components back to 1899 making use of the national income studies of King, Martin, and Kuznets.[6] Grant's concept of Z differs from the Commerce BGP series in that he excluded net rent, mortgage interest, depreciation of owner occupied non-farm dwellings, and employee compensation paid by government enterprises and Federal Reserve Banks, and included interest on brokers' loans which is excluded from BGP. Because of these differences Grant's Z was $89,008 million in 1929 while BGP was $94,801 million.[7]

[5] *Ibid.* p. 88.

[6] Arthur Grant, "Issues in Distribution Theory: The Measurement of Labor's Relative Share, 1899-1929," *Rev. Econ. & Stat.*, August 1963, **45**, p. 279. For the full treatment of Grant's methods and findings see his, *Wage and Non-Wage Shares in Business Gross Product* 1899-1929, a dissertation in Economics, Univ. of Pennsylvania 1961.

[7] For the reconciliation of Grant's Z and BGP see Grant, *Wage and Non-Wage Shares*, p. 95.

Table 1.1. Business Gross Product, Compensation of Business Employees, and Mark-Up Factor in the United States 1929-1964 (billions of dollars)

Year	Business Gross Product (Z)	Compensation of Employees (W_b)	Mark-Up Factor (k)
1929	$ 94.8	$ 43.8	2.16
1930	82.2	39.6	2.07
1931	68.0	32.8	2.07
1932	51.1	24.7	2.07
1933	48.7	23.2	2.10
1934	56.7	26.9	2.11
1935	63.7	29.5	2.16
1936	72.4	33.6	2.15
1937	80.5	38.7	2.08
1938	74.3	35.2	2.11
1939	80.1	38.2	2.09
1940	89.1	41.9	2.13
1941	112.5	52.8	2.13
1942	139.9	67.2	2.08
1943	162.8	80.8	2.02
1944	174.5	85.4	2.04
1945	173.4	83.9	2.07
1946	184.2	92.5	1.99
1947	210.7	107.0	1.97
1948	234.2	118.0	1.98
1949	230.3	115.6	1.99
1950	254.2	127.0	2.00
1951	291.2	146.2	1.99
1952	304.9	156.9	1.94
1953	321.4	169.5	1.90
1954	317.9	167.5	1.90
1955	349.0	181.3	1.93
1956	366.7	196.9	1.86
1957	386.3	206.7	1.87
1958	383.9	204.1	1.88
1959	418.9	222.7	1.88
1960	433.7	233.5	1.86
1961	444.6	238.0	1.87
1962	476.7	254.2	1.88
1963	499.0	266.7	1.87
1964	532.3	286.2	1.86

Source: Weintraub, *General Theory*, p. 14; *Survey of Current Business*, July 1962, p. 11; July 1964, p. 13; August 1965, p. 23.

See Table 1.2. for the values of Z, W_b, and k from 1899 to 1929.

Grant's series indicate that k was somewhat more variable in this earlier period. The total range of variation was from 2.33 in 1917 (wage share 42.9 per cent of gross product), to 1.92 in

Table 1.2. Gross Product of Business, Compensation of Employees, and the Mark-Up Factor in the United States 1899-1929.

Year	Gross Product (Z) (millions of dollars)	Compensation of Employees (W_b) (millions of dollars)	Mark-Up Factor (k)
1899	$14,614	$ 7,094	2.06
1900	15,793	7,565	2.09
1901	17,702	8,221	2.15
1902	18,281	8,980	2.04
1903	19,244	9,719	1.98
1904	18,955	9,857	1.92
1905	21,187	10,895	1.94
1906	24,575	11,830	2.08
1907	26,005	12,382	2.10
1908	23,151	11,083	2.09
1909	27,555	12,773	2.16
1910	28,487	13,710	2.08
1911	29,292	13,832	2.12
1912	32,194	14,618	2.20
1913	33,599	15,819	2.12
1914	30,655	15,384	1.99
1915	32,691	15,987	2.04
1916	43,350	19,160	2.26
1917	52,648	22,639	2.33
1918	66,055	27,611	2.39
1919	68,498	31,698	2.16
1920	78,047	38,422	2.03
1921	62,982	29,706	2.12
1922	62,265	31,029	2.01
1923	73,503	37,075	1.98
1924	74,165	36,817	2.01
1925	77,439	38,110	2.03
1926	83,624	40,756	2.05
1927	81,824	40,814	2.00
1928	83,325	41,502	2.01
1929	89,008	43,976	2.02

Source: Arthur Grant, *Wage and Non-Wage Shares in Business Gross Product 1899-1929*. Gross Product p. 84, Compensation of Employees p. 149, Mark-Up Factor, p. 280.

1904 (52.1 per cent), a change of about 22 percentage points. The largest one year change of .23, or 11 per cent, occurred between 1918 and 1919. In contrast to the k series after 1929, Grant's series displays no downward trend.

The remaining series of the WCM are derived as follows: Total Compensation of Business Employees (W_b) divided by the number of Full-Time Equivalent Employees of Business (N) equals Average Compensation of Employees (w). The Price Level (P) is the Commerce series "Implicit Price Deflators for Business Gross Product" used to develop their series BGP in 1954 dollars (Q). Output per man (A) is Q divided by N. The ratio R equals w divided by A, that is, Unit Wage Cost. All series are reduced to index numbers with the base period 1947-1949 equal to 100. The P' series is the result of computing the price level index by means of the WCM truism in the form P = kR. The fact that except for errors caused by rounding off it is identical to the Commerce P series indicates that no errors in computation and transcription have crept in. See Table 1.3. for the WCM component series from 1899 to 1964.[8]

THE EQUATION OF EXCHANGE

Dr. Richard T. Selden has provided us with an excellent series on the Income Velocity of Circulation, V_y, in the United States from 1899 to 1951.[9] With the assistance of a study of Drs. Eugene Smolensky and David Horlacher I have extended these figures to 1964.[10] Table 1.4. sets forth the numerical value of V_y, its index, and the k index. Figure 1.1. makes the comparison between these rival "constants" visual, and striking. In the 66 years for which we have data the V_y index has fluctuated between 164 and 66, a change of 85 per cent. Over the same period the k index has varied between 129 and 94, or 30 per cent. The largest one year change

[8]Since, as indicated above, Grant's measure of Z differs from Commerce' BGP, a decision must be made regarding how to "tack together" the two in a consistent series to contrast with Velocity for the same period. In Table 1.3. I have raised Grant's measure of k by 1.069, which is the ratio between his measure of Product and the Commerce figure in the year of overlap, 1929. Similar adjustments were also made to his Wb, Q, N series. If the two periods are joined without this "correction factor" the range of k index is 94-121, while with this factor the range of index k is 94 to 129.

[9]Richard T. Selden, "Monetary Velocity in the United States," *Studies in the Quantity Theory of Money*, Milton Friedman ed., (Univ. of Chicago Press, 1956). The figures for the period 1899-1919 are Selden's series "V-40," p. 220. The series for 1919-1951 are found on page 200.

[10]My figures for the most recent period may not be quite the same as Selden would have derived. In his very elaborate analysis he provides us with more than 40 alternative measures of V. My method was simply to reduce National Income to an index based on 1947-49 and divide through by the Money Supply Index, similarly based, supplied in the various issues of *International Financial Statistics*, (IMF, Washington).

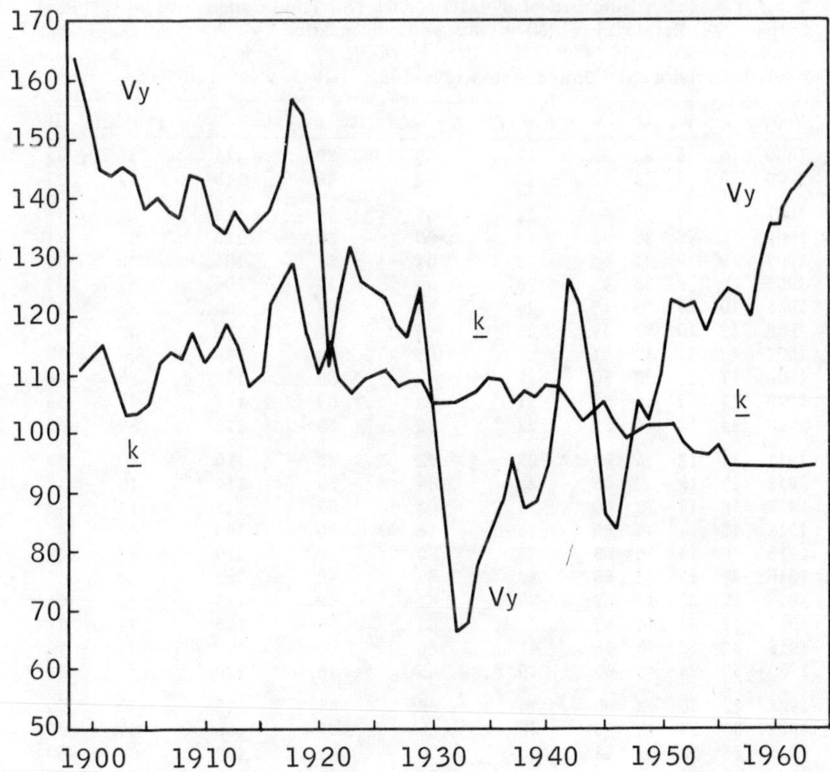

Fig. 1.1. Index of Income Velocity of Money (Vy = NI/M) and Wage Cost Mark-Up (k = BGP/Wb) in the United States 1899-1964. (1947-49 = 100)

in V_y was 23 per cent; the largest for k was 11 per cent.

Weintraub, after making the above comparison between k and V_y for 1929-1951, in order to avoid a show of strictly "no contest" contrasted V_y with less stable k_y

($k_y = \frac{\text{National Income}}{\text{Employee Compensation,}}$ *i.e.*, the reciprocal of the "wage share").[11]

Let us try a different tack in further comparisons. Rather than dull our tools, let us see if we can sharpen up Selden's for him by redefining Velocity as BGP/M (Money Supply) rather than NI/M. This is done in Table 1.5. From 1899 to 1964 the range of

[11] Weintraub, *General Theory*, pp. 78-82.

Table 1.3. Index Numbers of Total Product (Z), Total Compensation(W_b), Real Output (Q), Employment (N), Average Compensation ($\underline{w}$), Average Output per Employee (A), Unit Wage Cost (R), Mark-Up ($\underline{k}$), Price Level (P' = $\underline{k}$R), and Implicit Deflators (P) United States 1899-1961. (1947-1949 = 100)

Year	Z	W_b	Q	N	$\underline{w} = W_b/N$	A = Q/N	R = $\underline{w}$/A	$\underline{k} = Z/W_b$	P' = $\underline{k}$R	P
1899	7	6	22	38	17	58	28	111	31	32
1900	8	7	23	39	17	59	29	113	33	33
1901	9	7	26	40	18	65	28	116	32	33
1902	9	8	26	43	18	60	30	110	33	34
1903	9	9	27	44	20	61	31	104	32	34
1904	9	9	26	44	20	59	34	104	35	35
1905	10	10	28	47	20	60	34	105	35	36
1906	12	10	32	49	21	65	32	112	36	37
1907	12	11	32	51	21	63	33	114	38	38
1908	11	10	29	50	19	58	33	113	37	38
1909	13	11	33	53	21	62	34	117	40	39
1910	14	12	34	55	22	62	35	112	39	40
1911	14	12	35	56	22	63	35	115	40	40
1912	15	13	37	58	22	64	35	119	40	42
1913	16	14	38	60	23	63	37	115	43	42
1914	15	14	34	59	23	58	40	108	43	43
1915	16	14	36	60	23	60	40	110	42	44
1916	20	17	42	65	26	65	40	122	49	49
1917	25	20	41	67	30	61	49	126	62	61
1918	31	24	44	67	36	66	55	129	71	71
1919	32	28	45	68	41	66	62	117	73	72
1920	37	34	45	69	49	65	75	110	83	82
1921	30	26	43	65	40	66	61	115	70	70
1922	30	27	45	69	39	65	61	109	65	66
1923	35	33	51	73	45	70	64	107	68	68
1924	35	32	52	72	44	72	61	109	66	67
1925	36	33	54	74	45	73	62	110	68	69
1926	40	36	58	77	47	75	62	111	70	69
1927	38	36	58	77	47	75	63	108	68	67
1928	40	36	58	78	46	74	62	109	68	68
1929	42	39	62	80	49	78	63	109	68	68
1930	37	35	56	74	48	76	63	105	66	65
1931	30	29	52	67	44	78	56	105	59	59
1932	23	22	43	58	38	74	51	105	54	53
1933	22	20	41	58	36	71	51	106	54	52
1934	25	24	45	64	38	70	54	107	57	56
1935	28	26	50	67	40	75	53	109	58	56
1936	32	30	57	72	42	79	53	109	58	56
1937	35	34	62	76	45	82	55	105	58	58
1938	33	31	58	71	44	82	54	107	58	57
1939	36	34	63	74	46	85	54	106	57	56
1940	40	37	69	79	47	87	54	108	58	57

Source: 1899-1929 Grant, *Ibid.* Z p. 84, W_b p. 149, Q p. 84, N p. 273, P p. 37. Adjustments: Z = Grant's Z x 1.07, W_b = Grant's W_b x .996, Q = Grant's Q x 1.792, N = Grant's N x 1.12, $\underline{k}$ = Grant's $\underline{k}$ x 1.069, P = Grant's P x .68.

Note: Calculation of $\underline{w}$, A, $\underline{R}$, and $\underline{k}$ was carried out to additional decimal points. Because of rounding off the above indices will not check, particularly the earliest years.

Table 1.3. Continued

Year	Z	W_b	Q	N	$\underline{w} = W_b/N$	$A = Q/N$	$R = \underline{w}/A$	$\underline{k} = Z/W_b$	$P' = \underline{k}R$	P
1941	50	47	80	87	53	92	58	108	63	62
1942	62	59	88	94	63	94	70	105	73	71
1943	72	71	93	96	73	97	75	102	77	78
1944	78	75	98	94	80	104	77	103	79	79
1945	77	74	97	90	82	108	77	105	80	79
1946	82	81	95	95	86	100	86	101	87	86
1947	94	94	98	100	94	98	96	99	95	96
1948	104	104	102	102	102	100	102	100	102	102
1949	102	102	101	98	104	103	101	101	102	102
1950	113	112	110	101	111	109	102	101	103	103
1951	129	129	117	107	121	109	111	101	112	111
1952	135	138	120	108	128	111	115	98	113	113
1953	143	149	126	111	135	114	118	96	113	113
1954	141	148	124	107	137	116	118	96	113	114
1955	155	160	135	111	144	122	118	97	114	115
1956	163	173	138	114	151	121	125	94	117	118
1957	172	182	139	115	158	121	131	94	123	122
1958	171	180	137	111	162	123	132	94	124	125
1959	186	196	147	114	172	129	133	94	124	126
1960	193	206	151	113	182	134	136	94	129	128
1961	198	210	153	115	183	133	138	94	130	129
1962	212	224	163	118	190	138	138	94	130	130
1963	222	235	169	120	196	141	139	94	131	131
1964	237	251	177	123	204	144	142	94	133	133

Source: Weintraub, *Ibid.* pp. 20, 27, 47.
Survey of Current Business July 1962, pp. 11, 28-29; July 1964, pp. 13, 29-30; August 1965, p. 22.

V_y was 85 percent. Over the same period our new V series fluctuated a "mere" 69 per cent. The largest one-year change in V_y occurred in 1920-21 when the index fell .30, or 23 per cent. In the same year V fell .25, or 21 per cent. Also V has considerably less downward trend than V_y .

Table 1.5. also develops the remainder of the Equation of Exchange using the same Z, P, and Q series as in Table 1.3. The Money Supply (M) index is taken directly from Selden except for the last decade which are the International Monetary Fund series. The ratio $\underline{r}$ is the Money to Real Output, or M/Q, ratio. Again we compute the price level P' by means of the index numbers, this time in the EOE form $P = V\underline{r}$ and compare the result with the official Implicit Deflator of Business Gross Product (P) as a check against computational error.

The point of Tables 1.3. and 1.5. is not, however, to "prove that truisms are true," but to focus on the extent to which P and R, and P and $\underline{r}$, are or are not close to identical series. The fact that the WCM formulation yields an R series which is close to identical with the Price Level series is the basis of Weintraub's "Law of the Price Level" that P and R always move in the same direction. If k were *constant*, P and R would be the same series.

Table 1.4. Income Velocity of Circulation (Vy), Index of Vy, Index of k. United States 1899-1964. (1947-49 = 100)

Year	Vy	Vy Index	k Index	Year	Vy	Vy Index	k Index
1899	1.87	164	111	1931	0.97	85	105
1900	1.77	155	113	1932	0.75	66	105
1901	1.66	145	116	1933	0.77	67	106
1902	1.65	144	110	1934	0.88	77	107
1903	1.66	145	104	1935	0.95	83	109
1904	1.64	144	104	1936	1.00	88	109
1905	1.58	138	105	1937	1.10	96	105
1906	1.60	140	112	1938	0.99	87	107
1907	1.58	138	114	1939	1.01	88	106
1908	1.56	137	113	1940	1.06	93	108
1909	1.64	144	117	1941	1.23	108	108
1910	1.63	143	112	1942	1.44	126	105
1911	1.55	136	115	1943	1.39	122	102
1912	1.53	134	119	1944	1.22	107	103
1913	1.59	138	115	1945	1.01	86	105
1914	1.53	134	108	1946	0.95	83	101
1915	1.55	136	110	1947	1.08	95	99
1916	1.58	138	122	1948	1.20	105	100
1917	1.63	143	126	1949	1.15	101	101
1918	1.79	157	129	1950	1.24	109	101
1919	1.75	154	117	1951	1.39	122	101
1920	1.61	141	110	1952	1.38	121	98
1921	1.27	111	115	1953	1.39	122	96
1922	1.41	123	109	1954	1.32	116	96
1923	1.51	132	107	1955	1.38	121	97
1924	1.44	126	109	1956	1.41	124	94
1925	1.42	124	110	1957	1.40	123	94
1926	1.41	123	111	1958	1.35	118	94
1927	1.35	118	108	1959	1.47	129	94
1928	1.33	116	109	1960	1.53	134	94
1929	1.40	123	109	1961	1.50	132	94
1930	1.21	106	105	1962	1.59	139	94
				1963	1.60	140	94
				1964	1.64	144	94

Source: Vy from, Selden, R. T., "Monetary Velocity in the United States," *Studies in the Quantity Theory of Money*, Milton Friedman ed., 1899-1919 p. 220 "V-40," 1919-1951 p. 200. Extension from 1951-1957 by Smolensky, E., from 1958 by author. k Index, 1899-1929, Grant, A., *Ibid.* p. 280. 1929-1957, Weintraub, S., *Ibid.* p. 20. 1958-1964, *Survey of Current Business* July 1962, pp. 11, 28-29; July 1964, p. 13; August 1965, p. 22.

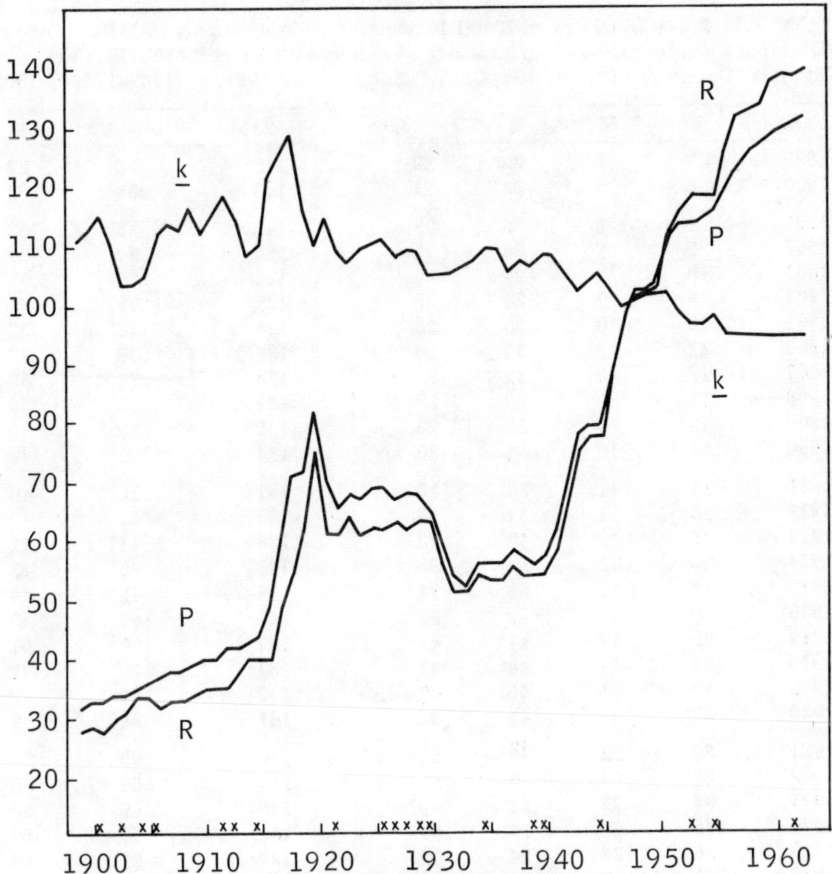

Fig. 1.2. Indices of Price (P), Unit Wage Cost (R), and Mark-Up Factor (k), in the United States from 1899 to 1964: x indicates an apparent exception to the "Law" that P and R indices move in the same direction. (1947-49 = 100)

Since k is merely *close* to constant, its all over variation since 1899 being some 30 per cent with a downward trend, the P and R series diverge.

Figure 1.2. is a graph of the WCM formulation P = kR, for the period 1899-1965. We see here the close correspondence between the P and R, or Unit Wage Cost, series throughout the entire 66 year period; this being the result of the near invariance of k. The small letter x at the bottom of the figure represents an apparent contradiction of the "law" that P and R always move in the

Table 1.5. Index Numbers of Total Product (Z), Money Supply (M), Real Output (Q), Money Supply to Real Output ratio ($\underline{r}$), Velocity (V), Price Level ($P' = V\underline{r}$), and Implicit Deflators (P) in the United States 1899-1961. (1947-1949 = 100)

Year	Z	M	Q	$\underline{r} = M/Q$	$V = Z/M$	$P' = V\underline{r}$	P
1899	7	5	22	22	146	32	32
1900	8	5	23	23	142	33	33
1901	9	6	26	23	142	33	33
1902	9	7	26	25	134	34	34
1903	9	7	27	26	133	35	35
1904	9	7	26	28	125	35	35
1905	10	8	28	28	128	36	36
1906	12	8	32	26	139	36	37
1907	12	9	32	28	138	39	38
1908	11	9	29	30	125	38	38
1909	13	9	33	28	139	39	39
1910	14	10	34	30	134	40	40
1911	14	11	35	30	131	39	40
1912	15	11	37	30	137	41	42
1913	16	12	38	30	138	41	42
1914	20	12	34	35	123	43	43
1915	16	12	36	34	126	43	44
1916	20	14	42	33	143	47	49
1917	25	17	41	41	147	60	61
1918	31	19	44	43	163	70	71
1919	32	21	45	47	152	71	72
1920	37	23	45	51	161	82	82
1921	30	22	43	51	136	69	70
1922	30	23	45	51	130	66	66
1923	35	25	51	49	140	69	68
1924	35	26	52	50	135	68	67
1925	36	28	54	52	129	67	69
1926	40	30	58	52	133	69	69
1927	38	31	58	53	123	65	67
1928	40	32	58	55	125	69	68
1929	42	32	62	52	131	68	68
1930	37	32	56	57	116	66	65
1931	30	30	52	58	100	58	59
1932	23	27	43	63	85	54	53
1933	22	25	41	61	88	54	52
1934	25	28	45	62	89	55	56
1935	28	31	50	62	90	56	56
1936	32	34	57	60	94	56	56
1937	36	35	62	56	103	58	58
1938	33	35	58	60	94	56	57
1939	36	38	63	60	95	57	56
1940	40	41	69	59	98	58	57

Table 1.5. Continued

Year	Z	M	Q	r = M/Q	V = Z/M	P' = Vr	P
1941	50	45	80	56	111	62	62
1942	62	51	88	58	122	71	71
1943	72	66	93	71	109	77	78
1944	78	81	98	83	96	80	79
1945	77	97	97	100	79	79	79
1946	82	102	95	107	80	86	86
1947	92	99	98	101	93	94	96
1948	104	101	102	99	103	102	102
1949	102	100	101	99	102	101	102
1950	113	103	110	94	110	103	103
1951	129	108	117	92	119	109	111
1952	135	117	120	98	115	113	113
1953	143	118	126	94	121	114	113
1954	141	121	124	98	117	115	114
1955	155	123	135	91	126	115	115
1956	163	126	138	91	129	117	118
1957	172	125	139	90	138	124	122
1958	171	130	137	95	132	125	125
1959	186	130	147	88	143	126	127
1960	193	130	151	86	148	127	128
1961	198	134	153	88	148	129	130
1962	212	137	163	84	155	130	130
1963	222	142	169	84	156	131	131
1964	237	148	177	84	160	134	133

Source: Grant, *Ibid.* Z, p. 84, Q, *ibid.* for years 1899-1929. Z, Q, and P 1929-1957 from Weintraub, *ibid.* pp. 14, 20, 27., Z, Q, and P 1958-1964 from *Survey of Current Business*, July 1964, pp. 13, 28-29; M, from Selden, *ibid.* p. 254 and *International Financial Statistics*, July 1965, p. 32.

same direction. We shall examine these cases in Table 1.6., but two interesting points are evident in Figure 1.2.

First, the exceptions are all small, P goes up or down a point or two and R either does not move or moves a point or two in the other direction. Second, no exceptions occurred during the period 1915-1921 when first k, then P, then R rose considerably during World War I and then fell back. There were, however, (small) exceptions in every one of the changes from 1925 through 1930 when k, P, and R were all changing only slightly.

Let us now see how the alternative EOE "law" that P and r

move together because V is constant performs.[12] Figure 1.3. is the graph of the equation P = V$\underline{r}$. Since V is so much more variable than $\underline{k}$, P and $\underline{r}$ are not "practically the same" series as are P and R. They diverge greatly on both sides of the base period 1947-1949, indeed, the greatest divergence has been the most recent experience. From 1947 $\underline{r}$ has steadily fallen while P has even more steadily risen, and the reason is not hard to see. The Federal Reserve Authorities in these years have deliberately held the growth of the money supply to a slower pace than the growth in Real Output after the great money creation in World War II years. However, instead of the fall in $\underline{r}$ bringing about a fall, or at least a leveling off, of P, their efforts have been offset by V rising to heights not seen since World War I!

One may even speculate that we might well have had just as much inflation if the "Fed" had merely followed Friedman's wishes and increased M at the same rate as Q. Velocity would have been

[12]Some quantity theorists may object to this recasting of the EOE as a "Law of the Price Level" holding that only "naive" theorists think that V is constant or close to constant. Indeed, Milton Friedman (in "The Quantity Theory of Money—A Restatement," *Studies in the Quantity Theory of Money*, Univ. of Chicago Press (Chicago 1956)) maintains that the quantity theory is "not a theory of the price level" but "a theory of the demand for money" (*ibid.* p. 4.). He then proceeds to derive the determinants of this demand and contends, not that income velocity is constant, but that it is a stable function of a few other variables. Having stated all this, however, Friedman reverts to the "naive" claim that income velocity is "extraordinarily" stable and regular. He writes:

"One of the chief reproaches directed at economics as an allegedly empirical science is that it can offer so few numerical "constants," that it has isolated so few fundamental regularities. The field of money is the chief example one can offer in rebutal: there is perhaps no other empirical relation in economics that has been observed to recur so uniformly under so wide a variety of circumstances as the relation between substantial changes in the stock of money and in prices ....There is an extraordinary empirical stability and regularity to such magnitudes as income velocity that cannot but impress anyone who works extensively with monetary data." (pp. 20-21).

Similarly, when Friedman turns to policy matters he forgets his "sophisticated" restatement of a quantity theory which is not a theory of the price level, and makes statements concerning the price level which are only necessarily true if V_y is constant. In a recent denial of "cost push" inflation he writes:

"Suppose....upward pressure on prices-ultimately of course reflecting an increase in the stock of money....History offers ample evidence that what determines the average level of prices and wages is the amount of money in the economy and not the greediness of businessmen or of workers." *Capitalism and Freedom*, p. 135.

Friedman, along with many other "naive" and "sophisticated" practitioners, therefore, does use the EOE as a "Law of the Price Level" and it is not a matter of knocking down straw men to show how poorly it performs.

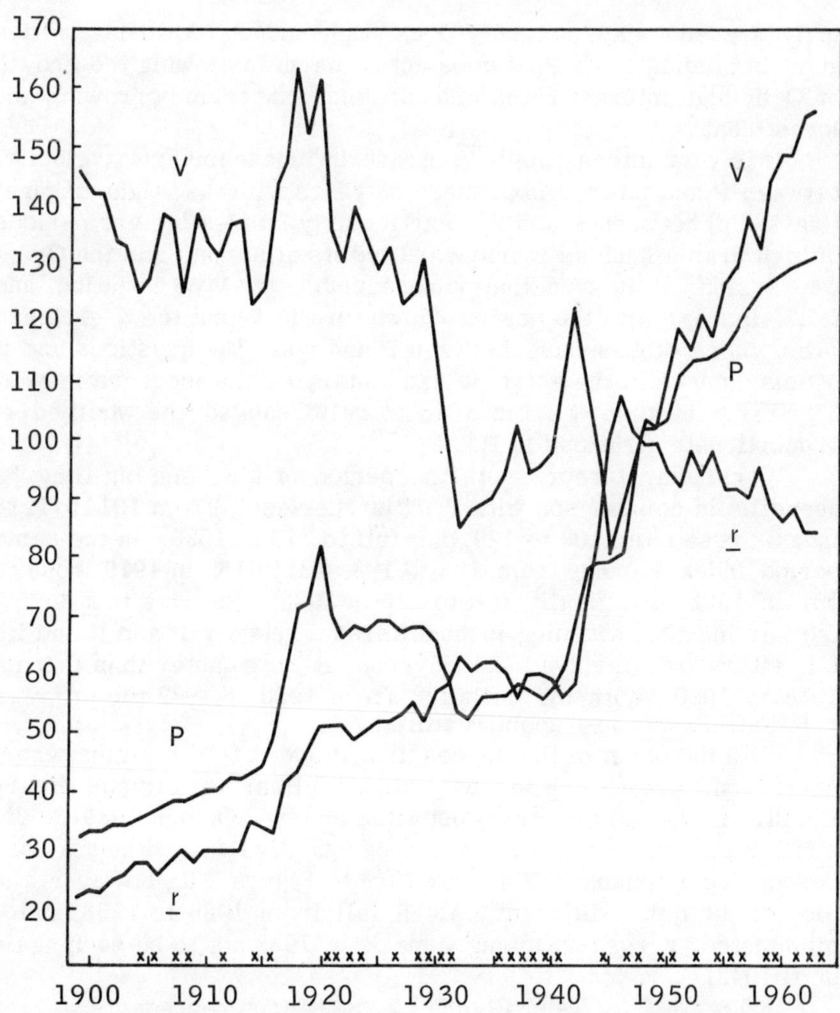

Fig. 1.3. Indices of Price (P), Money Supply to Real Output ratio (r), and Gross Product Velocity of Circulation (V) in the United States from 1899 to 1964: x indicates apparent exception to the "Law" that P and r indices move in the same direction (1947-49 = 100)

lower and total expenditures might well have been the same! Only as their actions indirectly influence the path of the R ratio, through employment effects of M on wage settlements, have the Federal Reserve Authorities acted on a factor with a fixed ratio - the Wage Cost Mark-Up - to the price level. Further, as is increasingly argued today, not only does "tight money" do little positive good in holding down P, it does actual harm in slowing the growth of Q by high interest rates discouraging long term borrowing and investment.

It is very interesting to contrast the "loose linkage" (velocity) between P and r throughout these 66 years with the "tight linkage" (Mark-Up) between P and R. Particularly interesting are periods of high drama such as World War I and its aftermath and the Great Depression. It is true that r rose during the WWI inflation, and fell (slightly) with the postwar down turn in P, but the *degree* and *promptness* of response between P and r are the questions and it seems dubious in the extreme to maintain that the increase in M at a faster rate than Q from 1916 to 1919 "caused" the wholly disproportionate girations in P.

World War I represents the period of k's "one big fling," a pecadillo in comparison with V's "lurcheries." From 1914 to 1918 index k rose from 108 to 129, then fell to 110 in 1920. In the same period index V rose from 123 to 163, fell to 152 in 1919, rose to 161 in 1920, and finally fell to 130 in 1922. The rise in k during the war meant a widening in the difference between P and R and its fall afterwards involved the reverse, R rose faster than P from 1918 to 1920. With the deflation from 1920 to 1922 the pre-war relationship was just about restored.

With the onset of the depression, P and R fell in almost exact correspondence (*i.e.* k fell only slightly) Henry C. Simons, Henry Hazlitt *et. al.* to the contrary not withstanding. Only in 1929-30 did k fall during the downswing, and consequently P fall without a corresponding R change. When we turn to Figure 1.3., however, the picture is quite different. As P fell from 1929 to 1933, and V plummeted, r *rose* reaching a peak in 1932 not to be seen again until 1942!

In Figure 1.3., as in Figure 1.2., a letter x represents a year of exception to the "law" under consideration. There are close to twice as many as in Figure 1.2, 36 out of 65 year-to-year changes as against 20 for the WCM, and the exceptions are not always small. Nor are the "confirmations" of the "law" that P and r are bound tightly together particularly persuasive; as 1917-18 when P rose 11 points and r rose 2, or 1946 when P rose 1 point and r rose 7.

Table 1.6. examines the exceptions to the rival price level laws in detail. The first thing noticable about the 20 WCM law exceptions is that 12 of the apparent exceptions are *not* exceptions, but

Table 1.6. Apparent Exceptions to Alternative Price Level Laws: 1. P and R Move in the Same Direction as k is Constant. 2. P and r Move in the Same Direction as V is Constant. United States 1899-1964, 65 Changes.

	1. P = kR			Size of Exception			2. P = Vr		
Year	ΔP	ΔR	Δk			Year	ΔP	Δr	ΔV
1900-01*	-0	-1	+3						
1902-03*	+0	+1	-6						
1904-05*	+1	+0	+0			1904-05*	+0	+1	-1
1905-06	+1	-1	+7	2	3	1905-06	+1	-2	+11
					2	1907-08	-0	+2	-13
					3	1908-09	+1	-2	+14
1911-12*	+2	+0	+4		2	1911-12	+2	0	+6
1912-13*	+0	+2	-4						
1914-15*	+1	+0	+2		2	1914-15	+1	-1	+3
					6	1915-16	+5	-1	+17
					37	1920-21	-12	+0	-25
1921-22*	-4	-0	-6			1921-22*	-4	-0	-6
					5	1922-23	+2	-3	+10
					2	1923-24	-1	+1	-5
1925-26	+0	-1	+1	1					
1926-27*	-2	-1	-3		3	1926-27	-2	+1	-10
1927-28	+1	-1	+1	2					
1928-29	+0	-0	+1	1	3	1928-29	+0	-3	+6
1929-30	-3	+0	-4	3	8	1929-30	-3	+5	-15
					7	1930-31	-6	+1	-16
					11	1931-32	-6	+5	-15
1934-35	+0	-1	+2	1					
					2	1935-36	+0	-2	+4
					6	1936-37	+2	-4	+9
					5	1937-38	-1	+4	-9
1938-39*	-1	-0	-1			1938-39*	-1	-0	+1
1939-40	+1	-0	+2	1	2	1939-40	+1	-1	+3
					8	1940-41	+5	-3	+13
1944-45	+0	-0	+2	1	17	1944-45	-0	+17	-17
					16	1946-47	+10	-6	+13
					8	1947-48	+6	-2	+10
					6	1949-50	+1	-5	+8
					10	1950-51	+8	-2	+9
1952-53*	+0	+3	-2		4	1952-53	+0	-4	+6
1954-55	+1	-0	+1	1	8	1954-55	+1	-7	+9
						1955-56*	+3	+0	+3
					5	1956-57	+4	-1	+9
					9	1958-59	+2	-7	+11
					3	1959-60	+1	-2	+5
1961-62*	+1	+0	+0		4	1961-62	+0	-4	+1
						1962-63*	+1	+0	+1
					3	1963-64	+3	-0	+4

*Indicates an apparent exception which has been resolved by taking the work to further decimal places.

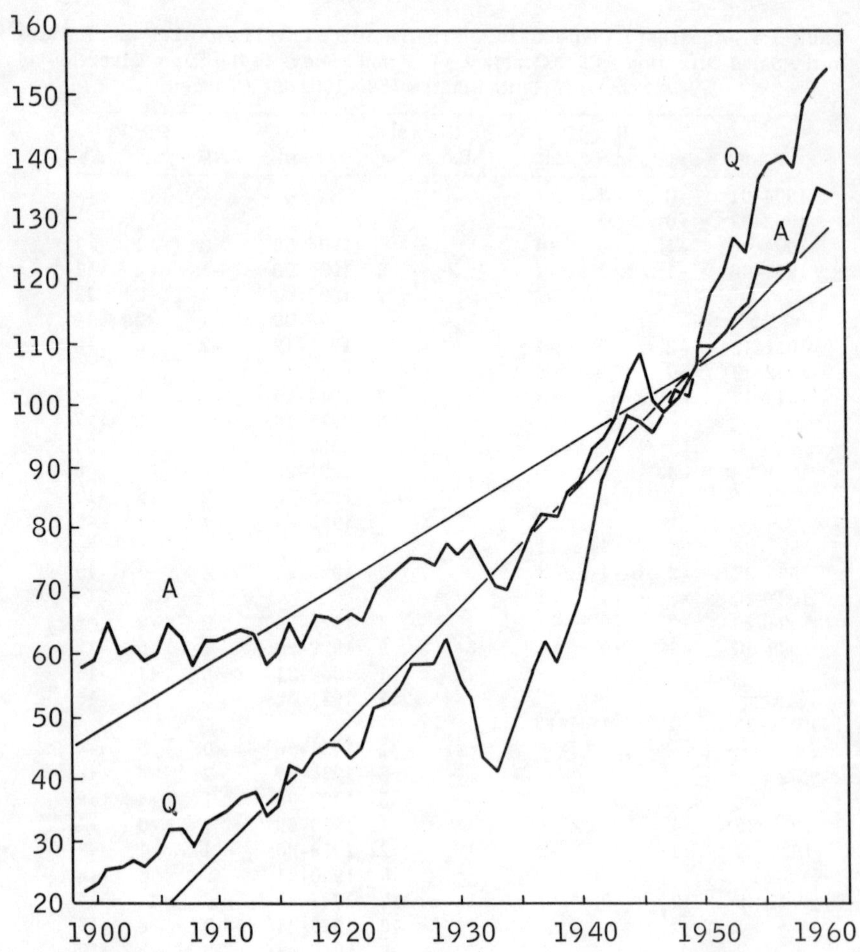

Fig. 1.4. Indices of Real Output (Q), and Average Output per Employee (A) in the United States from 1899 to 1961. (1947-49 = 100)

Analysis:

Q: Range 22-153, largest change 12.6%, slope b = +1.96231, sqt = 13.71, vt = 20.2%, R^2 = +.872.

A: Range 58-133, largest change 8.4%, b = +1.15827, sat = 7.78, vt = 9.4%, R^2 = +.876.

weak confirmations. When one series moved, the other moved in the same direction, but less than one-half an index point. The second point to note about the exceptions is that in no case do ΔP and ΔR diverge by more than 3 index points.

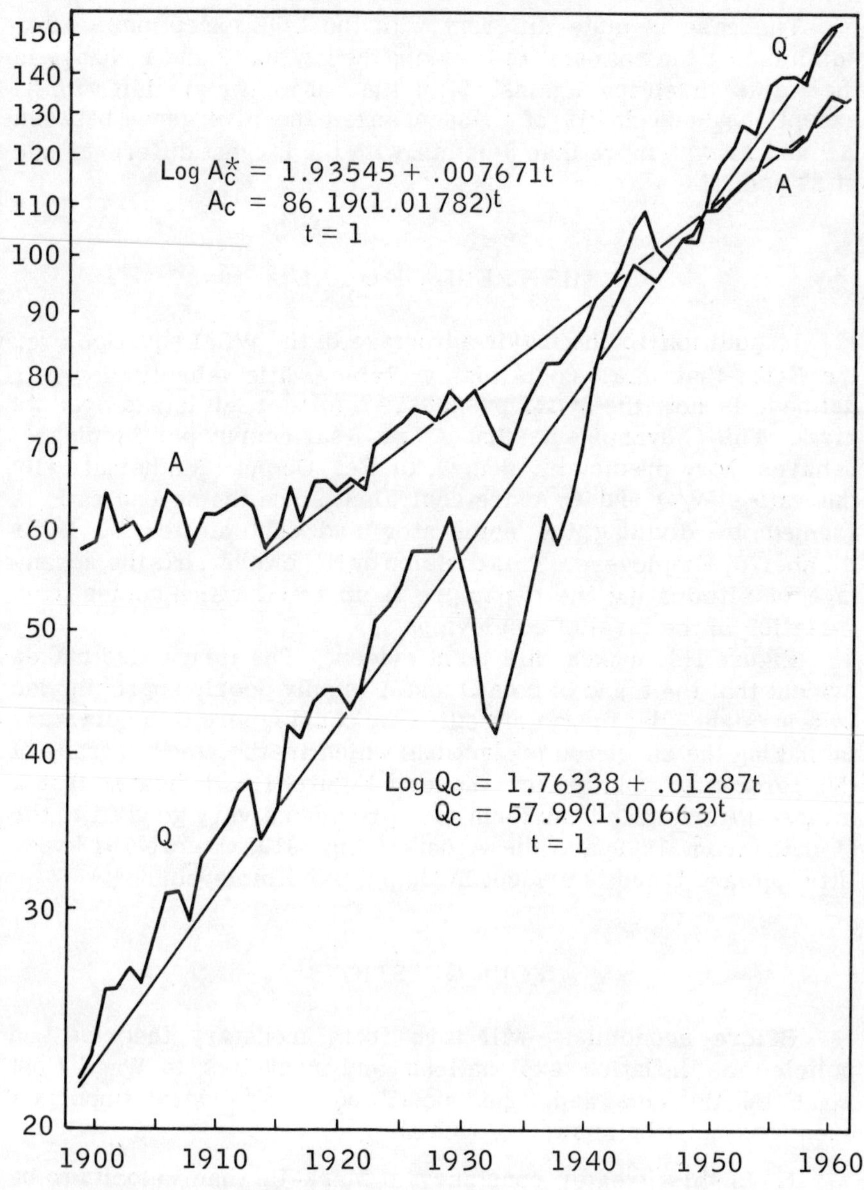

Fig. 1.5. Indices of Real Output (Q), and Average Output per Employee (A), in the United States from 1899 to 1961. (1947-49 = 100) Ratio Scale.

*Log trend of A calculated for the period 1913-1961.

The case is quite different with the EOE exceptions. After "dismissing the charges" of breaking the law that P and r change in the same direction against 5 of the cases, we are left with 31 exceptions, and in 19 of these changes the divergence between ΔP and Δr was more than 3 points, with the largest difference one of 37 points!

THE TREND OF Q AND A

In addition to the major advantage of the WCM equation over the EOE, that mark-up is highly stable, while velocity, however defined, is not, the WCM possesses a further advantage over its rival. This advantage is that A, or Real Output per Employee, behaves more predictably than Q, or Real Output. Mathematically the ratios W/Q and w/A are equivalent since the second ratio is formed by dividing the numerator and denominator by N, or Number of Employees. This division by N, however, has the advantage of eliminating the departure from trend which comes from variation in the level of employment.

Figure 1.4. makes this point evident. The figure also makes evident that the trend of both Q and A is only poorly approximated by a straight line, though of course we could ignore this curvature in making the short run projections which are the stock in trade of the forecaster and policy maker. Figure 1.5. indicates that a simple logarithmic transformation provides a very good fit to the Q data from 1899 and the A data from 1913. Before 1913 very little upward trend is evident in Output per Employee.

FOUR QUESTIONS

Before economists will turn from monetary theories and policies as inflation explanations and remedies to Wage Cost Mark-Up theories and "guidepost" policies several important questions must be answered such as:

1. Is this greater constancy of Mark-Up than Velocity to be found in other national economies?

2. Is the near constancy of Mark-Up merely the net resultant of offsetting shifts within and between industries, shifts which may not occur in the future, or is k also stable at lower levels of aggregation?

3. Is the trend in Output per Employee (A) stable at disaggregated as well as aggregated levels in various countries?

4. Can we account theoretically for the varying degrees of fluctuation in Mark-Up in different countries, time periods and levels of aggregation?

The remaining chapters of this study are attempts to answer these questions. Chapter Two deals with question 1. Chapters Three and Four attempt answers to questions 2 and 3, and Chapter Five suggests some partial answers to question 4.

Chapter 2

INTERNATIONAL COMPARISONS OF MARK-UP AND VELOCITY

Let us turn to international comparisons to see whether the generalization that mark-up is more stable than velocity, and consequently that the WCM Price Level Law will be confirmed more frequently than the EOE Law, is valid.

We can calculate Weintraub's measure of mark-up, (Business Gross Product/ Business Employee Compensation), only for those countries whose published national accounts enable us to separate the private from the public and foreign sector. Table 2.1. summarizes the countries and time periods for which k data have been derived. We shall discuss presently the use of GNP/W and NI/W ratios as "standins" for k where it is not available.

Table 2.1. Countries and Time Periods for which the Wage Cost Mark-Up Ratio (k) has been Derived.

Australia	1938-1961
Canada	1926-1964
Finland	1948-1963
India	1949-1963
Ireland	1938, 1947-1963
Netherlands	1938, 1946-1963
Norway	1930-1939, 1946-1963
Sweden	1938, 1946-1964
United Kingdom	1948-1963
United States	1899-1964

For each of the countries in Table 2.1. we can also develop a corresponding velocity index (V =BGP/M) and compare the stability of these key ratios.

Table 2.2. *Australia* 1. Outlay of Trading Enterprises, 2. Product of Financial Enterprises, 3. Business Gross Product (Z), 4. Wages of Trading Enterprises, 5. Wages of Finacial Enterprises, 6. Wages of Business, W_b, 7. Wage Cost Mark-Up (k), 8. k Index 1949 = 100. (millions of pounds)

Year	1. +	2.	= 3. (Z)	4. +	5. =	6. (W_b)	7. (k)	8.
1938	824	67	891	358	11	369	2.44	94
1939	908	82!	990	361	14	375	2.64	102
1940	949	84!	1,025	396	14	410	2.50	97
1941	1,073	86!	1,159	463	14	477	2.43	94
1942	1,189	90!	1,279	503	15	518	2.47	95
1943	1,178	95!	1,273	511	15	526	2.42	93
1944	1,145	101!	1,246	503	16	519	2.40	93
1945	1,258	105!	1,363	533	19	522	2.47	95
1946	1,464	112	1,576	617	20	637	2.47	95
1947	1,835	126	1,961	731	23	754	2.60	100
1948	2,072	140	2,212	872	26	898	2.46	95
1949	2,489	155	2,644	992	30	1,022	2.59	100
1950	3,326	174	3,500	1,241	36	1,277	2.74	106
1951	3,475	204	3,678	1,552	45	1,597	2.30	89
1952	3,771	228	3,999	1,650	49	1,650	2.35	91
1953	4,099	254	4,353	1,792	53	1,845	2.36	91
1954	4,413	281	4,694	1,947	58	2,005	2.34	90
1955	4,758	313	5,071	2,123	64	2,187	2.32	90
1956	5,149	346	5,495	2,233	70	2,303	2.39	92
1957	5,206	389	5,595	2,307	74	2,375	2.36	91
1958	5,568	413	5,981	2,383	79	2,462	2.43	94
1959	6,155	465	6,620	2,618	93	2,711	2.44	94
1960	6,464	512	6,976	2,788	99	2,887	2.42	93
1961	6,484	564	7,048	2,809	106	2,915	2.42	93

! extrapolation 1939-1945

Source: *National Income and Expenditure* 1938-1948, pp. 29-33; 1954-55, pp. 4-8; 1961-62, pp. 4-8.

AUSTRALIA

Table 2.2. sets forth the derivation of the wage cost mark-up ratio in Australia. Business Gross Product is taken as the sum of the Commonwealth Bureau of Census and Statistics categories, "Outlay (Product) of Trading Enterprises" and "Outlay of Financial Enterprises." Trading enterprises include public authority undertakings, farms, professional business, and ownership of dwellings in addition to manufacturing and distributing. Financial institutions include banks, insurance companies, retirement funds and mortgage lending societies.

Table 2.3. *Australia* Business Gross Product Index (Z), Money Supply Index (M), Gross Product Velocity Index (V). 1949 = 100

Year	(Z)	÷	(M)	=	(V)
1938	34		18		189
1939	37		19		195
1940	39		24		163
1941	44		27		163
1942	48		38		126
1943	48		48		100
1944	47		58		81
1945	52		62		84
1946	60		67		90
1947	74		70		106
1948	84		84		100
1949	100		100		100
1950	132		124		106
1951	139		142		98
1952	151		136		111
1953	165		153		108
1954	178		157		113
1955	192		159		121
1956	208		160		130
1957	212		168		126
1958	226		163		139
1959	250		171		146
1960	264		173		153
1961	267		168		159

Source: Z Index, Table 2.2.; M Index, *International Financial Statistics*, June 1953; pp. 20-21, July 1957, pp. 24-25, July 1963, pp. 34-35.

Table 2.3. sets forth the derivation of Gross Product Velocity of Circulation of Money in Australia. Figure 2.1. compares mark-up and velocity. As money supply increased more rapidly than output during the years of World War II velocity fell sharply. In the post war period M grew more slowly than Z and V rose again. In the middle to late 1950s the money supply increased but little and V rose sharply.

No such vagaries mar the path of mark-up. The largest one year change was the 17 index point fall from 1950 to 1951. This may be traced to windfall gains and losses in Australian agricultural export income at the time of the Korean War. In 1949 farm income was 448 million pounds, it rose to 756 million pounds in 1950, then fell to 441 million in 1951.[1]

[1] *National Income and Expenditure* 1954-55, Bureau of the Census and Statistics, Canberra, p. 8.

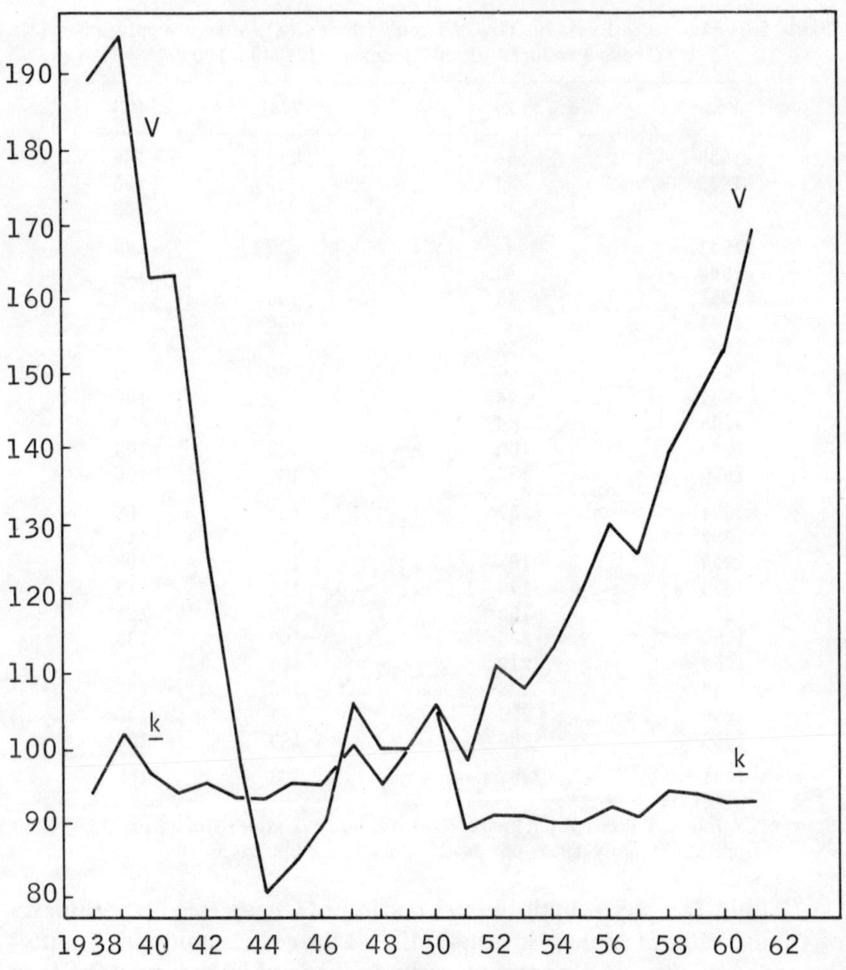

Fig. 2.1. *Australia* Mark-Up Index (k), and Gross Product Velocity Index (V), 1949 = 100.

CANADA

The excellent Canadian *National Accounts* do not set forth the Business Gross Product account explicitly, but since BGP equals Gross National Product less income originating in the personal and general government sectors the figures can be readily ascertained. Table 2.4. shows the derivation of BGP from 1926 through 1964.

Thanks to the labors of George Macesich we are provided with

Table 2.4. *Canada* 1. Gross National Product (GNP), 2. Public Administration & Defense, 3. Personal Sector, 4. Business Gross Product (Z), 5. Employee Compensation, 6. Business Employee Compensation (W_b), 7. Mark-Up Factor (k). (millions of dollars)

Year	1. GNP	- (2.	+ 3.)	= 4. Z	5.-(2. +3). W	= 6. W_b	7. k
1926	$ 5,152	$ 165	$ 139	$ 4,848	$ 2,373	$ 2,069	2.34
1927	5,549	177	143	5,229	2,513	2,193	2.38
1928	6,046	189	154	5,703	2,722	2,379	2.40
1929	6,134	205	169	5,760	2,948	2,574	2.24
1930	5,728	224	170	5,334	2,794	2,400	2.22
1931	4,699	225	151	4,323	2,416	2,040	2.12
1932	3,827	205	124	3,498	1,983	1,654	2.11
1933	3,510	183	112	3,215	1,796	1,501	2.14
1934	3,984	203	118	3,663	1,947	1,626	2.25
1935	4,315	206	121	3,988	2,088	1,761	2.26
1936	4,653	212	123	4,318	2,250	1,915	2.25
1937	5,257	227	133	4,897	2,547	2,187	2.24
1938	5,278	246	137	4,895	2,524	2,141	2.29
1939	5,636	266	137	5,233	2,633	2,230	2.35
1940	6,743	443	139	6,161	3,152	2,570	2.40
1941	8,328	644	144	7,540	3,994	3,206	2.35
1942	10,327	951	136	9,240	4,923	3,836	2.41
1943	11,088	1,260	130	9,698	5,722	4,332	2.24
1944	11,850	1,440	135	10,275	6,066	4,491	2.29
1945	11,835	1,514	147	10,174	6,154	4,493	2.26
1946	11,850	782	168	10,900	5,827	4,877	2.23
1947	13,165	554	191	12,420	6,482	5,737	2.16
1948	15,120	629	230	14,261	7,496	6,637	2.15
1949	16,343	740	262	15,341	8,115	7,113	2.16
1950	18,006	809	276	16,921	8,766	7,681	2.20
1951	21,170	995	318	19,857	10,304	8,991	2.21
1952	23,995	1,196	356	22,443	11,478	9,926	2.26
1953	25,020	1,314	396	23,310	12,419	10,709	2.18
1954	24,871	1,478	433	22,960	12,799	10,888	2.11
1955	27,132	1,590	460	25,082	13,617	11,567	2.17
1956	30,585	1,738	502	28,345	15,314	13,074	2.17
1957	31,909	1,928	551	29,430	16,494	14,015	2.10
1958	32,894	2,100	616	30,178	17,012	14,297	2.11
1959	34,915	2,201	680	32,034	17,955	15,074	2.13
1960	36,287	2,342	789	33,161	18,754	15,623	2.12
1961	37,471	2,516	903	34,052	19,546	16,127	2.11
1962	40,561	2,661	1,001	36,899	20,819	17,151	2.15
1963	43,180	2,806	1,113	34,261	22,144	18,225	2.15
1964	47,003	2,923	1,243	42,837	23,999	19,833	2.16

Source: *National Accounts*: *Income and Expenditure* 1926-1956, pp. 50-51, 56-57. 1964 pp. 27, 30.

a consistent series of the Income Velocity of Circulation (Vy) in Canada for the period 1926-1958.[2] Table 2.5. presents Macesich's Vy series with my extension to 1964, an index of this series with 1949 taken as the base year, and the k index from Table 2.4. From 1926 through 1964 the Vy index fluctuated between 138 and 88 a range of 44.2 per cent. The largest one year change of 20 index points, or 17.7% of the range, occurred in 1930-31. The Mark-Up index, in comparison, from 1926 to 1964 fluctuated between 112 and 97 or 14.3%. The largest one year change of 8 index points, or 7.7%, occurred in 1942-43.

Figure 2.2. graphs Table 2.5. As in the United States and Australia, there was a strong upsurge in Vy in Canada from World

Fig. 2.2. *Canada* Mark-Up Index (k), and Income Velocity Index (V_y), 1949 = 100

[2] George Macesich, "Determinants of Monetary Velocity in Canada, 1926-58," *The Canadian Journal of Economics and Political Science*, XXVIII (May 1962), pp. 246-47. Macesich's definition of income is Personal Disposable Income rather than National Income.

Table 2.5. *Canada* Income Velocity of Circulation (Vy) Index of Vy, Index of Mark-Up (k), 1949 = 100.

Year	Vy	Vy Index	k Index
1926	1.99	127	108
1927	2.03	129	110
1928	2.01	128	111
1929	2.02	129	104
1930	2.01	128	103
1931	1.69	108	98
1932	1.51	96	98
1933	1.38	88	99
1934	1.55	99	104
1935	1.55	99	105
1936	1.54	98	104
1937	1.63	104	104
1938	1.62	103	106
1939	1.62	103	109
1940	1.75	111	111
1941	1.85	118	109
1942	2.02	129	112
1943	1.81	115	104
1944	1.66	106	106
1945	1.50	96	105
1946	1.42	90	103
1947	1.45	92	100
1948	1.57	100	100
1949	1.57	100	100
1950	1.61	103	102
1951	1.83	117	102
1952	1.89	120	105
1953	1.89	120	101
1954	1.81	115	98
1955	1.75	111	100
1956	1.87	119	100
1957	1.87	119	97
1958	2 01	128	98
1959	2.17!	138	99
1960	2.16	138	98
1961	2.00	127	98
1962	2.10	134	100
1963	2.06	131	100
1964	2.01	128	100

Source: Vy from, Macesich, George, "Determinants of Monetary Velocity in Canada, 1926-1958," *The Canadian Journal of Economics and Political Science* XXVIII. (May 1962), pp. 246-7. k Index from Table 2.4.
! Vy from 1958 from *National Accounts: Income and Expenditure*, 1964, p. 19, and *International Financial Statistics* July 1965 p. 32.

War II lows, while k has trended slowly downward. Also, as in these other two economies, year-to-year fluctuations in k have been steadily decreasing in applitude since the war while no such dampening is discernible in the velocity indices.

FINLAND

Our data on mark-up in Finland is derived as shown in Table 2.6. From Gross Domestic Product is deducted Public Administration and Defense to obtain Business Domestic Product (Z), while wages and salaries of public service are deducted from total wages and salaries to derive Compensation of Business Employees., Table 2.7. shows the derivation of velocity for Finland and Figure 2.3. again contrasts k and V with the expected result: k shows a mild downward trend with little fluctuation about it while V has increased greatly since 1949.

Table 2.6. *Finland* 1. Gross Domestic Product at Market Price,(GDP),2. Public Administration and Defense, 3. Business Gross Product(Z),4. Total Wages and Salaries (W), 5. Government Wages and Salaries, 6. Business Wages and Salaries (W_b), 7. Wage Cost Mark-Up(k), 8. k Index. (millions of marks) 1949 = 100.

Year	1. GDP	- 2.	= 3. Z	4. W	- 5.	= 6. W_b	7. k	8.
1948	3,731	250	3,481	1,690	220	1,470	2.06	100
1949	4,008	300	3,708	1,800	240	1,560	2.06	100
1950	4,990	406	4,584	2,549	315	2,234	2.05	100
1951	7,293	513	6,780	3,599	367	3,232	2.10	102
1952	7,431	560	6,871	3,800	376	3,424	2.01	98
1953	7,506	602	6,904	3,813	406	3,407	2.03	99
1954	8,234	639	7,595	4,188	405	3,783	2.01	98
1955	9,092	746	8,346	4,705	468	4,237	1.97	96
1956	10,279	911	9,368	5,394	620	4,774	1.96	95
1957	11,092	1,023	10,069	5,698	662	5,036	2.00	97
1958	11,825	1,141	10,684	5,990	748	5,242	2.04	99
1959	12,559	1,263	11,296	6,486	838	5,648	2.00	97
1960	14,294	1,365	12,929	7,262	852	6,410	2.02	98
1961	15,901	1,516	14,385	8,096	978	7,118	2.02	98
1962	17,062	1,690	15,372	8,934	1,115	7,819	1.97	96
1963	18,599	1,952	16,647	9,947	1,350	8,597	1.94	94

Source: *The Economic Review of Finland* 1958; *Statistical Yearbook of Finland* 1960; *Yearbook of National Accounts Statistics* 1964, pp. 86-87.

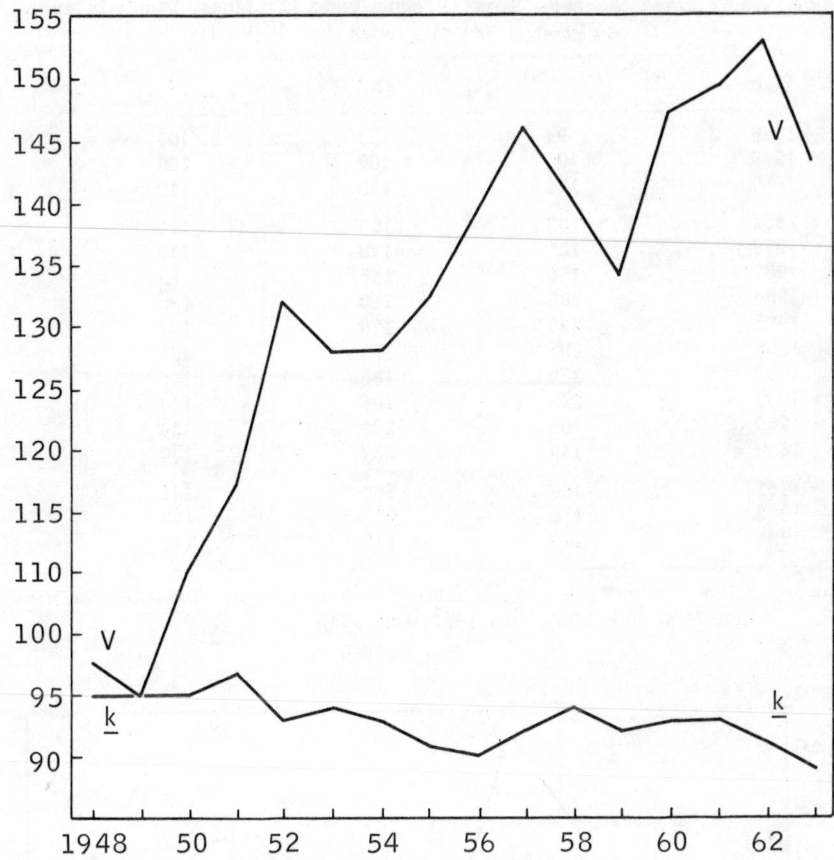

Fig. 2.3. *Finland* Mark-Up Index (k), and Gross Product Velocity Index (V), 1949 = 100.

INDIA

Sidney Weintraub's labors during his recent sojourn there have resulted in our being able to add India to the list of countries in which k can be calculated, and be shown to be far more stable than V. Table 2.8. presents the derivation of k together with V and Figure 2.4. makes the invidious comparison visible. From 1948-49 to 1962-63 the V index fluctuated between 100 and 141.5, while the k index moved between 100 and 103.6.

Table 2.7. *Finland* Business Gross Product Index (Z), Money Supply Index (M), Gross Product Velocity Index (V). 1949 = 100

Year	(Z)	÷	(M)	=	(V)
1948	94		91		103
1949	100		100		100
1950	124		113		110
1951	183		157		117
1952	185		140		132
1953	186		145		128
1954	205		160		128
1955	225		170		132
1956	253		182		139
1957	272		186		146
1958	288		206		140
1959	305		228		134
1960	349		237		147
1961	388		260		149
1962	415		272		153
1963	449		315		143

Source: Z Index from Table 2.6.; M Index from *International Financial Statistics*, June 1953, July 1957, July 1963, July 1965.

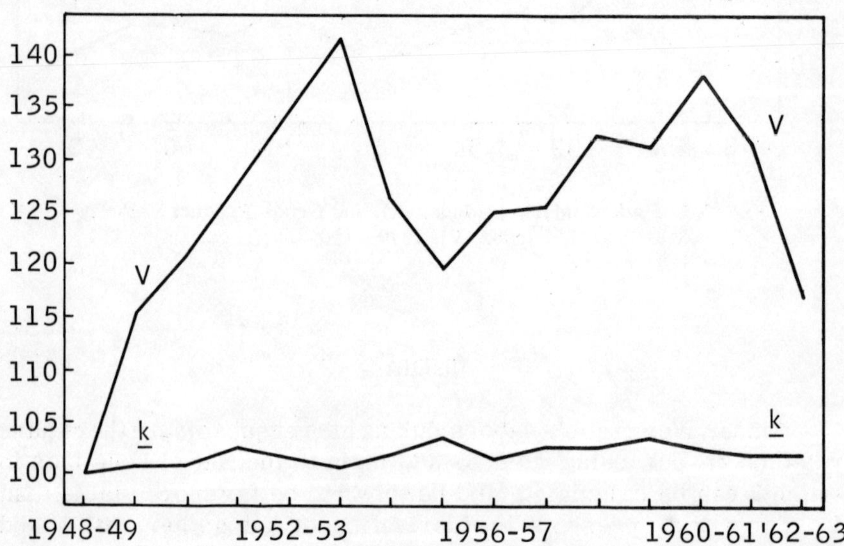

Fig. 2.4. *India* Mark-Up Index k, and Gross Product Velocity Index (V), 1948-49 = 100

Table 2.8. *India* 1. Gross National Market Product(GNMP),2. Earnings of Persons Engaged in GNMP Sector(W_b),3. Mark-Up Factor(k),4. k Index, 5. Velocity Index (V), 1948-49 = 100 (millions of rupees)

Year	1. GNMP	÷	2. W_b	=	3. k	4. k Index	5. V Index
1948-49	77, 700		31, 062		2.50	100.0	100.0
1949-50	81, 200		32, 247		2.52	100.8	115.4
1950-51	85, 300		33, 770		2.52	100.8	120.6
1951-52	90, 400		35, 318		2.56	102.4	127.7
1952-53	88, 801		34, 992		2.54	101.6	134.5
1953-54	93, 900		37, 175		2.52	100.8	141.5
1954-55	88, 499		34, 682		2.55	102.0	126.1
1955-56	92, 500		35, 743		2.59	103.6	119.8
1956-57	103, 000		40, 600		2.54	101.6	125.1
1957-58	106, 501		41, 470		2.57	102.8	125.8
1958-59	115, 700		45, 068		2.57	102.8	132.4
1959-60	120, 300		46, 527		2.59	103.6	131.3
1960-61	130, 701		51, 028		2.56	102.4	138.1
1961-62	137, 801		53, 943		2.55	102.0	131.6
1962-63	143, 500		56, 236		2.55	102.0	116.7

Source: S. Weintraub, *Growth Without Inflation*, National Council of Applied Economic Research (New Delhi 1965) pp. 61, 88.

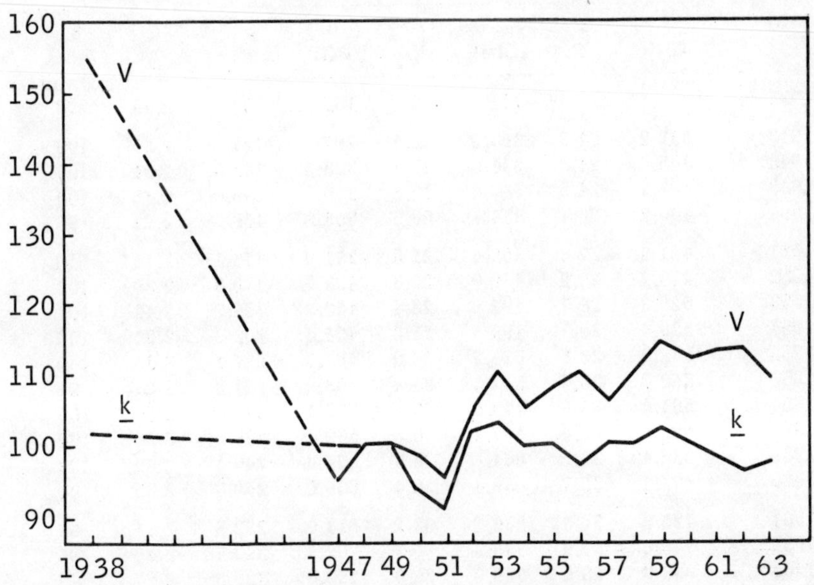

Fig. 2.5. *Ireland* Mark-Up Index k, and Gross Product Velocity Index (V), 1949 = 100

IRELAND

Mark-up statistics for Ireland in 1938 and in 1948 through 1963 are derived as shown in Table 2.9. Rest of the World and Public Administration and Defense are deducted from Gross National Product to obtain Business Gross Product and Government Wages are deducted from total wages to get Compensation of Business Employees.

Table 2.10. uses the BGP index (Z) derived from Table 2.9. together with the money supply index from the International Monetary Fund series to develop velocity in Ireland. The k and V indices are contrasted in Figure 2.5. It is notable that except for its initial fall, V in Ireland was nearly as stable as k for these years. This is the first country we have studied in which this has been the case.

Table 2.9. *Ireland* 1. Gross National Product, 2. Rest of the World, 3. Gross Domestic Product, 4. Public Administration and Defense, 5. Business Gross Product, 6. Compensation of Business Employees, 7. Mark-Up (k), 8. k Index. 1949 = 100 (millions of pounds)

Year	1. GNP -	2. F =	3. GDP -	4. G =	5. BGP ÷	6. W_b =	7. k	8. Index
1938			171	12	160	67	2.39	102
1947	332.2	24.3	307.9	16.1	291.8	124.1	2.35	100
1948	365.6	24.6	341.0	17.7	323.3	138.0	2.34	100
1949	392.7	24.9	367.8	17.3	350.5	149.0	2.35	100
1950	400.2	26.1	374.1	20.3	353.8	159.1	2.22	94
1951	421.3	27.8	393.5	21.6	371.9	173.1	2.15	91
1952	479.2	27.2	452.0	23.3	428.7	179.0	2.39	102
1953	526.3	28.7	497.6	25.4	472.2	194.2	2.43	103
1954	529.3	29.7	499.6	25.2	474.4	202.9	2.34	100
1955	552.3	28.6	523.7	26.0	497.7	212.1	2.35	100
1956	560.0	28.7	531.3	27.4	503.9	221.8	2.27	97
1957	581.4	31.9	549.5	27.4	522.1	220.9	2.36	100
1958	599.8	32.4	567.4	28.3	539.1	228.6	2.36	100
1959	636.4	31.6	604.8	28.4	576.4	240.1	2.40	102
1960	673.1	33.7	639.4	30.4	609.0	259.0	2.35	100
1961	722.3	36.1	686.2	33.2	653.0	282.8	2.31	98
1962	776.6	37.8	738.8	36.7	702.1	310.1	2.26	96
1963	838.0	39.0	789.0	39.0	750.0	330.0	2.27	97

Source: *Irish Statistical Survey* 1958; *National Income and Expenditure*, 1963.

Table 2.10. *Ireland* Business Gross Product Index (Z), Money Supply Index (M), Gross Product Velocity Index (V). (1949 = 100)

Year	(Z)	÷	(M)	=	(V)
1938	46		30		153
1947	83		87		95
1948	92		92		100
1949	100		100		100
1950	101		103		98
1951	106		112		95
1952	122		117		104
1953	135		123		110
1954	135		129		105
1955	142		131		108
1956	144		131		110
1957	149		140		106
1958	154		140		110
1959	164		144		114
1960	174		155		112
1961	186		164		113
1962	200		177		113
1963	214		197		109

Source: Z Index, Table 2.9.; M Index, *International Financial Statistics*, June 1953, July 1957, July 1965.

NETHERLANDS

Since Table 2.11. is pieced together from four sources it may contain errors from changes in concept between sources. Particularly dubious seems the initial rise in k from the 1938 level as in most countries studied prewar mark-up was higher than postwar. Attempts were made to allow for changed concepts by use of the relationship between series in years of overlap and the general picture shown is probably correct. Table 2.12. gives the derivation of Velocity in the Netherlands and Figure 2.6. brings k and V together. Again, while k moderately declines V rises and fluctuates widely.

Table 2.11. *Netherlands* 1. Gross Domestic Product (GDP), 2. Public Administration & Defense, 3. Ownership of Dwellings, 4. Business Gross Product, (Z), 5. Employee Compensation (W), 6. Business Employee Compensation (W_b), 7. Wage Cost Mark-Up (k), 8. k Index 1949 = 100. (million guilders)

Year	1. - GDP	(2.	+ 3.) =	4. Z	5. - 2. = W	6. W_b	7. k	8.
1938				3, 745		2, 106	1.80	83
1946				8, 745		4, 184	2.09	96
1947				10, 506		5, 027	2.07	95
1948				11, 722		5, 718	2.05	94
1949				13, 265		6, 085	2.18	100
1950	16, 639	1, 225	444	14, 970	8, 267	6, 749	2.22	102
1951	18, 931	1, 414	528	16, 989	8, 992	7, 578	2.24	103
1952	19, 820	1, 430	563	17, 827	9, 313	7, 883	2.26	104
1953	21, 115	1, 496	587	19, 022	10, 304	8, 394	2.27	104
1954	23, 787	1, 763	825	21, 199	11, 260	9, 497	2.23	102
1955	26, 744	1, 948	722	24, 074	13, 151	10, 656	2.26	104
1956	29, 184	2, 102	771	26, 311	14, 660	11, 879	2.21	101
1957	32, 149	2, 377	846	28, 926	16, 476	13, 180	2.19	100
1958	32, 590	2, 429	1, 008	29, 153	17, 100	13, 460	2.17	100
1959	34, 538	2, 493	1, 054	30, 991	17, 826	14, 493	2.14	98
1960	38, 686	2, 731	1, 291	34, 664	19, 886	16, 167	2.14	98
1961	40, 663	2, 976	1, 360	36, 327	21, 839	17, 755	2.05	94
1962	43, 360	3, 290	1, 430	38, 640	24, 080	19, 577	1.97	90
1963	46, 780	3, 680	1, 490	41, 610	26, 720	21, 723	1.92	88

Source: *National Accounts Studies: Netherlands*, OEEC 1951; *Statistical Yearbook of the Netherlands*, 1951-52, pp. 232-33; 1957-58, pp. 236-37; *Yearbook of National Accounts Statistics*, 1964, pp. 207-08.

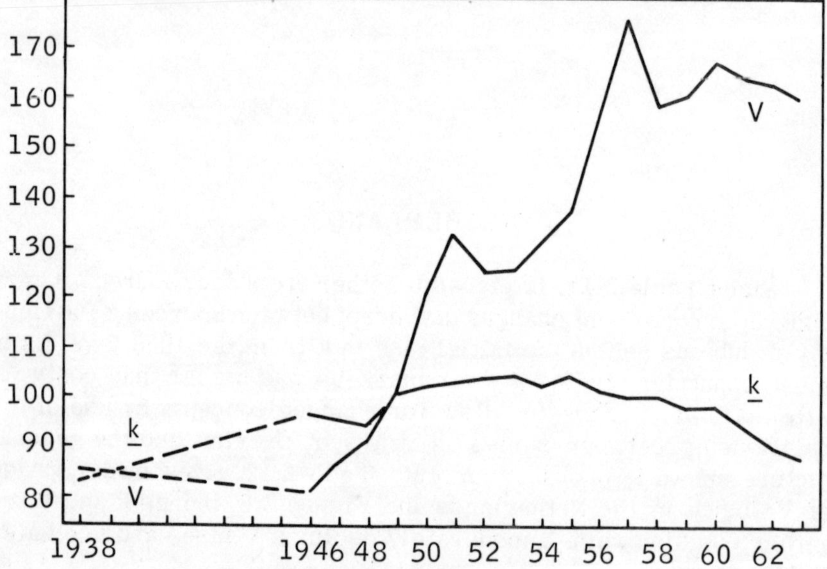

Fig. 2.6. *Netherlands* **Mark-Up Index (k), and Gross Product Velocity Index (V), 1949 = 100.**

Table 2.12. *Netherlands* Gross Product Index (Z), Money Supply Index (M), and Gross Product Velocity Index (V). (1949 = 100)

Year	(Z)	÷	(M)	=	(V)
1938	29		34		85
1946	66		82		80
1947	79		92		86
1948	88		97		91
1949	100		100		100
1950	113		94		120
1951	128		97		132
1952	134		107		125
1953	143		114		125
1954	160		122		131
1955	181		132		137
1956	198		127		156
1957	218		124		176
1958	220		139		158
1959	234		146		160
1960	261		156		167
1961	274		167		164
1962	291		179		163
1963	314		196		160

Source: Z Index, Table 2.11.; M Index, *International Financial Statistics*, June 1953, July 1957, July 1965.

NORWAY

The derivation of k in Norway for 1930-1939 and 1946-1963 is given in Table 2.13. Similarly to the U. S., the contribution of the government sector is regarded as entirely labor income. Therefore this sector is deducted from both Gross Domestic Product and total Labor Income in developing Business Domestic Product and Income of Business Employees. Similarly, Wages Paid Domestic Servants is deducted from GDP and Labor Income.

Unfortunately, our IMF series on money supply commences only in 1937. Table 2.14. presents the derivation of V in Norway and Figure 2.7. brings together k and V. Velocity nose dived between the prewar and postwar period and then climbed steeply after World War II. Mark-up showed only a slight downward trend with small fluctuations around it.

Table 2.13. *Norway* 1. Gross Domestic Product (GDP), 2. Government Product, 3. Wages Paid Domestic Servants, 4. Business Gross Product (Z), 5. Total Labor Income (W), 6. Income of Business Employees (W_b), 7. Mark-Up (k), 8. k Index. 1949 = 100 (million kroner)

Year	1.	2.	3.	4.	5.	6.	7.	8.
1930	4,411	89	98	4,224	1,734	1,547	2.73	113
1931	3,874	83	91	3,700	1,547	1,373	2.69	111
1932	3,891	75	87	3,729	1,540	1,379	2.70	112
1933	3,892	70	84	3,738	1,536	1,382	2.70	112
1934	4,092	72	84	3,936	1,591	1,435	2.74	113
1935	4,386	79	87	4,220	1,686	1,520	2.78	115
1936	4,875	86	91	4,698	1,859	1,684	2.79	115
1937	5,609	87	98	5,424	2,094	1,910	2.84	117
1938	5,857	91	104	5,662	2,297	2,103	2.69	111
1939	6,285	125	109	6,051	2,490	2,256	2.68	111
1946	10,760	404	174	10,182	4,698	4,120	2.47	102
1947	12,667	368	181	12,118	5,467	4,918	2.46	102
1948	13,897	386	188	13,323	6,077	5,503	2.42	100
1949	14,917	429	199	14,289	6,546	5,918	2.42	100
1950	16,425	429	195	15,801	7,035	6,411	2.46	102
1951	20,456	533	206	19,717	8,021	7,282	2.71	112
1952	22,564	660	210	21,694	9,221	8,351	2.60	107
1953	22,884	733	209	21,942	9,838	8,896	2.47	102
1954	24,806	807	215	23,784	10,556	9,534	2.49	103
1955	26,376	893	215	25,268	11,309	10,201	2.48	102
1956	29,747	1,006	216	28,525	12,399	11,177	2.55	105
1957	31,775	1,087	210	30,478	13,365	12,068	2.53	105
1958	31,919	1,154	216	30,549	14,170	12,800	2.39	99
1959	33,946	1,250	219	32,477	15,182	13,713	2.37	98
1960	36,101	1,315	219	34,567	16,084	14,550	2.38	98
1961	39,245	1,375	226	37,644	17,509	15,908	2.37	98
1962	42,148	1,547	226	40,375	19,484	17,711	2.28	94
1963	44,821	1,684	233	42,904	20,867	18,950	2.26	93

Source: *National Accounts* 1930-1939, *and* 1946-1951; 1938 *and* 1946-1958 (mimeographed); 1949-1962 (mimeographed); *Yearbook of National Accounts Statistics* 1964.

SWEDEN

Table 2.15. sets forth the derivation of k in Sweden in 1938 and in 1946-1964. From Gross National Product is deducted Government and Local Authorities Wages and Salaries, and Net Income

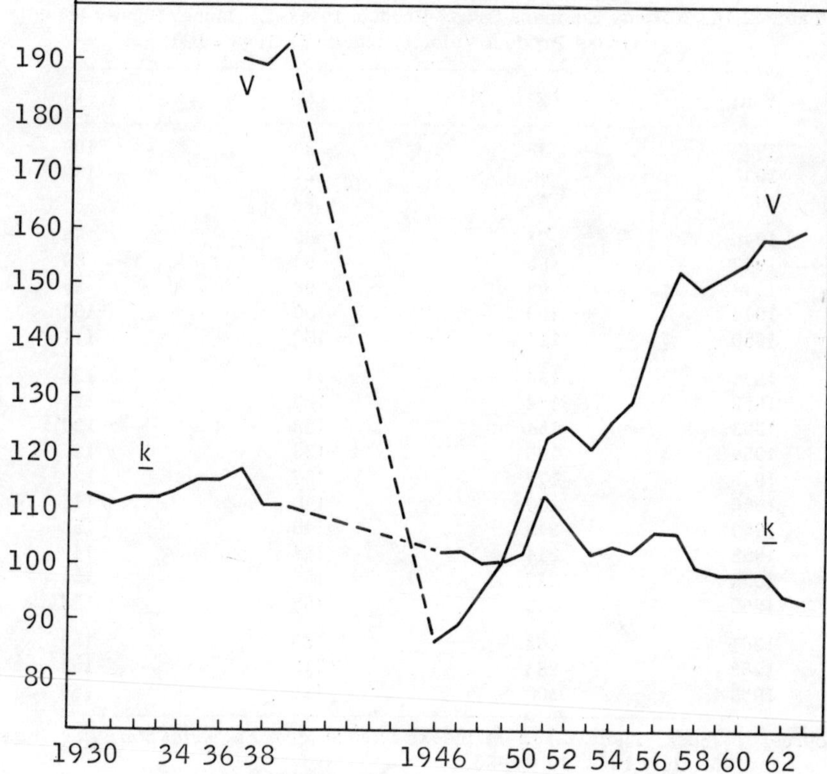

Fig. 2.7. *Norway* Mark-Up Index k, and Gross Product Velocity Index (V), 1949 = 100

from Abroad, to obtain Business Gross Product. Similarly, Government and Local Authority Wages and Salaries are deducted to obtain Business Compensation.

A change in statistics supplied by Sweden made it necessary to extrapolate Government and Local Authority Wages and Salaries from 1959 to 1964. Since, however, *The Swedish Economy* contains a "Consumption Index" for these sectors it was merely assumed that their employee compensation rose at the same rate as did their consumption. Any distortion imparted to the figures should be small.

Table 2.16. shows the derivation of velocity in Sweden and Figure 2.8. contrasts it with mark-up. Again, k is clearly more stable, but its superiority is less marked than in many countries studied.

Table 2.14. *Norway* Business Gross Product Index (Z), Money Supply Index (M), Gross Product Velocity Index (V). 1949 = 100

Year	(Z)	÷	(M)	=	(V)
1937	38		20		190
1938	40		21		189
1939	42		22		193
1946	71		83		86
1947	85		95		89
1948	93		98		95
1949	100		100		100
1950	111		100		111
1951	138		113		122
1952	152		123		124
1953	154		128		120
1954	166		133		125
1955	177		137		129
1956	200		140		143
1957	213		140		152
1958	214		144		149
1959	227		150		151
1960	242		158		153
1961	263		166		158
1962	283		179		158
1963	300		189		159

Source: Z Index, Table 2.13.; M Index, *International Financial Statistics*, June 1953, July 1957, July 1965.

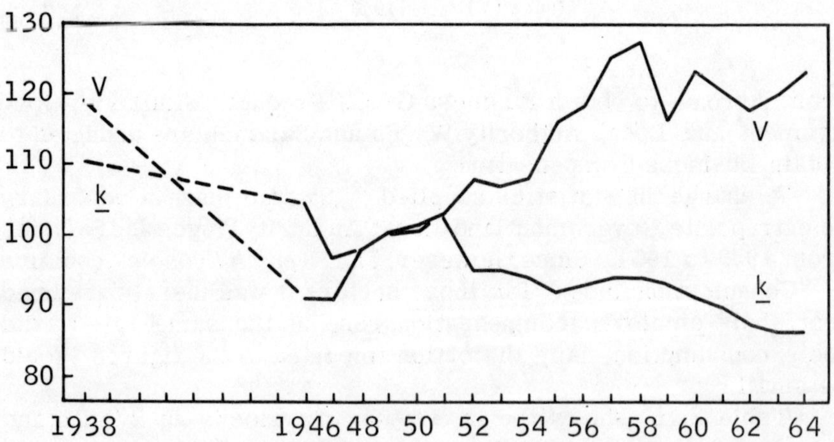

Fig. 2.8. *Sweden* Mark-Up Index k, and Gross Product Velocity Index V. 1949 = 100

Table 2.15. *Sweden* 1. Gross National Product (GNP), 2. Government Wages and Salaries, 3. Local Authorities Wages and Salaries, 4. Net Income from Abroad, 5. Business Gross Product (Z), 6. Wages and Salaries (W), 7. Compensation of Business Employees (W_b), Mark-Up (k), 9. k Index 1949 = 100 (millions of kroner)

Year	1. -	(2. +	3. +	4.) =	5. (BGP)	6. - (2 + 3) = (W)	7. (W_b)	8. k	9. Index
1938	12,713	316	457	43	11,897	5,613	4,840	2.46	111
1946	23,131	838	803	52	21,438	11,102	9,461	2.27	105
1947	24,818	910	997	145	22,766	12,688	10,781	2.11	97
1948	27,839	1,011	1,151	108	25,569	14,162	12,000	2.13	98
1949	29,223	1,031	1,227	8	26,957	14,676	12,418	2.17	100
1950	31,171	1,082	1,287	14	28,788	15,384	13,015	2.21	102
1951	38,145	1,299	1,594	52	35,200	18,653	15,760	2.23	103
1952	41,671	1,597	1,986	70	38,018	21,992	18,409	2.04	95
1953	42,990	1,691	2,119	65	39,115	22,844	19,034	2.06	95
1954	45,140	1,704	2,284	95	41,057	24,263	20,275	2.03	94
1955	48,983	1,823	2,599	90	44,471	26,607	22,185	2.00	92
1956	53,154	1,950	2,841	130	48,233	28,612	23,821	2.02	93
1957	57,453	2,152	3,181	152	51,968	30,812	25,179	2.04	94
1958	59,581	2,324	3,425	152	53,680	31,965	26,216	2.05	94
1959	63,355	2,484	3,661	142	57,068	34,432	28,287	2.02	93
1960	68,808	2,658	3,990	152	62,008	38,050	31,402	1.97	91
1961	75,087	2,931	4,359	146	67,653	42,030	34,742	1.95	90
1962	81,302	3,328	4,942	194	72,838	47,021	38,751	1.88	87
1963	88,147	3,701	5,711	184	78,551	51,864	42,452	1.86	86
1964	97,052	4,099	6,224	194	86,531	56,629	46,306	1.87	86

Source: *The Swedish Economy* 1964, p. 542. Columns 2 and 3 from 1959 are extrapolations which assume that wages and salaries of Government and Local authorities grew as did their consumption index. Years prior to 1959 from *Konjunktur Laget Hosten* 1959, pp. 8, 44-50.

UNITED KINGDOM

Table 2.17. presents the mark-up series from 1948-1963. The U. K. Central Statistics Office account Gross Product of "Total Production and Trade" is a close equivalent of the U. S. BGP account and is therefore used as "Z". Again in Britain we see mark-up's characteristic slight downward trend.

Table 2.18. gives the derivation of our corresponding velocity measure in the U. K. and Figure 2.9. presents the k and V indices together. Again the near constancy of mark-up is in sharp contrast to the strong upsurge in velocity from early postwar lows, as Z grew more rapidly than M from the invocation of "tight money" to banish the inflationary spector.

Table 2.16. *Sweden* Business Gross Product Index (Z), Money Supply Index (M), Gross Product Velocity Index (V). 1949 = 100

Year	(Z)	÷	(M)	=	(V)
1938	44		37		119
1946	80		88		91
1947	84		92		91
1948	95		97		98
1949	100		100		100
1950	107		106		101
1951	131		127		103
1952	143		132		108
1953	147		138		107
1954	152		141		108
1955	165		142		116
1956	179		152		118
1957	193		155		125
1958	199		157		127
1959	212		182		116
1960	233		190		123
1961	251		209		120
1962	270		228		118
1963	291		242		120
1964	321		261		123

Source: Z Index, Table 2.15.; M Index, *International Financial Statistics*.

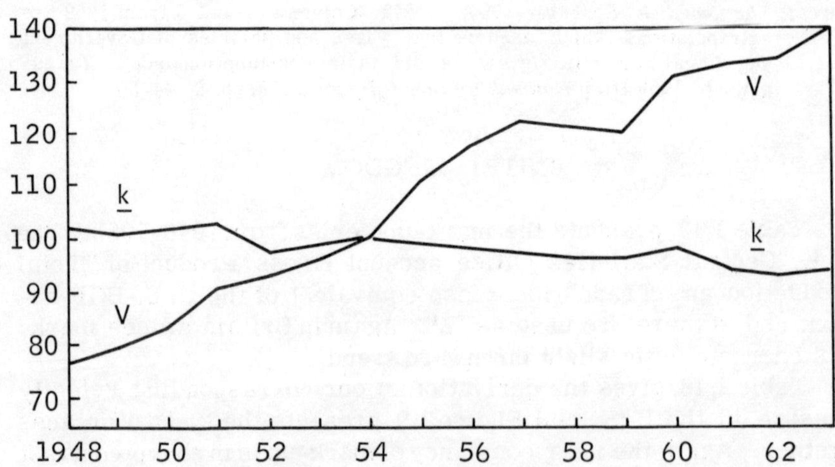

Fig. 2.9. *United Kingdom* Mark-Up Index (k), and Gross Product Velocity Index (V), 1954 = 100.

Table 2.17. *United Kingdom* Gross Product of Total Production and Trade (Z), Compensation of Business Employees (W_b), Mark-Up Factor (k), k Index 1954 = 100. (million pounds)

Year	(Z)	÷	(W_b)	=	k	Index k
1948	9,111		5,629		1.62	104
1949	9,667		6,045		1.60	103
1950	10,371		6,371		1.63	104
1951	11,527		7,069		1.63	104
1952	11,747		7,586		1.55	99
1953	12,447		8,022		1.55	99
1954	13,413		8,591		1.56	100
1955	14,683		9,472		1.55	99
1956	15,722		10,316		1.52	97
1957	16,504		10,885		1.52	97
1958	16,880		11,286		1.50	96
1959	17,890		11,740		1.52	97
1960	19,324		12,683		1.52	97
1961	20,560		13,799		1.49	96
1962	21,405		14,561		1.47	94
1963	22,526		15,220		1.48	95

Source: *National Income and Expenditure* 1959, 1961, pp. 6, 11-12, 1964, pp. 9, 11.

Table 2.18. *United Kingdom* Gross Product Index (Z), Money Supply Index (M), and Gross Product Velocity Index (V). (1954 = 100)

Year	(Z)	÷	(M)	=	(V)
1948	68		90		76
1948	72		91		79
1950	77		93		83
1951	86		94		91
1952	88		95		93
1953	93		97		96
1954	100		100		100
1955	109		98		111
1956	117		99		118
1957	123		101		122
1958	125		103		121
1959	131		109		120
1960	145		111		131
1961	153		115		133
1962	160		119		134
1963	168		121		139

Source: Z Index, Table 2.17.; M Index, *International Financial Statistics*, June 1953, July 1957, July 1965.

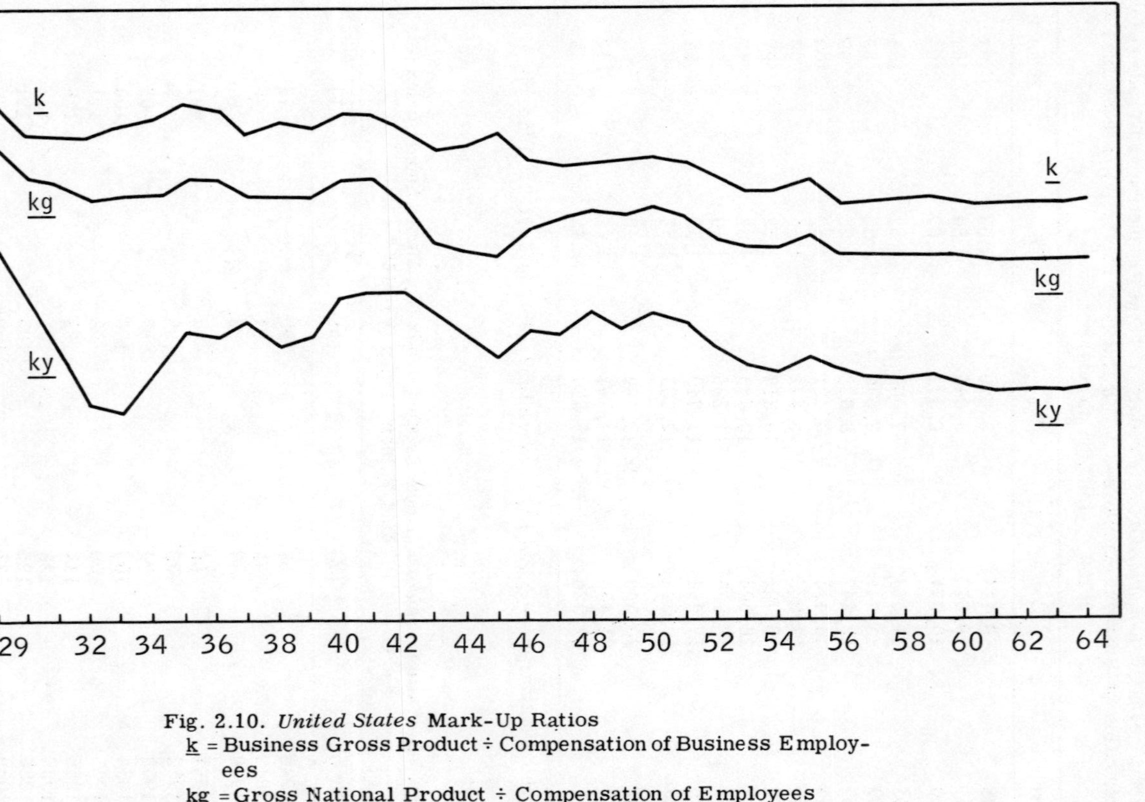

Fig. 2.10. *United States* Mark-Up Ratios
k = Business Gross Product ÷ Compensation of Business Employees
kg = Gross National Product ÷ Compensation of Employees
ky = National Income ÷ Compensation of Employees

MARK-UP IN GROSS NATIONAL PRODUCT AND NATIONAL INCOME

A major problem in carrying out this study is that most countries do not use the sector accounts system which enable one to study Business Gross Product relative to Compensation of Business Employees. Most countries which report national income statistics today follow the United Nations system.[3] This system enables us to get comparable data on Gross National Product, Gross Domestic Product, National Income, and Employee Compensation. From these we can compute what we shall call kg, (Gross National Product, or Gross Domestic Product/Employee Compensation) and ky, (National Income/Employee Compensation, *i.e.* the reciprocal of the "wage share"), but can not study the private sector only.

The question therefore becomes, how much can we learn about the fluctuations in k, which we cannot study in many countries, by studying kg and ky? Perhaps the best way to answer it is to examine k, kg, and ky in countries where we can calculate all three. Let us examine all three in the United States, Canada, and Australia where we have fairly long series with which to work.

THE UNITED STATES

Table 2.19. sets forth k, kg, and ky in the U. S. from 1929 to 1964, and Figure 2.10. is a semi-logarithmic graph of these series. The figure indicates that in the U. S. kg would have been a very good "standin" for k in all but the years of World War II. In these years the 100 per cent wages and salaries government sector expanded markedly causing a sag in kg not affecting k itself. On the other hand, ky had a marked cyclical movement absent from the gross product ratios and considerably greater year-to-year fluctuation.

CANADA

The k, kg, and ky ratios for Canada are presented for the period 1926-1964 in Table 2.20. and graphed in Figure 2.11. As in

[3] *A System of National Accounts and Supporting Tables, Series F, No.* 2, United Nations, New York.

Table 2.19. *United States* 1. The k Ratio (BGP ÷ W_b), 2. The kg Ratio (GNP ÷ W), 3. The ky Ratio (NI ÷ W).

Year	1. (k)	2. (kg)	3. (ky)
1929	2.16	2.04	1.75
1930	2.07	1.95	1.64
1931	2.07	1.92	1.51
1932	2.07	1.88	1.39
1933	2.10	1.89	1.37
1934	2.11	1.89	1.45
1935	2.16	1.94	1.54
1936	2.15	1.93	1.53
1937	2.08	1.89	1.56
1938	2.11	1.89	1.51
1939	2.09	1.89	1.53
1940	2.13	1.93	1.62
1941	2.13	1.94	1.64
1942	2.08	1.87	1.64
1943	2.02	1.76	1.58
1944	2.04	1.74	1.53
1945	2.07	1.73	1.48
1946	1.99	1.79	1.54
1947	1.97	1.82	1.54
1948	1.98	1.84	1.59
1949	1.99	1.83	1.55
1950	2.00	1.85	1.58
1951	1.99	1.82	1.56
1952	1.94	1.77	1.50
1953	1.90	1.75	1.46
1954	1.90	1.75	1.45
1955	1.93	1.78	1.48
1956	1.86	1.73	1.45
1957	1.87	1.73	1.43
1958	1.88	1.73	1.43
1959	1.88	1.73	1.44
1960	1.86	1.72	1.42
1961	1.87	1.72	1.41
1962	1.87	1.72	1.41
1963	1.87	1.72	1.41
1964	1.88	1.72	1.42

Source: 1. Column 3 Table 1.1.
2. & 3. *National Income* 1954, pp. 162-163, 168-169; *Survey of Current Business*, July 1962 pp. 6-7; July 1964 p. 8; July 1965 p. 4.

Table 2.20. *Canada* 1. The k Ratio (BGP ÷ W_b), 2. The kg Ratio (GNP ÷ W), 3. The ky Ratio (NI ÷ W).

Year	1. (k)	2. (kg)	3. (ky)
1926	2.34	2.17	1.75
1927	2.38	2.21	1.74
1928	2.40	2.22	1.74
1929	2.24	2.08	1.60
1930	2.22	2.05	1.58
1931	2.12	1.94	1.40
1932	2.11	1.93	1.34
1933	2.14	1.95	1.32
1934	2.25	2.05	1.44
1935	2.26	2.07	1.49
1936	2.25	2.07	1.50
1937	2.24	2.06	1.50
1938	2.29	2.09	1.59
1939	2.35	2.14	1.63
1940	2.40	2.14	1.65
1941	2.35	2.09	1.66
1942	2.41	2.10	1.71
1943	2.24	1.94	1.61
1944	2.29	1.95	1.63
1945	2.26	1.92	1.59
1946	2.23	2.03	1.63
1947	2.16	2.03	1.62
1948	2.15	2.02	1.62
1949	2.16	2.01	1.61
1950	2.20	2.05	1.64
1951	2.21	2.05	1.64
1952	2.26	2.09	1.66
1953	2.18	2.01	1.59
1954	2.11	1.94	1.53
1955	2.17	1.99	1.57
1956	2.17	2.00	1.56
1957	2.18	2.00	1.50
1958	2.19	1.99	1.52
1959	2.20	2.00	1.52
1960	2.20	1.99	1.51
1961	2.18	1.97	1.49
1962	2.22	2.00	1.52
1963	2.22	2.00	1.51
1964	2.22	2.01	1.50

Source: *National Accounts*: *Income and Expenditure* 1926-1956, pp. 50-51, 56-57. 1962, pp. 26, 38. 1964, 18, 27.

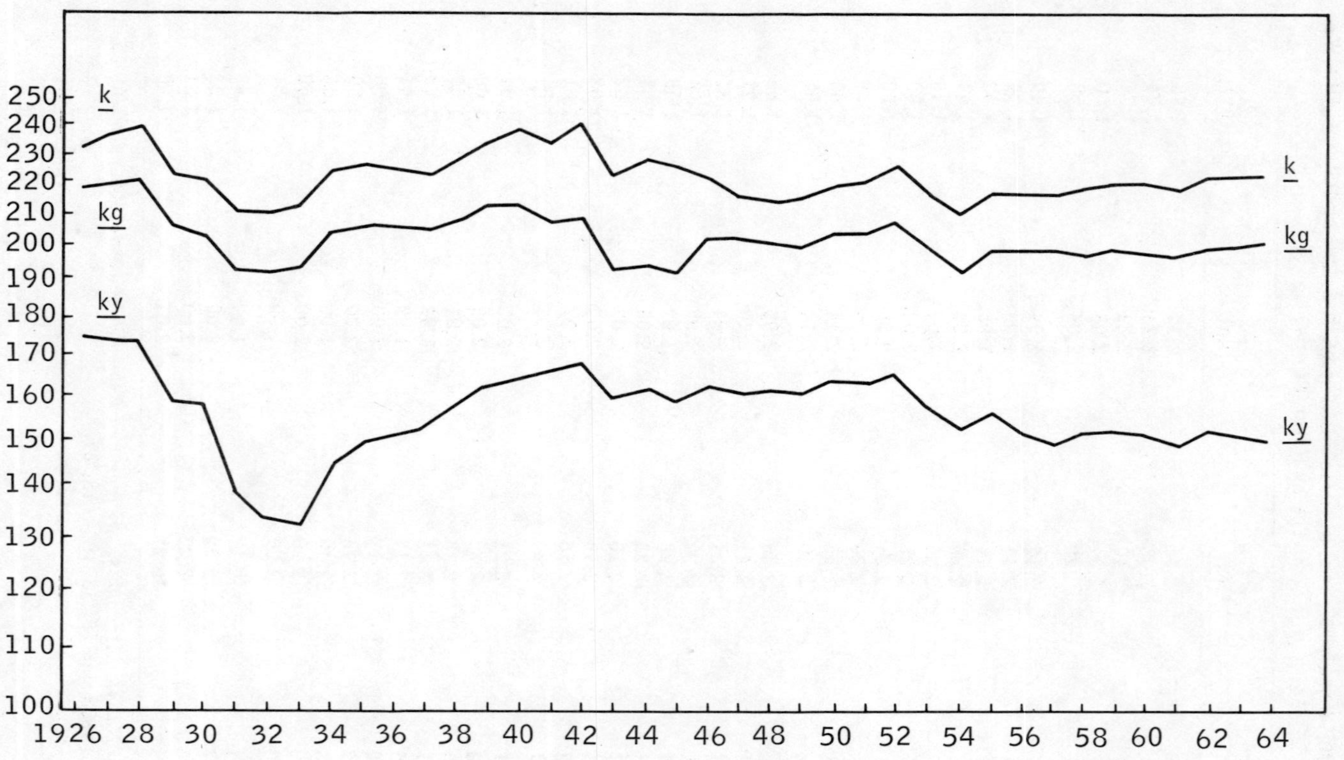

Fig. 2.11. *Canada* Mark-Up Ratios. $\underline{k} = BGP \div \overline{W}b$, $\underline{kg} = GNP \div W$, $\underline{ky} = NI \div \overline{W}$.

the United States, we see that kg fluctuates very much as does k except for the World War II period. We also see that ky fell more drastically in the great depression and then rose more than did either of the gross product ratios. Furthermore, the downward trend of ky after the war is greater than that in k and kg. Except for the greater variability of these ratios than their equivalent in the United States, their fluctuations are quite synchronous with the U. S. ratios.

AUSTRALIA

Finally, Table 2.21. sets forth the derivation of k, kg, and ky in Australia from 1938 to 1961 and Figure 2.12. compares the three ratios. Here again we see the wartime fall in kg and ky not affecting business mark-up and the greater downward trend in ky after the war. Again, except for wartime, kg is a good "standin" for k while ky is considerably more variable.

We may conclude then, on the basis of the data from the United States, Canada, and Australia, that we may use kg in place of k in countries where k may not be calculated with only a small increase in variability. Let us continue the study of mark-up and velocity by means of kg and equivalent Vg, (Vg =GNP/M, or Gross Domestic Product/M).

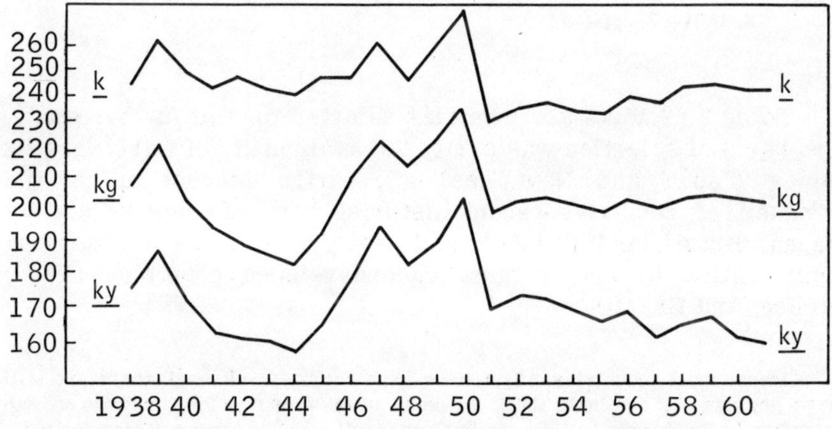

Fig. 2.12. Mark-Up Ratios in Australia 1938-1961.

Table 2.21. *Australia* 1. Gross National Product (GNP), 2. National Income (NI), 3. Employee Compensation (W) 4. Gross National Product Mark-Up (kg), 5. National Income Mark-Up (ky), 1938-1961. (millions of pounds)

Year	1.	2.	3.	4.	5.
1938	912	780	445	2.07	1.75
1939	1, 025	877	448	2.22	1.87
1940	1, 110	949	478	2.03	1.72
1941	1, 283	1, 099	548	1.95	1.64
1942	1, 458	1, 253	588	1.88	1.62
1943	1, 496	1, 309	607	1.85	1.61
1944	1, 455	1, 274	600	1.83	1.58
1945	1, 471	1, 284	632	1.92	1.65
1946	1, 624	1, 383	776	2.09	1.78
1947	2, 013	1, 759	908	2.23	1.94
1948	2, 283	1, 966	1, 081	2.14	1.82
1949	2, 729	2, 318	1, 230	2.22	1.88
1950	3, 633	3, 141	1, 546	2.30	2.03
1951	3, 869	3, 303	1, 943	1.99	1.70
1952	4, 213	3, 617	2, 090	2.02	1.73
1953	4, 561	3, 871	2, 252	2.04	1.72
1954	4, 918	4, 137	2, 449	2.01	1.69
1955	5, 321	4, 442	2, 675	1.99	1.67
1956	5, 754	4, 772	2, 828	2.02	1.68
1957	5, 852	4, 735	2, 919	2.00	1.63
1958	6, 231	5, 047	3, 041	2.03	1.65
1959	6, 894	5, 592	3, 352	2.04	1.67
1960	7, 255	5, 864	3, 573	2.03	1.61
1961	7, 327	5, 932	3, 646	2.01	1.60

Source: *National Income and Expenditure* 1938-1948, pp.29-33; 1954-1955, pp. 4-8; 1961-62, pp. 4-8.

Table 2.22. lists six countries selected for this further study. The basis of selection was partly the availability of fairly long kg series (Japan and New Zealand), partly interest in how the stresses of countries recent histories have affected kg and Vg (Japan, Brazil, and France), and partly in interest in observing these ratios in low income, underdeveloped countries (Peru, Greece, and Brazil).[4]

[4]Many more countries might have been included, although there are still large gaps in the available data. In many of the less developed nations we can calculate kg back only to 1951, as in Greece. If we wish longer series for most countries we must be content with ky, which we have just seen fluctuates much more than k.

Table 2.22. Selected Countries and Time Periods for Comparison of the kg and Vg Ratios

Brazil	1947-1963	Japan	1930-1944, 1946-1963
France	1938, 1946-1963	New Zealand	1938-1963
Greece	1951-1963	Peru	1942-1959

BRAZIL

As is well known, Brazil has in recent decades achieved a high growth in real output accompanied by a rapid inflation. How has the distribution of income and velocity of circulation reacted to this situation? Table 2.23. gives data necessary to calculate kg for the period 1947-1960 and Vg from 1947 to 1963. Figure 2.13. makes the comparison visual. It is interesting that kg and Vg both were quite stable during these years, and the superiority of kg in this respect was rather slight.

Table 2.23. *Brazil* Gross Domestic Product (GDP), Employee Compensation (W), Mark-Up (kg), kg Index, GDP Index, Money Supply Index (M), Velocity Index (Vg). 1953 = 100 (billions of cruzeiros)

Year	GDP ÷	W =	kg	kg Index	GDP Index ÷	M Index =	Vg Index
1947	165.6	58.4	2.84	99	38.2	38	100
1948	187.6	67.5	2.78	97	43.3	40	108
1949	215.5	78.2	2.76	96	49.7	47	106
1950	254.1	91.6	2.77	97	58.6	63	93
1951	309.4	105.0	2.95	103	71.4	73	98
1952	354.0	124.9	2.83	99	81.7	84	97
1953	433.4	150.9	2.87	100	100	100	100
1954	560.4	188.7	2.97	104	129	122	106
1955	697.1	254.4	2.72	95	161	143	113
1956	887.8	348.3	2.54	89	205	175	117
1957	1,056.5	414.6	2.67	93	267	234	114
1958	1,310.0	501.4	2.61	91	302	285	106
1959	1,788.9	665.1	2.69	94	413	403	102
1960	2,385.6	885.3	2.70	94	551	558	98
1961	3,449.6				796	841	95
1962	5,419.3				1,258	1,374	92
1963	9,451.3				2,181	2,254	97

Source: *Statistics of National Income and Expenditure*, p. 20; *Yearbook of National Accounts Statistics*, 1958, pp. 27-28, 1964 p. 30; *Statistical Yearbook* 1953, p. 484, 1962, p. 523; *International Financial Statistics*, July 1965, p. 32.

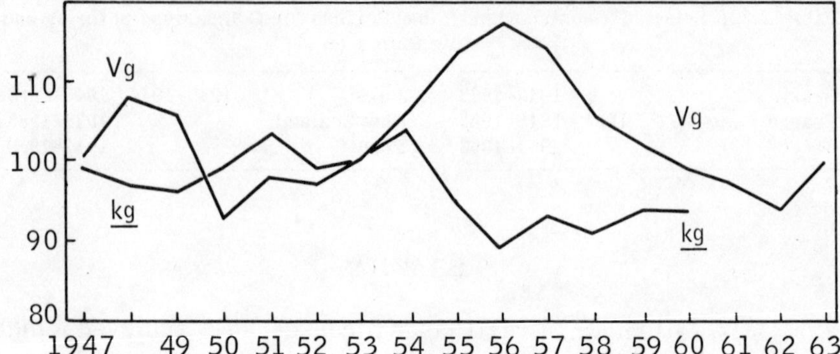

Fig. 2.13. *Brazil* Mark-Up Index (kg), and Gross Product Velocity Index (Vg). (1953 = 100)

Table 2.24. *France* Gross National Product (GNP), Employee Compensation (W), Mark-Up (kg), kg Index, GNP Index, Money Supply Index (M), Velocity Index (Vg). 1953 = 100 (billions of new francs)

Year	GNP	÷ W	kg	kg Index	GNP Index	÷ M Index	= V Index
1938	4.46	1.84	2.42	103	2.99	4.1	73
1946	32.7	11.5	2.85	122	21.9	29.1	75
1947	41.3	16.1	2.54	109	27.6	36.2	76
1949	86.6	35.8	2.42	103	58.0	58.4	99
1950	100.8	40.3	2.50	105	66.3	67.4	98
1951	122.3	51.0	2.40	101	80.5	79.4	101
1952	145.4	61.4	2.37	100	95.7	90	106
1953	151.9	64.1	2.37	100	100	100	100
1954	159.9	69.6	2.30	97	105	114	92
1955	172.2	75.6	2.28	96	113	128	88
1956	191.3	84.1	2.27	96	126	141	89
1957	213.0	95.0	2.24	95	140	153	92
1958	244.7	109.2	2.24	95	161	163	99
1959	267.4	120.7	2.22	94	176	181	97
1960	296.2	137.3	2.24	95	195	205	95
1961	319.7	147.5	2.17	92	210	238	88
1962	356.3	165.3	2.16	91	235	282	83
1963	391.8	186.0	2.11	89	259	323	80

Source: *Annuaire Statistique de la France Retrospectif* 1961, p. 356; *Statistical Yearbook* 1953, p. 407; *Yearbook of National Accounts Statistics* 1964, pp. 92, 94; *International Financial Statistics*, July 1965 p. 32.

FRANCE

Table 2.24. presents the data to calculate mark-up and velocity in France in 1938, 1946-1947, and 1949-1963. Figure 2.14. graphs the kg and Vg indices. Mark-Up in France, which has a pronounced downward trend, is clearly more stable about that trend than is Vg after 1949. In the immediate postwar years both indices girated fairly widely.

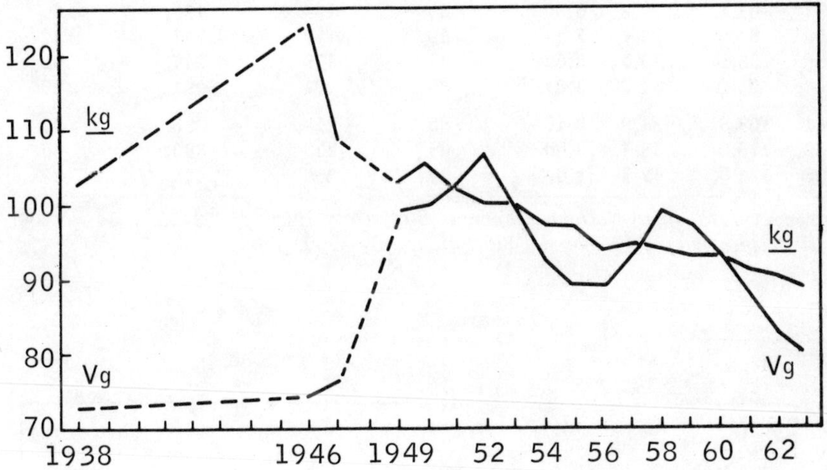

Fig. 2.14. *France* Mark-Up Index (kg), and Gross Product Velocity Index (Vg) 1938-1963. 1953 = 100

GREECE

The data for Greece from 1951 through 1963 are presented in Table 2.25. and sketched in Figure 2.15. Both kg and Vg had pronounced downward trends during this period as Employee Compensation and money supply both increased more rapidly than total output. Mark-up decreased less and with less oscilation than velocity. It is unfortunate that the series are too short to tell whether these downward movements are part of a long trend or a retreat from Korean War highs.

Table 2.25. *Greece* Gross Domestic Product (GDP), Employee Compensation (W), Mark-Up (kg), Mark-Up Index, Money Supply Index (M), Gross Product Velocity Index (Vg). 1953 = 100 (billions of drachmas)

Year	GDP	÷ W =	kg	kg Index	GDP Index	÷ M Index	= Vg Index
1951	35.1				70	66	106
1952	37.2				75	71	106
1953	49.8	14.2	3.51	100	100	100	100
1954	56.6	16.3	3.47	99	114	113	101
1955	65.6	21.1	3.11	89	132	143	92
1956	76.2	25.0	3.05	87	153	161	95
1957	81.7	27.2	3.00	85	164	193	85
1958	85.9	27.4	3.14	89	172	211	82
1959	88.9	29.0	3.07	87	179	247	72
1960	95.2	31.6	3.01	86	191	291	66
1961	108.3	34.9	3.10	88	217	335	65
1962	116.0	38.7	3.00	85	233	386	60
1963	128.3	42.2	3.04	87	258	449	57

Source: *Yearbook of National Accounts Statistics*, 1958, pp. 92-93, 1964, p. 109; *International Financial Statistics*, July 1965, p. 32.

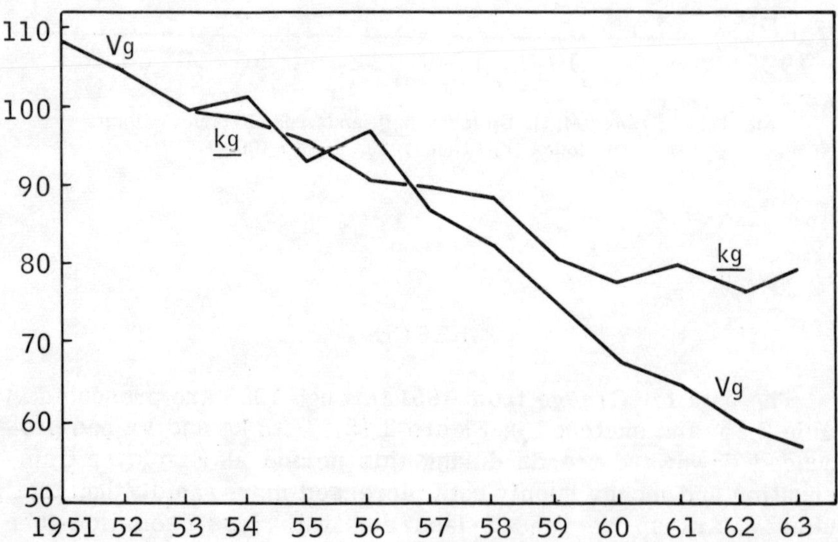

Fig. 2.15. *Greece* Mark-Up Index (kg), and Gross Product Velocity Index (Vg). 1951-1963 (1953 = 100)

JAPAN

The experiences of Japan from 1930 to 1963 make her a special, and especially interesting, case. The figures in Table 2.26. and Figure 2.16. tell an aspect of the dramatic story. With the beginning of the "China Incident" the kg ratio rose from 2.95

Table 2.26. *Japan* Gross National Product (GNP), Employee Compensation (W), Mark-Up (kg), kg Index, Money Supply Index (M), Gross Product Velocity Index (Vg). (1949 = 100) (billions of yen)

Year	GNP	÷	W	=	kg	kg Index	GNP	÷	M	=	Vg
1930	13.0		4.9		2.84	96					
1931	12.5		4.5		2.78	94					
1932	13.1		4.5		2.91	99					
1933	14.3		4.8		2.97	101					
1934	15.7		5.3		2.96	100					
1935	16.7		5.5		3.04	103					
1936	17.7		6.0		2.95	100					
1937	23.4		6.8		3.44	117	.69		1		69
1938	26.8		7.8		3.44	117	.79		1		79
1939	33.0		9.6		3.44	117	1.0		1		100
1940	39.4		11.4		3.46	117	1.2		2		60
1941	44.9		13.8		3.25	110	1.3		2		65
1942	54.3		16.2		3.35	114	1.6		3		53
1943	63.8		20.8		3.07	104	1.9		4		48
1944	74.5		26.6		2.80	95	2.2		5		44
1946	474		111		4.27	145	14		22		64
1947	1, 309		315		4.15	141	39		46		84
1948	2, 666		828		3.22	109	79		87		91
1949	3, 375		1, 144		2.95	100	100		100		100
1950	3, 947		1, 415		2.79	95	117		120		98
1951	5, 168		1, 852		2.79	95	153		155		99
1952	5, 886		2, 317		2.54	86	174		188		93
1953	6, 854		2, 679		2.56	87	203		290		70
1954	7, 355		2, 931		2.51	85	218		301		72
1955	8, 171		3, 180		2.57	87	242		348		70
1956	8, 997		3, 612		2.49	84	267		406		66
1957	10, 123		4, 075		2.48	84	300		423		71
1958	9, 973		4, 383		2.28	77	295		475		62
1959	12, 039		4, 935		2.44	83	357		556		64
1960	14, 065		5, 776		2.44	83	417		660		63
1961	17, 203		6, 925		2.48	84	510		784		65
1962	19, 004		8, 162		2.33	79	563		917		61
1963	21, 482		9, 502		2.26	77	637		1, 230		52

Source: *Economic Statistics of Japan*; *Yearbook of National Accounts Statistics*, 1958, 1964; *International Financial Statistics*, June 1958, July 1965.

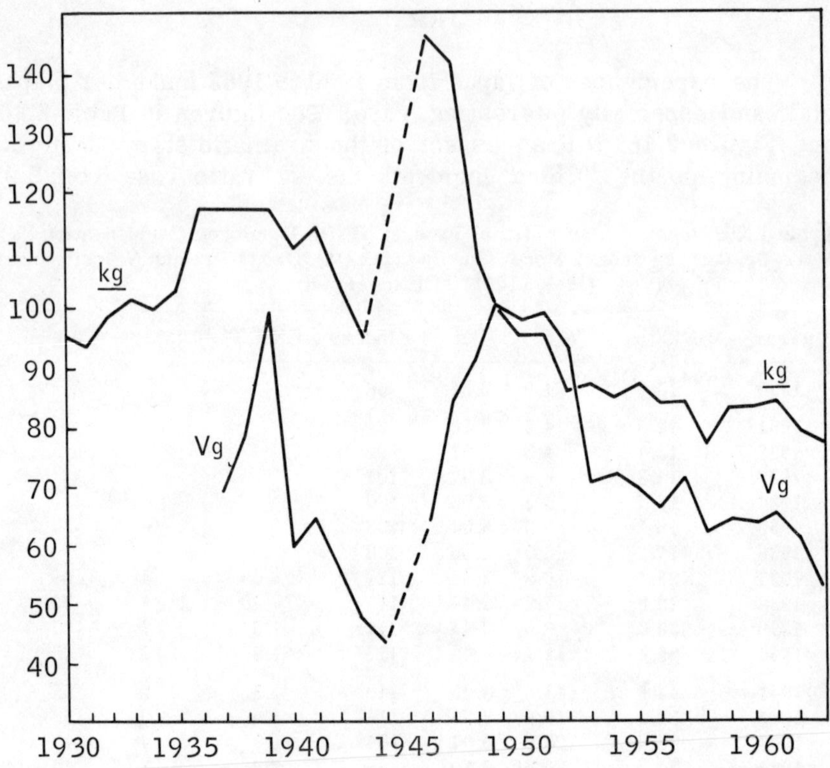

Fig. 2.16. *Japan* Mark-Up Index (kg), and Gross Product Velocity Index (Vg). (1949 = 100)

(wages 33.9 per cent of GNP) in 1936 to 3.44 (wages 29.1%) in 1937 where it remained until 1940. Mark-up had fallen to its 1931 level by Japan's defeat. In 1946 kg was a remarkable 4.27 (wages only 23.4 per cent of GNP) and it was 1949 before it fell to its 1936 level. The inflation, which had been present in every year since 1931, became hyperinflation with defeat. The wholesale price index which averaged 100 in 1934-36 stood at 232 in 1944. Its value in a few postwar years are given in Table 2.27.

Table 2.26. and Figure 2.16, which compares kg and Vg, indicate that what ever the forces are which work for mark-up stability they are not strong enough to keep it constant in the face of war, great destruction and disorganization of industry, atomic bombs, defeat, hyperinflation, and occupation. The swings in kg and Vg in Japan and France (Figure 2.14.) in the immediate postwar years are quite similar, and also similarly, except for this period mark-up instability is not marked. Because of the extreme rounding of the money supply series in prewar years velocity was not calculated prior to 1937. There is little to choose between kg and Vg in stability in the postwar period.[5]

Table 2.27. *Japan* Wholesale Price Index, Selected Years 1934-36 = 100

Year	Index
1946	1,627
1947	4,815
1949	20,876
1951	34,253
1957	36,877

Source: *Economic Statistics of Japan*, p. 27; *Japan Statistical Yearbook* 1958, p. 392.

NEW ZEALAND

Table 2.28. presents the data necessary to calculate kg and Vg in New Zealand from 1938 to 1963 and Figure 2.17. compares the two ratios. The strong rise in kg here during WWII contrasts with the fall in this ratio in the U. S., Canada, and Australia. Apparently the rise in mark-up in the private sector, especially the dominant industry, agriculture, was great enough to outweigh the rise in the government sector. The fall and rise in Vg is analogous to that in many other countries, as is the finding that kg is far more stable than Vg. As in Australia, kg jumped with the Korean War then sagged.

PERU

Our final kg and Vg series are those available for Peru from 1942 to 1959. Mark-up and velocity both slumped during WWII, as is characteristic of these series in developed countries, and rose in the late 1940s. Also, as in developed countries, kg is considerably more stable than Vg. Table 2.29. and Figure 2.18. present the data.

[5] I am indebted to my friend Dr. Herbert M. Bernstein for making available to me his study, "An Analysis of the Constancy of the Wage Mark-Up Factor in the Japanese Economy, 1947-1959," an unpublished paper written at the Graduate School of Western Reserve University in May 1962. His study shows that not only was kg not very stable, but productivity (A Index) gains were also irregular.

Table 2.28. *New Zealand* Gross National Product (GNP), Employee Compensation (W), Mark-Up (kg), kg Index, GNP Index, Money Supply Index (M), Gross Product Velocity Index (Vg). (1949 = 100) (millions of pounds)

Year*	GNP	÷ W	= kg	kg Index	GNP	÷ M	Vg
1938	232	111	2.09	95	42	23	183
1939	249	111	2.24	101	45	27	163
1940	268	118	2.27	103	49	32	152
1941	290	121	2.40	109	52	36	146
1942	335	127	2.64	119	61	47	129
1943	375	141	2.66	120	68	56	121
1944	379	147	2.58	117	69	61	112
1945	399	162	2.46	111	72	70	103
1946	425	187	2.27	103	77	78	99
1947	481	210	2.29	104	87	82	106
1948	489	227	2.15	97	88	90	98
1949	553	250	2.21	100	100	100	100
1950	698	279	2.50	113	126	113	112
1951	723	328	2.20	100	131	116	113
1952	758	348	2.18	99	137	114	120
1953	838	384	2.18	99	152	135	113
1954	930	431	2.16	98	168	147	114
1955	982	468	2.10	95	178	145	123
1956	1,029	495	2.08	94	186	147	127
1957	1,085	534	2.03	92	196	147	133
1958	1,135	558	2.03	92	205	139	147
1959	1,217	603	2.02	91	220	156	141
1960	1,311	652	2.01	91	237	198	120
1961	1,357	696	1.95	88	245	195	121
1962	1,453	737	1.97	89	263	193	136
1963	1,595	791	2.02	91	288	200	144

*Data are for fiscal years beginning July 1.

Source: *Official Yearbook of New Zealand*, 1959, 1962; *Yearbook of National Accounts Statistics*, 1964; *International Financial Statistics*, June 1958, July 1965.

SUMMARY

In 10 of the 16 countries k or kg were clearly more stable than V or Vg, in most of these cases mark-up's superiority in this regard was overwhelming. In no case was the velocity index clearly more stable than the mark-up index. In 5 countries; Brazil, France, Greece, Ireland, and Sweden mark-up's superior stability was less marked. Only in Japan, however, did Vg appear to be slightly more stable than kg. Thus, at best velocity of money

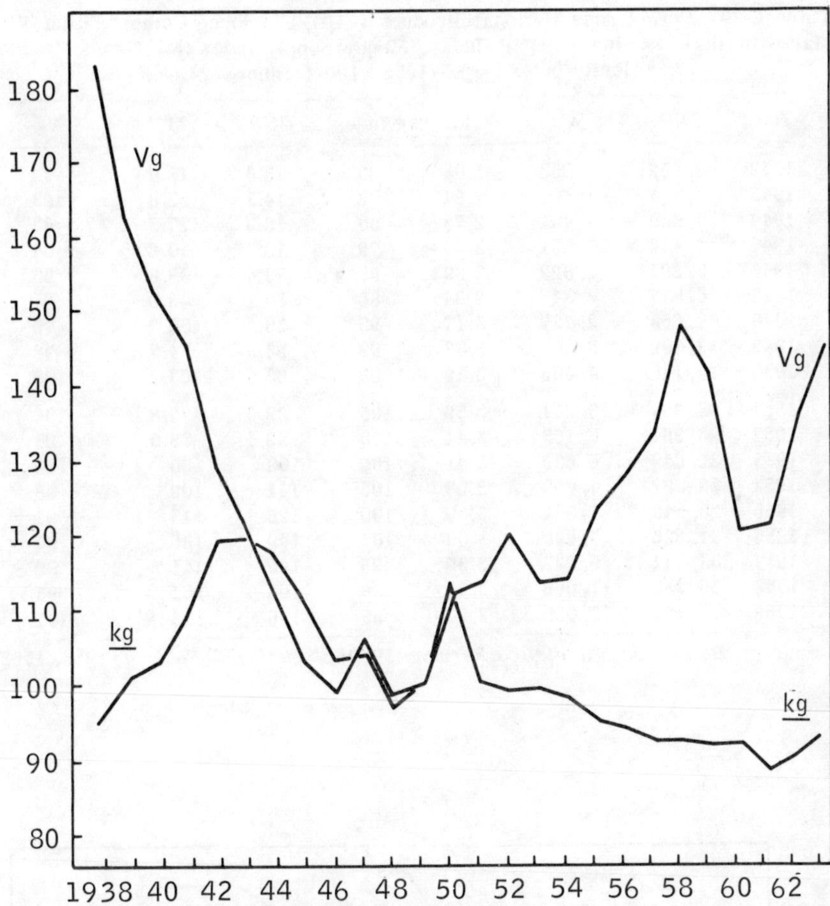

Fig. 2.17. *New Zealand* Mark-Up Index (kg), and Gross Product Velocity Index (Vg). (1949 = 100)

circulation may approach or equal mark-up in stability, or putting it the other way, under the most unfavorable conditions encountered, Japan, mark-up was as unstable as velocity.

LONG RUN TRENDS

Except for the U. S. series produced by Arthur Grant, we have no mark-up series commencing earlier than 1926, and many series are considerably shorter than that. These short series have well

Table 2.29. *Peru* Gross National Product (GNP), Employee Compensation (W), Mark-Up (kg), kg Index, GNP Index, Money Supply Index (M), Gross Product Velocity Index (Vg). (1953 = 100) (millions of soles)

Year	GNP	÷ W	= kg	kg Index	GNP	÷ M	= Vg
1942	2, 952	958	3.08	90	13.0	18.0	72
1943	3, 241	1, 101	2.94	86	14.3	22.8	63
1944	3, 829	1, 401	2.73	80	16.9	27.3	62
1945	4, 454	1, 651	2.70	79	19.7	30.6	64
1946	5, 291	1, 829	2.89	85	23.4	38.8	60
1947	6, 817	2, 317	2.94	86	30.1	45.0	67
1948	8, 653	2, 727	3.17	93	38.2	50.7	75
1949	12, 189	3, 604	3.38	99	53.8	54.7	98
1950	15, 148	4, 465	3.39	99	66.9	63.2	106
1951	18, 707	5, 211	3.59	105	82.6	77.8	106
1952	20, 964	6, 153	3.41	100	92.6	88.0	95
1953	22, 646	6, 639	3.41	100	100	100	100
1954	25, 082	7, 007	3.58	105	111	109	98
1955	28, 540	7, 954	3.59	105	126	115	91
1956	31, 626	8, 830	3.58	105	140	136	97
1957	33, 741	9, 932	3.39	99	149	141	95
1958	36, 936	11, 069	3.34	98	163	151	93
1959	42, 196	13, 050	3.23	95	186	188	101

Source: *Boletin de Estadistica Peruana* 1959; *Statistical Yearbook*, 1956, 1962.

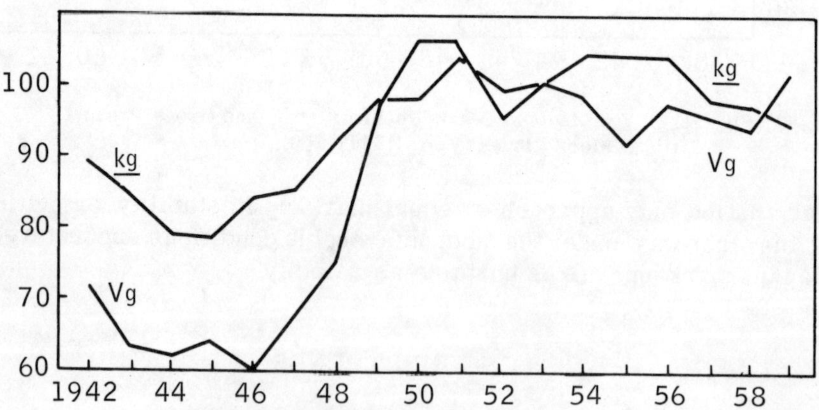

Fig. 2.18. *Peru* Mark-Up Index (kg), and Gross Product Velocity Index (Vg). (1953 = 100)

established that in most countries in most years mark-up is very stable. What, however, of the long run trend of this "near constant"? A review of the various tables and figures in the above two chapters indicate that the long run trend of mark-up is down, (*i.e.* a long run rise in the wage share in gross product). This is confirmed by Table 2.30. where we have focused on long term trend by use of overlapping decade averages of the annual data. In all but 4 of the 16 series shown here the trend appears to be down; the exceptions being India, Ireland, Netherlands, and Peru.

To obtain really long series we must turn to the ky series available for the United Kingdom and United States which are pre-

Table 2.30. Long Run Trends in Mark-Up, k or kg, in 16 Countries by Overlapped Decades. Years as Noted.

Country	U.S.	Canada	U.K.	Aus.	Fin.	Ireland	Nether.	Norway
Series	k	k	k	k	k	k	k	k
Years	1899-1964	1926-1964	1948-1963	1938-1961	1948-1963	1938*, 1963	1938, 1963	1930-1963
1899-08	2.04							
1904-13	2.08							
1909-18	2.16							
1914-23	2.12							
1924-33	2.05	2.25						2.71
1929-38	2.11	2.24						2.74
1934-43	2.11	2.31				2.39	1.80	2.76
1939-48	2.05	2.25		2.47		2.35	2.07	2.52
1944-53	1.98	2.18	1.56	2.48	2.05	2.32	2.17	2.50
1949-58	1.93	2.16	1.54	2.45	2.02	2.32	2.22	2.50
1954-63	1.88	2.13	1.52	2.39	1.99	2.33	2.13	2.41

Country	India	Sweden	Brazil	France	Greece	Japan	N.Z.	Peru
Series	k	k	kg	kg	kg	kg	kg	kg
Years	1948-1962	1938-1964	1947-1961	1938, 1963	1951-1963	1930-1963	1938-1963	1942-1959
1924-33						2.88		
1929-38						3.04		
1934-43		2.46		2.42		3.24	2.09	3.01
1939-48		2.12	2.81	2.75		3.45	2.40	2.92
1944-53	2.53	2.16	2.83	2.49	3.51	3.06	2.30	3.16
1949-58	2.55	2.10	2.77	2.31	3.31	2.58	2.17	3.47
1954-63	2.56	1.98	2.70	2.23	3.10	2.43	2.03	3.45

*1938 and postwar years: Ireland 1948-, Netherlands 1946-, France 1946-47, 1949-.

Source: All sources noted above with individual country's series.

sented in Table 2.31. According to Kuznet's figures, ky had virtually no trend in the U. K. during the 19th century. In 1800 ky is estimated as 2.13 (wages 47 per cent of national income) and in the decade centered on 1900 it was 2.02 (wages 49.6 per cent of N. I.). The World War I era, however, reduced mark-up to 1.68 in the decade centered on 1925, and the World War II period saw another drop of ky to 1.45. It is probable that the k index for the U. K. for the same period, if we had it, would show less downward

Table 2.31. Long Run Trends in National Income Mark-Up ky, in the United Kingdom and the United States. Years as Indicated.

Years	United Kingdom	Years	United States: King's data	United States: Martin's data	United States: Kuznets' data	United States: U.S.D.C. data
1688	2.70	1850-59	2.74			
c1798	2.14	1860-69	2.33			
c1800	2.13	1870-79	1.99			
		1880-89	1.90			
1860-69	2.11	1890-99	1.98			
1865-74	2.10	1900-09	2.12			
1870-79	2.05					
1875-84	2.05	1899-08		1.68		
1880-89	2.07	1909-18		1.68	1.64	
1885-94	2.03	1919-28		1.54	1.64	
1890-00	2.01	1929-38			1.50	1.52
1895-04	2.02	1939-48				1.57
1900-09	2.07	1949-58				1.49
1905-14	2.12	1959-64				1.42
1920-29	1.68					
1925-34	1.64					
1930-39	1.61					
1935-44	1.56					
1940-49	1.45					
1945-54	1.39					
1950-59	1.38					
1955-63	1.36					

Source: U. K. years 1688-c1800 from Phylis Deane, "The Implication of Early National Income Estimates for the Measurement of Long Term Economic Growth in the United Kingdom," *Econ. Dev. & Cult. Change*, Vol. IV, No. 1. Nov. 1955. Years 1860-1954 from S. Kuznets, "Distribution of National Income by Factor Shares," *Econ. Dev. & Cult. Change*, Vol. VII, No. 3, April 1959. 1955-1959 from *National Income and Expenditure*, 1960. 1950-1960 from *National Income and Expenditure*, 1960.

U. S. 1850-1951 from D. Gale Johnson, "The Functional Distribution of Income in the United States, 1850-1952,"*R.E.S.*, Vol. XXXVI, May 1954. 1952-1964 *National Income* 1954, *Survey of Current Business*, July 1960, 1965.

trend than does ky because part of this trend in ky is attributable to the rise in the importance of the government sector. This sector enters the national accounts as 100 per cent wages and salaries, but it is excluded from the calculation of k.

In the United States from 1899-1908 to 1954-63 k fell from 2.04 to 1.88, a fall of .16 or 8.9 per cent. From 1899-1908 to 1959-64 ky fell from 1.68 to 1.42, a fall of .26 or 16.7 per cent. From 1929-38 to 1954-63, where we have Department of Commerce data throughout, k fell from 2.11 to 1.88 or 11.5 per cent while over the same period ky fell from 1.52 to 1.42, or only 7 per cent. This differing result comes from the fact that ky fell considerably during the great depression while k did not.

These qualifications noted, however, the evidence that mark-up, gross product or net income, falls over time as a nation develops appears conclusive. The time series above can here be supplemented by cross sectional studies of countries arranged in order of per capita income and percentage of the labor force engaged in agriculture. As Table 2.32. shows: low mark-up and a low per-

Table 2.32. Cross Sectional Association of National Income Mark-Up (ky), c1955, Per Capita Income c1949, and Percentage of the Labor Force Engaged in Agriculture c1950.

	ky	Per Capita Income ($)	Agricultural Labor Force (%)
I High Income (over $700) Average of 12 countries	1.64	$931	11.9
II Upper Middle ($350-699) Average of 9 countries	1.70	444	18.7
III Lower Middle ($150-349) Average of 16 countries	2.17	224	27.7
IV Low Income (below $150) Average of 13 countries	2.50	104	44.0

Source: Adapted from Paul Studenski, *Income of Nations*; *Yearbook of National Accounts Statistics*, 1958.

centage of the labor force engaged in agriculture are associated with a high per capita income.

This is, of course, eminently reasonable. Rising per capita income means demand for urban produced goods expands more rapidly than that for agricultural produce as demand for food is income inelastic, while demand for durable goods is income elastic. This, combined with rising productivity, fosters a massive shift of the labor force from agriculture to urban occupations. In the lowest income countries studied in Table 2.32. an average of 44 per cent of the labor force is in agriculture while in the highest income group only 11.9 per cent are so engaged. Institutional arrangements are such that this transfer of occupation also means a great shift from proprietor to employee status, which is reflected in a high mark-up in agriculture and a lower one in industry. In Chapter 3 where we disaggregate mark-up in three countries we shall investigate the extent to which we can account for the fall in mark-up by the relative decline of agriculture with development.

The conclusion that mark-up over contractual employee compensation falls as development proceeds, is as far as the published data will take us. Since our study is of the contractual shares question, that is enough. We shall therefore only touch on the further question of distribution between "labor", or "earned income", and all "property" or "capital" income, concerning which a considerable literature exists.

Depending on how one imputes "mixed incomes" of unincorporated enterprise between labor and property one can arrive at the finding that the labor share has increased, decreased, or remained constant.[6] It is interesting that if all of this mixed income is allocated to labor, as has been done by Kuznets,[7] and Klein & Kosobud,[8] it is found that from the highest to lowest per capita income countries this "participation income" is almost constant at 82 to 85 per cent.

[6] See E. C. Budd, "United States Factor Shares 1850-1910," *Studies in Income and Wealth*, 24, Princeton 1960, 365-406. D. G. Johnson, "The Functional Distribution of Income in the United States 1850-1952," *Rev. Econ. Stat.*, May 1954, 34 175-182. W. I. King, *National Income and Its Purchasing Power*, N.B.E.R. New York 1930. I. Kravis, "Relative Income Shares in Fact and Theory," *Am. Econ. Rev.*, Dec. 1959, 49, 917-949. L. R. Klein and R. F. Kosobud, "Some Econometrics of Growth: Great Ratios of Economics," *Quart. Jour. Econ.*, May 1961, 75, No. 2. 180-185. S. Kuznets, "Distribution of National Income by Factor Shares," *Econ. Develop. and Cult. Change*, April 1959, Pt. II, 7, 1-100.

[7] Kuznets, p. 9.

[8] Klein and Kosobud, pp. 183-184.

The difficulty with imputation is that it is hard to know where to stop. Kuznets[9] points out that all wages larger than that received by an unskilled laborer might well be attributed to an asset return on the investment made in education. He estimates that at least half of the wages received in a high income country could be so allocated and in consequence of so allocating we would conclude that economic development has meant a very large rise in the property share!

[9]Kuznets, *Ibid.*, p. 44.

Chapter 3

DISAGGREGATION OF MARK-UP IN THE UNITED STATES, CANADA, AND THE UNITED KINGDOM

INTRODUCTION

It is beyond the scope of this effort at international comparisons of mark-up and related price level phenomena to attempt an exhaustive disaggregation down to the level of the firm. Rather it is intended to supplement the aggregate mark-up analysis with disaggregations to the next highest level, the major industries which produce Business Gross Product. Further disaggregation of the dominant industry, Manufacturing, is then carried out culminating, in the U. S. only, with a few studies of mark-up in leading manufacturing firms.

These disaggregations are developed to explore whether the small variability of aggregate mark-up reflects similar mark-up rigidity in component firms and industries or whether we are in need of a special macro theory to account for this macro stability. Disaggregation should also give us considerable insight into the reasons for the downward trend of $\underline{k}$ seen in many countries. As a useful byproduct of these disaggregations we shall be able to study the degree of stability in productivity gains in the various industries.

Weintraub has held that his Wage Cost Mark-Up formulation focuses on "behavioral or structural relationships,"[1] while the Equation of Exchange, "only indicates the movement in components and not the causal factors."[2] The behavioral relationships on which

[1]Weintraub, *The General Theory*, p. 5.

[2]*Ibid.* Many would not concede this, of course, holding that velocity or cash balance phenomena do reflect liquidity preference behavior and the three motives for desiring liquidity; transactions, precaution, and speculation, the third accounting for instability.

Table 3.1. Wage Cost Mark-Up in the United States in the Aggregate and in 11 Industry Disaggregation.

Year	Aggregate	Industries 1.	2.	3.	4.	5.
1947	1.97	6.87	2.03	1.48	1.50	1.97
1948	1.98	7.18	2.31	1.50	1.50	1.95
1949	1.99	6.22	2.26	1.53	1.54	1.91
1950	2.00	7.07	2.41	1.52	1.56	1.91
1951	1.99	7.56	2.38	1.46	1.56	1.93
1952	1.94	7.38	2.28	1.46	1.51	1.89
1953	1.90	6.81	2.32	1.45	1.48	1.83
1954	1.90	6.60	2.59	1.44	1.46	1.80
1955	1.93	6.44	2.68	1.47	1.52	1.84
1956	1.86	6.18	2.62	1.46	1.47	1.79
1957	1.87	6.00	2.47	1.47	1.47	1.78
1958	1.88	6.43	2.50	1.45	1.44	1.76
1959	1.88	5.89	2.52	1.44	1.48	1.78
1960	1.88	6.00	2.56	1.43	1.46	1.72
1961	1.87	5.95	2.74	1.42	1.45	1.73
1962	1.88	6.05	2.81	1.42	1.47	1.74
1963	1.87	6.13	2.77	1.40	1.47	1.74

Year	Industries 6.	7.	8.	9.	10.	11.
1947	4.70	1.42	1.65	2.50	2.30	1.30
1948	4.66	1.45	1.61	2.44	2.29	1.23
1949	4.98	1.45	1.67	2.55	2.29	1.16
1950	4.89	1.52	1.80	2.62	2.32	1.08
1951	4.88	1.50	1.82	2.78	2.30	1.03
1952	4.92	1.50	1.84	2.76	2.25	1.14
1953	4.86	1.48	1.85	2.72	2.25	1.23
1954	4.75	1.44	1.86	2.86	2.19	1.19
1955	4.63	1.50	1.84	2.90	2.25	1.11
1956	4.44	1.45	1.81	2.94	2.18	.95
1957	4.56	1.45	1.89	3.00	2.19	1.05
1958	4.51	1.45	2.00	2.92	2.17	1.02
1959	4.45	1.42	2.11	3.03	2.18	1.10
1960	4.41	1.41	2.10	3.10	2.09	1.08
1961	4.33	1.43	2.14	3.14	2.08	1.00
1962	4.33	1.45	2.17	3.17	2.06	1.03
1963	4.29	1.45	2.20	3.17	2.04	1.11

Source: "GNP by Major Industries," *Survey of Current Business*, October 1962, September 1964.

Industries

1. Agriculture, forestry, and fishing
2. Mining
3. Contract construction
4. Manufacturing
5. Wholesale and retail trade
6. Finance, insurance, and real estate
7. Transportation
8. Communications
9. Public utilities
10. Services
11. Government enterprises

the WCM would focus are accounting, engineering, and managerial conventions in individual firms and industries which result in "formula," "full-cost," or "mark-up" pricing. Later we shall have more to say about these conventions. First let us look at the available data.

THE UNITED STATES

Consistent series enabling us to analyze gross, rather than net, mark-up at disaggregated levels in the United States are available only for the period 1947-1963. This shortcoming is partially made up for by the fact that the data are complete enough so that we can develop complete matrices for 11 industries and most of 8 sub-industries to study productivity gains as well. Table 3.1. presents the mark-up factor in the aggregate and in 11 industries. Table 3.1. makes it evident that mark-up varies greatly between industries, averaging 6.19 (wages 16.1 per cent of gross product) in Agriculture and 1.45 (68.9%) in Transportation. In 7 of the 11 industries mark-up declined from 1947 to 1963 as it did in the aggregate. However, in industry 2. Mining, 8. Communications, and 9. Public utilities, mark-up rose rather steeply, while in industry 7. Transportation, it was virtually unchanged.

Eight of the industries appear to be somewhat more variable than aggregate mark-up, the greatest variability being shown by Agriculture and Communications. In Chapter Four we shall analyze this variability closely and check the statistical significance of the degree of variability encountered at differing levels of aggregation. Figure 3.1. depicts the aggregate mark-up and 10 of the 11 industrial $\underline{k}$ factors. Industry 11. Government Enterprises, was not graphed as they are not "firms producing for profit," and their unstable mark-ups are not germane to our discussion, except to the small extent that their instability affects $\underline{k}$ in the aggregate. Ratio scale is used in Figure 3.1. so that equal vertical distances represent equal percentage changes. Three low, stable mark-up industries; Contract construction, Manufacturing, and Transportation, have virtually indistinguishable mark-up series with slight downward trends. High, widely fluctuating Agriculture and Finance, insurance and real estate likewise have downward trends, while the three series with upward trends are all intermediate in height of mark-up.

The idea of a constancy of relative shares has been examined recently by R. M. Solow, who asks what it means to say that the

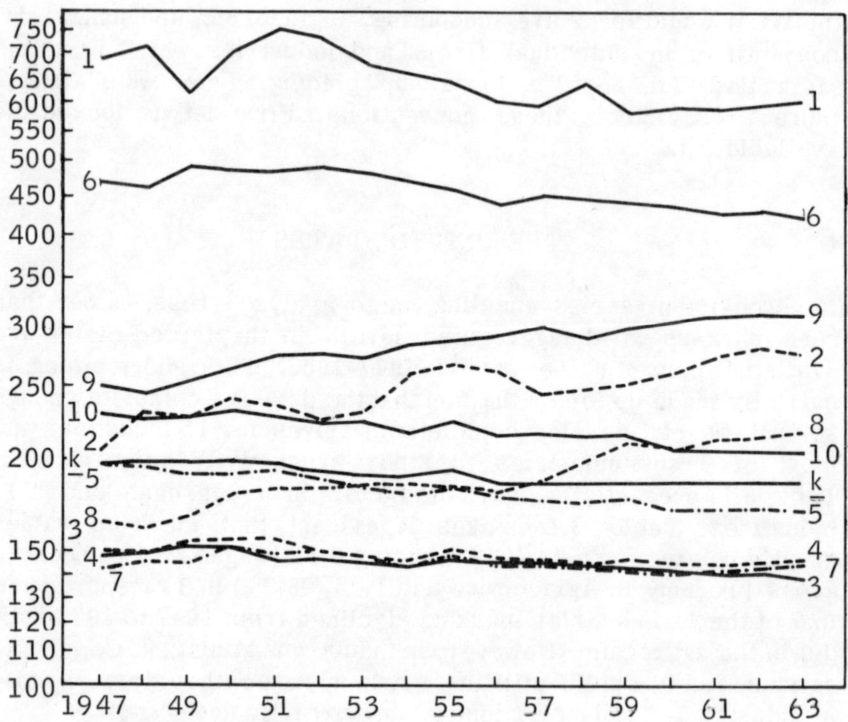

Fig. 3.1. Mark-Up in the Aggregate (k), and in 10 Industries Producing BGP in the United States.* Ratio Scale

*Government Enterprises not graphed.

wage share has been relatively stable.[3] He holds that the statement is meaningless unless we have some standard to distinguish between "wide" and "narrow" fluctuations and suggests three possible sources of such a standard.

1. If we had a tightly quantifiable distribution theory it would suggest to us how much fluctuation in shares to expect, but we don't.[4]

2. "A second possible source . . . is . . . the past behavior of the process itself. Clearly if the wage share had once oscillated between 50 and 80 per cent and now moved only in the range from

[3] R. M. Solow, "A Skeptical Note on the Constancy of Relative Shares," *A. E. R.*, XLVIII (September 1958) pp. 618-631.

[4] See, however, the discussion on p. 158 below.

60 to 70 per cent, we could speak of relative stability. But it is not claimed that this is the case."[5]

3. An internal standard can be formulated, "if wide swings within industries yield only narrow swings in the aggregate, this points to some specifically interindustrial or macroeconomic force."[6]

To test for the presence of such a force Solow calculates a "theoretical variance" for aggregate wage shares to compare with the variance through time actually obtained. The formula $\sigma^2 = \Sigma \underline{w}_i{}^2 \sigma_i^2$ where $\underline{w}_i$ represents sector weights and σ_i^2 represents sector variances, expresses the aggregate variance, σ^2, which would obtain if in each sector wage shares fluctuated independently with neither positive or negative correlation with the other sectors. If the correlation between sectors is positive a rise in a sector wage share will be reinforced by a rise in that sector's weight in the aggregate and the observed aggregate variance will be greater than the theoretical variance. On the other hand, if correlation is negative a rise in a sector wage share will be partially offset by a fall in that sector's weight and observed variance can properly be called "unexpectedly small."

Solow looks for such stabilizing negative correlation in two ways; comparison of theoretical and actual variance, and comparison of actual variance with variance of sector wage shares tied to fixed sector weights. He finds that the observed variance is not significantly different from either the theoretical variance or the fixed weight variance and concludes:

> "if by the 'historical constancy' of labor's share it is meant that the share of the total social product imputed to wages has shown a marked absence of fluctuation as compared with the fluctuations of its industrial components, then this belief is probably wrong. Whatever exceptional stability there has been in the pattern of relative shares appears attributable to the components. This in turn suggests that there is no need for a special theory to explain how a number of unruly microeconomic markets are willy-nilly squeezed into a tight-fitting size .65 strait-jacket. A theory which

[5] *Ibid.* p. 621. I would not agree with the final sentence. Aggregate mark-up *has* become increasingly stable over time in the U. S. and Canada, (see Figure 1.1. and 2.2. above and statistical verification p. 135). Furthermore, we shall show that $\underline{k}$'s increasing stability in Canada is largely attributable to the decreasing weight of the agricultural industry (p. 105).

[6] *Ibid.*

Table 3.2. Percentage of Business Gross Product Produced by the 11 Industries in the United States

Year	1.	2.	3.	4.	5.	6.
1947	10.11	2.99	4.27	31.61	22.07	10.49
1948	10.43	3.46	4.74	31.25	21.75	10.56
1949	8.64	3.04	4.87	30.76	21.94	12.12
1950	8.34	3.23	4.96	32.22	21.24	11.92
1951	8.34	3.19	5.22	33.44	20.67	11.40
1952	7.74	2.99	5.41	33.30	20.47	11.78
1953	6.78	2.95	5.32	34.36	20.02	12.10
1954	6.70	3.02	5.44	32.65	20.45	12.99
1955	5.90	3.15	5.42	34.01	20.31	12.61
1956	5.56	3.22	5.73	33.62	20.48	12.60
1957	5.28	3.00	5.67	33.42	20.35	13.10
1958	5.86	2.74	5.63	31.47	20.60	13.99
1959	5.06	2.53	5.59	32.73	20.60	13.82
1960	5.11	2.53	5.48	32.43	20.51	14.11
1961	5.08	2.58	5.46	31.46	20.58	14.59
1962	4.82	2.47	5.43	32.20	20.51	14.34
1963	4.66	2.38	5.41	32.14	20.62	14.44

Year	7.	8.	9.	10.	11.	Check %
1947	6.55	1.57	1.90	7.21	1.23	100.00
1948	6.37	1.58	1.88	6.84	1.55	100.00
1949	6.26	1.74	2.22	7.17	1.26	100.02
1950	6.22	1.77	2.16	6.84	1.10	100.00
1951	6.18	1.75	2.20	6.56	1.06	100.01
1952	6.14	1.87	2.26	6.73	1.31	100.00
1953	6.03	1.96	2.36	6.78	1.34	100.00
1954	5.66	2.04	2.61	7.11	1.35	100.02
1955	5.67	2.01	2.58	7.11	1.20	99.97
1956	5.67	2.07	2.65	7.36	1.04	100.00
1957	5.64	2.15	2.72	7.53	1.14	100.00
1958	5.44	2.29	2.89	7.85	1.22	99.99
1959	5.23	2.32	2.89	7.97	1.27	100.01
1960	5.16	2.37	2.99	8.03	1.29	100.01
1961	5.03	2.45	3.10	8.34	1.25	99.92
1962	4.82	2.47	3.06	8.41	1.25	99.93
1963	4.90	2.46	3.04	8.51	1.40	99.96

Source: *Survey of Current Business*, October 1962, September 1964.

Industries

1. Agriculture, forestry and fisheries
2. Mining
3. Contract construction
4. Manufacturing
5. Wholesale and retail trade
6. Finance, insurance, and real estate
7. Transportation
8. Communications
9. Public utilities
10. Services
11. Government enterprises

wishes to produce the magic number among its consequences may have to say something about the component sectors among its premises."[7]

Let us check Solow's results with our $\underline{k}$ data, which, as we have seen, are less variable than the $1/\underline{k}y$ data he used; being wary of a verbal trap on the way. A rise in the wage share is the same thing as a fall in mark-up, but if a rise in a wage share accompanies a rise in that sector's (industry's) weight Solow would call this positive association while in our terms it would be negative.

The theoretical variance computed from the data in Tables 3.1. and 3.2., which gives the weights of the 11 industries, is .002070.[8] The actually observed variance of aggregate mark-up from 1947 to 1963 was .002568. An "F" test shows the difference to be clearly nonsignificant. (See Figure 3.2.)

In Figure 3.3. and Table 3.3. $\underline{k}$ is observed mark-up, $\underline{k}_1$ is what "would have happened" if fluctuations in industry mark-ups had been neither amplified nor damped by weight shifts, and $\underline{k}_2$ traces the effect of the weight shifts alone.[9] Both stabilizing and destabilizing weight shifts can be seen in the figure. Between 1949 and 1951 fixed weight $\underline{k}_1$ rose greatly while $\underline{k}$ rose to a lesser extent because of the weight shifts. However, in 1951-52 no weight shifts occurred, *i.e.* $\underline{k}_2$'s value remained unchanged, to dampen the fall of industry mark-ups, and in 1952-53 the weight shifts reinforced the fall in mark-ups with a destabilizing weight shift. Furthermore, the fact that $\underline{k}_2$ shows some downward trend ($\underline{b}$ = -.00137) as does $\underline{k}_1$ ($\underline{b}$ = -.00846) resulted in an observed mark-up $\underline{k}$ with a greater downward trend than either "might have been;" ($\underline{b}$ of $\underline{k}$ was -.00892).

The standard deviation (s) of $\underline{k}_1$ is larger than that for $\underline{k}$, indicating some stabilizing effect of weight shifts, but the difference is so slight ($\underline{s}$ of $\underline{k}_1$ = .0524, $\underline{s}$ of $\underline{k}$ = .0507) as to be clearly nonsignificant. This confirms Solow's finding that stabilizing and destabilizing shifts about cancel out so that aggregate mark-up

[7] *Ibid.* p. 628.

[8] Industry variances were calculated for 1947-1960 and weighted by the percentage of BGP produced by each of the industries in 1953. Whenever variance is referred to in this study the notation $\underline{s}^2$ will be used rather than σ^2.

[9] Each industry mark-up factor was converted to its reciprocal wage share percentage and weighted by the percentage of BGP produced by that industry. Weighted products were then summed and the result converted back into mark-up. Working with $\underline{k}$ directly results in becoming entangled in the harmonic mean.

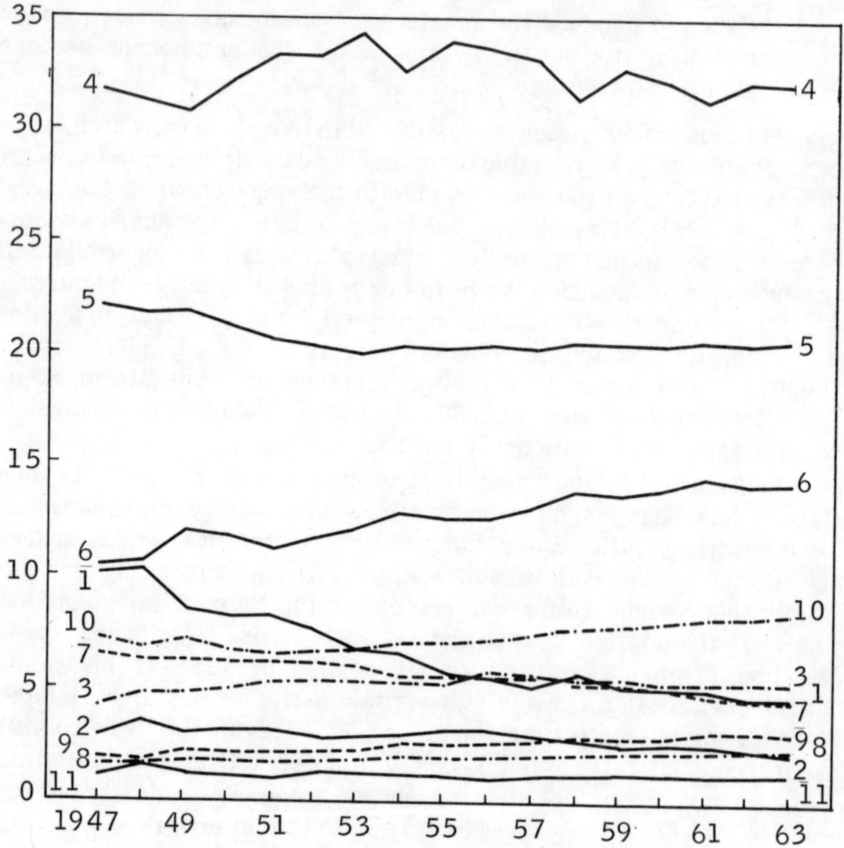

Fig. 3.2. Percentage of Business Gross Product produced by the 11 Industries in the United States

Industries

1. Agriculture, forestry, and fisheries
2. Mining
3. Contract construction
4. Manufacturing
5. Wholesale and retail trade
6. Finance, insurance, and real estate
7. Transportation
8. Communications
9. Public utilities
10. Services
11. Government enterprises

fluctuates about as it "should" given the fluctuation of its constituent parts. The small variability of these aggregate mark-up measures is best seen in the figure for relative variability, $\underline{v} = \underline{s}/\underline{k}$. The remaining statistical measures of Table 3.3. are des-

Table 3.3. Numerical Values of $\underline{k}$, $\underline{k}_1$, and $\underline{k}_2$ in the United States.

Year	$\underline{k}$	$\underline{k}_1$	$\underline{k}_2$
1947	1.97	1.97	1.97
1948	1.98	1.97	1.98
1949	1.99	1.99	1.97
1950	2.00	2.02	1.96
1951	1.99	2.02	1.94
1952	1.94	1.98	1.94
1953	1.90	1.94	1.92
1954	1.90	1.92	1.94
1955	1.93	1.97	1.92
1956	1.96	1.86	1.92
1957	1.87	1.91	1.92
1958	1.88	1.89	1.95
1959	1.88	1.91	1.93
1960	1.86	1.88	1.94
1961	1.87	1.87	1.96
1962	1.88	1.89	1.95
1963	1.87	1.89	1.95

Source: *Survey of Current Business*, October 1962, September 1964.

		Statistical Analysis	
Variation	7.3%	8.2%	3.1%
Largest change	3.6%	5.7%	1.5%
Mean of $\underline{k}$	1.92	1.93	1.94
$\underline{b}$	-.00892	-.00846	-.00137
$\underline{s}$	.0507	.0524	.0197
$\underline{s}_{\underline{k}t}$	.0262	.0301	.0177
$\underline{v}$	2.7%	2.8%	1.0%
$\underline{v}t$	1.4%	1.6%	0.9%
R^2	-.745	-.661	-.194

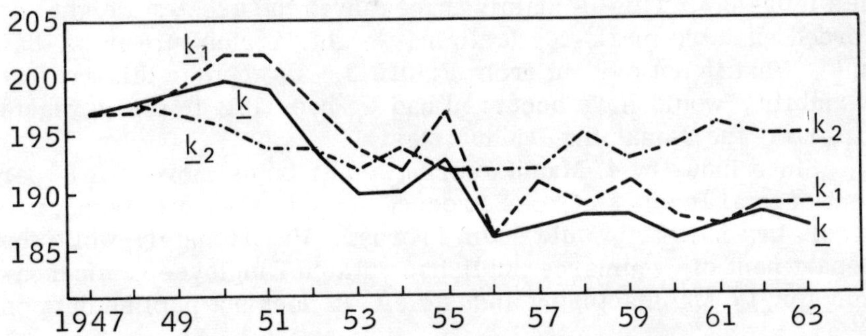

Fig. 3.3. Graph of $\underline{k}$, $\underline{k}_1$, and $\underline{k}_2$ in the United States
$\underline{k}$ = BGP/Wb $\underline{k}_1 = 1/\underline{k}it$. BGPi1947/BGP $\underline{k}_2 = 1/\underline{k}i1947$.
BGPit/BGP (i = industries 1 to 11, t = yearly data)

criptive of mark-up's downward trend (b), and variability about that trend, (s_{kt} , vt, and R^2).

Let us disaggregate further and check again. Industries 1. Agriculture, 4. Manufacturing, 6. Finance, insurance, and real estate, and 7. Transportation are presented in Table 3.4. divided into 8 sub-industries. As Figure 3.4. makes evident sub-industries 1a. Farms, and 6b. Real Estate, have high, unstable mark-ups while the other six sub-industries have low, stable mark-ups. The extreme smallness of 1b. Agricultural Services, forestry, and fisheries, undoubtedly accounts for most of the fluctuation in mark-up in that industry as the data are heavily rounded off.[10]

Table 3.5. gives the changing percentage of these 8 sub-industry outputs and Figure 3.5. presents the data visually. A steady decline in the percentage of output of farms is evident as well as a steady rise in the percentage contribution of real estate. There is also evident a cyclical pattern by which 1a. and 6b. "gain weight" in recession years (1949, 1954, 1958, 1961) at the expense, mainly, of 4a. Durable goods manufacturing. Since 1a. and 6b. have high mark-ups and Durables manufacturing mark-up is low, these weight shifts should be stabilizing.

When we repeat the calculation of fixed weight ks_1 and fixed mark-up ks_2 we find, however, that weight shifts were, on balance, somewhat destabilizing. This is shown in Table 3.6. by the fact that the standard deviation, s, of ks (mark-up in sub-industries 1a. to 7b.) is larger than in fixed weight ks_1, (.0627 vs .0503). Although the stabilizing shifts we are looking for occurred in 1954 in most other years ks_2 contributed to the downward trend and variability of ks rather than damping it.

There is also a greater variability evident in Figure 3.6. than in Figure 3.3. This is mainly traceable to the greater weight accorded unstable mark-up, declining weight, Agriculture in ks than in k. What is not evident from Figure 3.6. is whether this greater variability would have occurred had we been able to disaggregate similarly the remaining 7 industries.

Since Industry 4. Manufacturing, contributes more than 30 per cent of total Business Gross Product some further disaggregation of this key industry would seem in order. Unfortunately, while the Department of Commerce publishes data on Employee Compensation for 17 Manufacturing Industries, it does not publish data on

[10]Thus in 1948 BGP in lb. is given as $.6 billion and W as $.3 billion giving a k factor of 2.00. In 1949 Z was still given as $.6 billion but W was $.4 billion, so k fell to 1.50 while additional decimal points might show it was actually unchanged.

Table 3.4. Wage Cost Mark-Up in the United States in 8 Sub-Industries.

Year	1a	1b	4a	4b	6a	6b
	Sub-Industries					
1947	7.39	2.00	1.34	1.70	1.47	18.33
1948	7.93	1.50	1.37	1.68	1.50	16.73
1949	6.66	2.00	1.44	1.64	1.69	18.45
1950	7.59	2.33	1.51	1.63	1.56	18.75
1951	8.43	1.75	1.48	1.68	1.62	18.69
1952	8.14	2.00	1.41	1.66	1.62	21.67
1953	7.46	2.25	1.39	1.62	1.66	21.38
1954	7.52	2.00	1.38	1.58	1.62	21.07
1955	7.26	2.00	1.44	1.66	1.56	19.81
1956	7.15	1.83	1.37	1.62	1.48	19.59
1957	6.93	1.67	1.38	1.61	1.50	21.47
1958	7.34	2.00	1.33	1.62	1.51	21.33
1959	6.67	2.00	1.37	1.64	1.53	21.53
1960	6.97	1.86	1.34	1.63	1.52	21.15
1961	6.84	2.00	1.34	1.62	1.51	20.91
1962	6.94	2.14	1.37	1.64	1.48	21.35
1963	7.00	2.29	1.37	1.63	1.40	20.84

Year	7a	7b
	Sub-Industries	
1947	1.37	1.49
1948	1.40	1.51
1949	1.37	1.56
1950	1.45	1.60
1951	1.42	1.59
1952	1.45	1.55
1953	1.45	1.52
1954	1.37	1.50
1955	1.46	1.54
1956	1.41	1.49
1957	1.41	1.49
1958	1.39	1.49
1959	1.37	1.46
1960	1.38	1.43
1961	1.36	1.46
1962	1.37	1.50
1963	1.40	1.48

1a Farms
1b Agricultural services, forestry, and fisheries
4a Durable goods manufacturing
4b Nondurable goods manufacturing
6a Finance and insurance
6b Real estate
7a Railroads
7b Other transportation

Source: "GNP by Major Industries," *Survey of Current Business*, October 1962, September 1964.

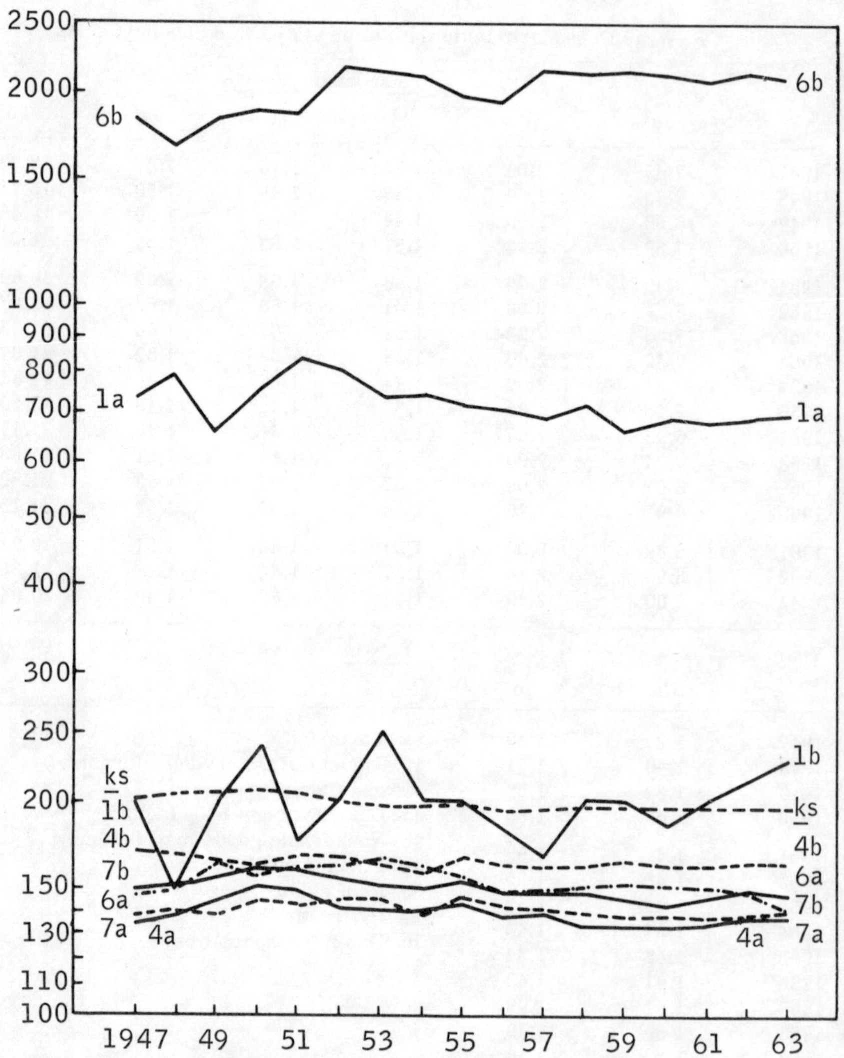

Fig. 3.4. Mark-Up in the Aggregate of 8 Sub-Industries (ks), and in the 8 Sub-Industries in the United States

Sub-Industries

1a Farms	6a Finance and insurance
1b Agricultural services, forestry, and fisheries	6b Real estate
4a Durable goods manufacturing	7a Railroads
4b Nondurable goods manufacturing	7b Other transportation

Table 3.5. Percentage of the Business Gross Product Produced by Industries 1, 4, 6, and 7 which is Produced by each of the 8 Sub-Industries in the U. S.

Year	Sub-Industries 1a	1b	4a	4b	6a	6b
1947	16.72	.48	27.23	26.57	4.52	13.33
1948	17.36	.44	27.43	25.89	4.60	13.42
1949	14.51	.45	27.44	25.79	5.71	15.26
1950	13.74	.47	30.23	24.66	5.23	15.08
1951	13.65	.40	31.98	24.35	5.15	14.05
1952	12.69	.45	32.39	24.10	5.51	14.47
1953	10.97	.47	34.12	23.83	5.83	14.59
1954	11.01	.54	32.32	23.97	6.40	16.00
1955	9.65	.49	34.12	24.32	6.06	15.61
1956	9.16	.53	34.08	24.44	6.12	15.80
1957	8.74	.45	34.20	23.97	6.35	16.45
1958	9.78	.55	31.12	24.32	7.02	17.62
1959	8.40	.50	33.12	24.46	7.14	17.18
1960	8.47	.53	32.58	24.51	7.33	17.50
1961	8.48	.56	31.46	24.53	7.56	18.81
1962	8.00	.55	32.82	24.30	7.18	18.27
1963	7.74	.51	33.12	24.08	7.13	18.58

Year	7a	7b	Check %	Output of Industries 1, 4, 6, and 7 as % of BGP
1947	5.98	5.17	100.00	58.76
1948	5.91	4.96	100.01	58.61
1949	5.56	5.26	99.98	57.78
1950	5.43	5.17	100.01	58.70
1951	5.26	5.15	99.99	59.36
1952	5.23	5.18	100.02	58.96
1953	4.93	5.25	99.99	59.27
1954	4.39	5.37	100.00	58.00
1955	4.38	5.37	100.00	58.19
1956	4.41	5.46	100.00	57.45
1957	4.19	5.63	99.98	57.44
1958	3.90	5.69	100.00	56.76
1959	3.57	5.63	100.00	56.84
1960	3.40	5.67	99.99	56.81
1961	3.16	5.80	99.96	56.19
1962	3.01	5.84	99.97	56.37
1963	2.88	5.85	99.97	56.17

Source: *Survey of Current Business*, October 1962, September 1964.

Sub-Industries

- 1a Farms
- 1b Agricultural service, forestry, and fisheries
- 4a Durable goods manufacturing
- 4b Nondurable goods manufacturing
- 6a Finance and insurance
- 6b Real estate
- 7a Railroads
- 7b Other transportation

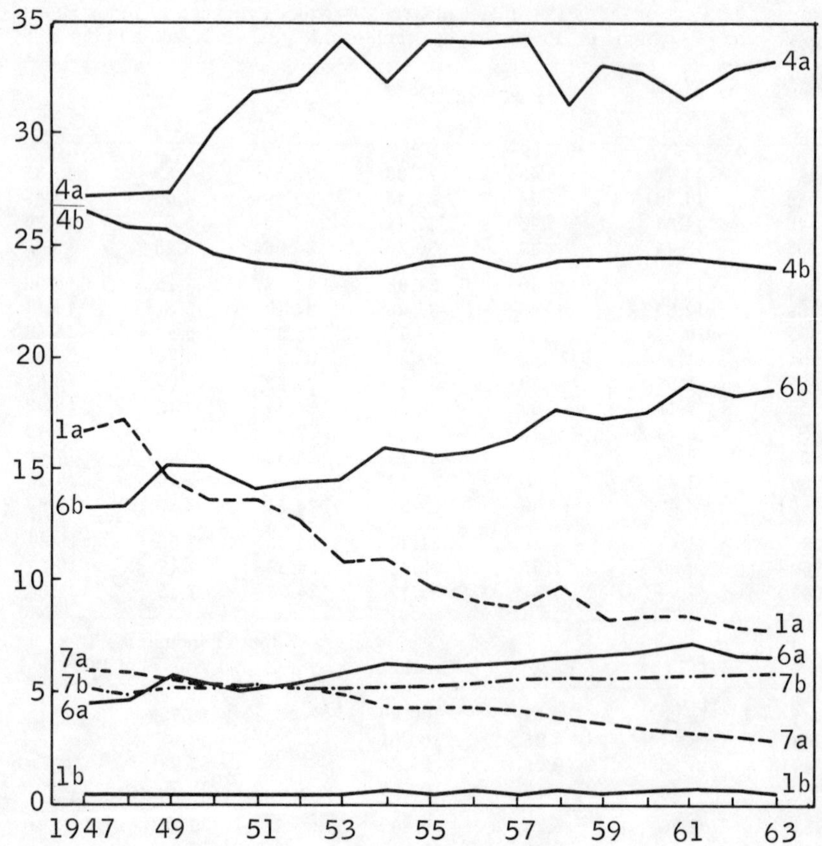

Fig. 3.5. Percentage of Business Gross Product Produced by Industries 1, 4, 6, and 7 which is Produced by each of 8 Sub-Industries.

Sub-Industries

1a Farms
1b Agricultural services, forestry, and fisheries
4a Durable goods manufacturing
4b Nondurable goods manufacturing
6a Finance and insurance
6b Real estate
7a Railroads
7b Other transportation

Gross Output of these 17 Industries. A close approximation of the missing gross output series can be constructed, however, by adding the disaggregated series "Profits of Manufacturing Corporations" and "Depreciation Charges of Manufacturing Corporations" to "Compensation of Manufacturing Employees." Since Unincorpor-

Table 3.6. Numerical Values of ks, ks_1, and ks_2 in the United States with Statistical Analysis

Year	ks	ks_1	ks_2
1947	2.00	2.00	2.00
1948	2.03	2.02	2.02
1949	2.05	2.05	2.00
1950	2.07	2.10	1.97
1951	2.04	2.11	1.94
1952	1.99	2.06	1.93
1953	1.92	2.03	1.89
1954	1.93	1.99	1.93
1955	1.95	2.06	1.89
1956	1.88	1.99	1.89
1957	1.89	1.95	1.89
1958	1.92	1.97	1.95
1959	1.91	1.97	1.93
1960	1.90	1.96	1.93
1961	1.91	1.96	1.94
1962	1.91	1.99	1.92
1963	1.91	1.98	1.92
Variation	9.6%	7.9%	6.6%
Largest Change	3.5%	3.4%	3.1%
Mean of ks	1.95	2.01	1.94
b	-1.00245	-.00637	-.00471
s	.0627	.0503	.0398
s_{kt}	.0368	.0378	.0328
v	3.2%	2.5%	2.1%
vt	1.9%	1.3%	1.7%
R^2	-.655	-.436	-.320

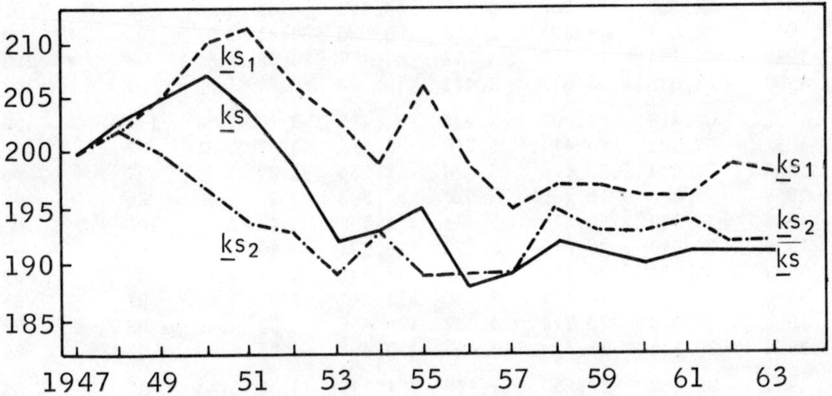

Fig. 3.6. Graph of ks, ks_1, and ks_2 in the United States.
ks = BGPs/Wbs ks1 = 1/kst . BGPs1947/BGPs
ks_2 = 1/ks1947 . BGPst/BGPs (s = Sub-industries 1a to 7b)

ated Enterprises produce only a small fraction of total manufacturing output the distortion from omitting profits and depreciation of these firms is slight. Table 3.7. presents the derivation of Disaggregateable Manufacturing Mark-Up (k.4i) and compares this series to Manufacturing Industry Mark-Up (k.4) from Table 3.1. As Figure 3.7. indicates the indices of k.4i and k.4 are close to the same.

Table 3.8. presents mark-up data for the 17 Manufacturing Industries from 1946 to 1961 and Table 3.9. gives the percentage of Manufacturing output produced by each. Most of the 17 Industries might be described as having fairly stable mark-ups although Industries b. Tobacco manufactures, f. Paper and allied products, h. Chemicals & allied products, i. Products of petroleum and coal, and q. Automobiles and automobile equipment show considerable fluctuation.

Table 3.10. shows the results obtained by again calculating

Table 3.7. Derivation of Disaggregateable Manufacturing Industry Mark-Up (k.4i) with Comparison to Manufacturing Industry Mark-Up (k.4). 1. Compensation of Mfg. Employees, 2. Profits of Mfg. Corporations, 3. Depreciation Charges of Mfg. Corporations, 4. Disaggregateable Gross Output of Mfg. (Z.4i), 5. Disaggregateable Mfg. Industry Mark-Up (k.4i), 6. Mfg. Industry Mark-Up (k.4), 7. k.4i Index, 8. k.4 Index. (1947-49 = 100) (million $)

Year	1. + (W.4)	2. +	3. =	4. (Z.4i) +	5. (W.4) =	6. k.4i)	7. k.4i Index	8. k.4 Index
1946	$38,178	$11,402	$ 1,916	$ 51,526	1.35		96	
1947	44,537	16,529	2,376	63,442	1.42	1.50	101	99
1948	48,604	18,233	2,818	69,655	1.43	1.50	101	99
1949	46,124	14,203	3,172	63,499	1.38	1.54	98	102
1950	52,535	23,579	3,444	79,558	1.51	1.56	107	103
1951	62,418	24,999	3,998	91,415	1.46	1.56	104	103
1952	67,391	20,411	4,710	92,512	1.37	1.51	97	100
1953	74,809	22,116	5,629	102,554	1.37	1.48	97	98
1954	71,089	18,703	6,510	96,302	1.35	1.46	96	96
1955	77,979	26,310	7,499	111,788	1.43	1.52	101	100
1956	83,943	26,018	8,372	118,333	1.40	1.47	99	97
1957	87,671	24,467	9,300	121,438	1.37	1.47	97	97
1958	83,726	18,481	9,440	111,647	1.33	1.44	94	95
1959	92,913	25,713	9,829	128,455	1.38	1.48	98	98
1960	96,334	23,674	10,450	130,458	1.34	1.46	95	96
1961	96,557	23,559	11,160	131,276	1.34	1.45	95	96
1962						1.47		97
1963						1.47		97

Source: *U. S. Income and Output*, 1958, pp. 200, 203, 216; *Survey of Current Business*, July 1962, July 1964.

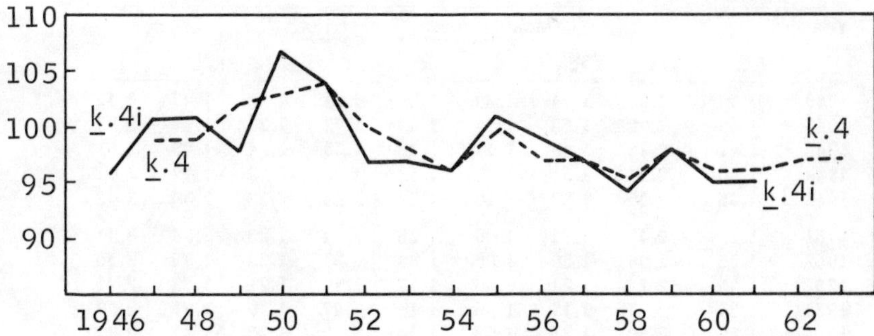

Fig. 3.7. Indices of Manufacturing Industry Mark-Up (k.4), and Disaggregatable Manufacturing Industry Mark-Up, (k.4i), in the United States. (1947-49 = 100)

fixed weight $k.4i_1$ and fixed mark-up $k.4i_2$ series and comparing them with k.4i. Here again weight shifts were somewhat destabilizing on balance as indicated by the standard deviation of k.4i being non-significantly longer than that for $k.4i_1$ (.0494 and .0463 respectively). As Figure 3.8. also indicates, weight shifts between Manufacturing industries were of very minor importance in accounting for the yearly movements or trend of Manufacturing mark-up.

Since Manufacturing Industry 4m. Metals, metal products, & misc., accounts for some 20 per cent of Manufacturing output it

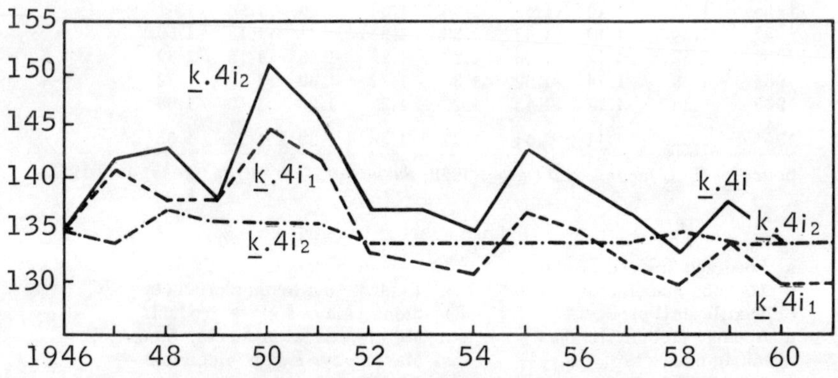

Fig. 3.8. Graph of k.4i, $k.4i_1$, and $k.4i_2$ in the United States. k.4i = BGP.4i/W.4 $k.4i_1$ = 1/k.4it . BGP.4i1946/BGP.4 $k.4i_2$ = 1/k.4i1946 . BGP.4it/BGP.4

(i = Manufacturing Industries a to q)

Table 3.8. Mark-Up in 17 Manufacturing Industries in the United States

Year	a	b	c	d	e	f	g	h	i
1946	1.60	1.91	1.54	1.20	1.26	1.54	1.35	1.77	2.42
1947	1.50	1.98	1.52	1.17	1.32	1.72	1.29	1.81	2.87
1948	1.41	2.18	1.46	1.11	1.28	1.56	1.24	1.73	3.51
1949	1.40	2.21	1.25	1.07	1.19	1.43	1.22	1.77	2.61
1950	1.45	2.30	1.38	1.10	1.32	1.64	1.23	2.08	3.02
1951	1.38	2.17	1.31	1.06	1.25	1.74	1.23	1.98	3.01
1952	1.36	2.08	1.20	1.06	1.20	1.53	1.22	1.75	2.55
1953	1.36	2.23	1.21	1.06	1.17	1.49	1.21	1.73	2.71
1954	1.34	2.11	1.17	1.06	1.19	1.47	1.19	1.71	2.67
1955	1.39	2.30	1.25	1.08	1.24	1.53	1.23	1.87	2.97
1956	1.36	2.33	1.25	1.07	1.20	1.56	1.24	1.78	3.03
1957	1.35	2.41	1.23	1.06	1.17	1.46	1.22	1.74	2.72
1958	1.39	2.58	1.22	1.07	1.18	1.42	1.20	1.67	2.46
1959	1.41	2.62	1.29	1.08	1.21	1.44	1.23	1.80	2.68
1960	1.39	2.54	1.26	1.08	1.16	1.40	1.21	1.70	2.76
1961	1.39	2.65	1.26	1.09	1.17	1.38	1.20	1.69	2.58

Year	j	k	l	m	n	o	p	q
1946	1.44	1.27	1.36	1.26	1.20	1.09	1.00	1.11
1947	1.29	1.24	1.37	1.35	1.33	1.30	1.02	1.56
1948	1.32	1.15	1.39	1.39	1.35	1.33	1.15	1.67
1949	1.24	1.11	1.39	1.32	1.33	1.30	1.14	1.79
1950	1.50	1.17	1.55	1.46	1.43	1.49	1.24	2.00
1951	1.52	1.13	1.48	1.46	1.41	1.42	1.17	1.71
1952	1.36	1.13	1.41	1.31	1.35	1.39	1.16	1.68
1953	1.35	1.12	1.45	1.34	1.31	1.34	1.18	1.63
1954	1.31	1.13	1.47	1.31	1.29	1.31	1.20	1.57
1955	1.38	1.15	1.58	1.39	1.32	1.30	1.19	1.88
1956	1.38	1.13	1.52	1.36	1.34	1.29	1.18	1.61
1957	1.34	1.13	1.47	1.33	1.31	1.31	1.18	1.66
1958	1.36	1.12	1.48	1.29	1.27	1.28	1.15	1.37
1959	1.38	1.14	1.52	1.30	1.32	1.30	1.12	1.72
1960	1.33	1.12	1.43	1.26	1.27	1.23	1.10	1.68
1961	1.31	1.11	1.41	1.27	1.28	1.23	1.12	1.65

Source: *U. S. Income and Output* 1958, *Survey of Current Business*, July 1962.

Manufacturing Industries

- a Food and kindred products
- b Tobacco manufactures
- c Textile mill products
- d Apparel & other finished fabric products
- e Lumber & furniture products
- f Paper & allied products
- g Printing, publishing & allied products
- h Chemicals & allied products
- i Products of petroleum & coal
- j Rubber products
- k Leather and leather products
- l Stone, clay, & glass products
- m Metals, metal products, & misc.
- n Machinery, except electrical
- o Electrical machinery
- p Transportation equipment, except automobiles
- q automobiles & automobile equipment

Table 3.9. Percentage of Total Manufacturing Output Produced by the 17 Manufacturing Industries in the U. S.

Year	a	b	c	d	e	f	g	h	i
1946	11.66	.73	8.37	5.96	5.34	3.54	5.19	7.12	3.86
1947	10.10	.64	7.69	5.08	5.75	3.82	4.76	6.82	4.49
1948	9.22	.67	7.66	4.67	5.41	3.53	4.66	6.22	5.81
1949	10.20	.78	6.47	4.86	5.04	3.47	5.27	6.85	4.88
1950	8.95	.68	6.50	4.32	5.35	3.66	4.51	7.20	4.61
1951	8.18	.64	5.50	3.80	4.92	3.90	4.26	7.21	4.79
1952	8.35	.64	4.87	3.91	4.78	3.53	4.46	6.80	4.34
1953	8.03	.66	4.45	3.73	4.28	3.44	4.33	6.74	4.54
1954	8.61	.69	4.14	3.86	4.39	3.72	4.75	7.33	4.80
1955	8.04	.66	4.05	3.59	4.44	3.65	4.54	7.37	4.71
1956	7.99	.67	3.93	3.62	4.28	3.85	4.66	7.44	4.85
1957	7.94	.69	3.65	3.55	3.86	3.66	4.75	7.61	4.61
1958	8.92	.84	3.72	3.75	4.10	3.91	5.15	7.98	4.52
1959	8.35	.79	3.82	3.63	4.11	3.81	4.91	8.09	4.35
1960	8.55	.83	3.71	3.69	3.86	3.83	5.13	8.07	4.41
1961	8.81	.88	3.65	3.77	3.78	3.99	5.27	8.35	4.18

Year	j	k	l	m	n	o	p	q	check%
1946	2.17	2.24	3.11	18.35	9.65	4.97	3.57	4.17	100.00
1947	1.76	1.91	3.03	19.03	10.54	5.88	2.68	6.00	99.98
1948	1.60	1.67	3.19	19.97	10.68	5.64	2.93	6.45	99.98
1949	1.52	1.70	3.36	19.16	9.98	5.49	3.10	7.87	100.00
1950	1.73	1.55	3.43	20.30	9.64	5.94	2.73	8.87	99.98
1951	1.81	1.31	3.43	21.47	11.25	6.29	3.82	7.42	100.00
1952	1.73	1.40	3.20	20.53	11.76	7.02	5.34	7.33	99.99
1953	1.69	1.29	3.26	21.67	10.98	7.14	5.83	7.93	99.99
1954	1.59	1.33	3.48	20.63	10.53	6.82	6.11	7.20	99.98
1955	1.72	1.27	3.64	21.33	9.94	6.42	5.44	9.18	99.99
1956	1.68	1.25	3.60	21.50	11.06	6.81	5.96	6.85	100.00
1957	1.66	1.24	3.49	21.53	10.90	7.27	6.54	7.06	100.01
1958	1.74	1.28	3.74	20.86	10.10	7.49	6.52	5.39	100.01
1959	1.78	1.25	3.78	20.57	10.45	7.84	5.68	6.81	100.02
1960	1.75	1.19	3.67	20.49	10.33	8.01	5.34	7.12	99.98
1961	1.75	1.20	3.58	20.47	10.30	8.35	5.36	6.30	99.99

Source: *U. S. Income and Output* 1958, *Survey of Current Business*, July 1962.

Manufacturing Industries

a Food and kindred products
b Tobacco manufactures
c Textile mill products
d Apparel & other finished fabric products
e Lumber & furniture products
f Paper & allied products
g Printing, publishing & allied
h Chemicals & allied products
i Products of petroleum & coal
j Rubber products
k Leather and leather products
l Stone, clay, & glass products
m Metals, metal products, & misc.
n Machinery, except electrical
o Electrical machinery
p Transportation equipment, except automobiles
q Automobiles & automobile equipment

seems useful to disaggregate it further into 4 sub-groups. Table 3.11. presents data on mark-up and weights for these sub-groups from 1948 to 1961. All of the sub-groups have mark-up factors of about the same stability as does 4m itself and all series except that for 4mc. Instruments, show a declining mark-up trend from Korean War highs.

Table 3.12. gives the values of fixed weight $\underline{k}.4\bar{m}_1$ and fixed mark-up $\underline{k}.4m_2$ together with $\underline{k}.4m$. As Figure 3.9. shows visually $\underline{k}.4m$ and $\underline{k}.4m_1$ are virtually the same series, weight shifts being insignificantly destabilizing ($\underline{s}$ = .0632 and .0618 respectively).

This concludes our study of weight shifts as accounting for, or rather, failing to account for, aggregate mark-up stability in the United States. Before turning to similar studies in Canada and the United Kingdom let us take a brief look at mark-up in several leading manufacturing firms. Four corporations were selected for this study: United States Rubber, United States Steel, General

Table 3.10. Numerical Values of $\underline{k}.4i$, $\underline{k}.4i_1$, and $\underline{k}.4i_2$ in the United States with Statistical Analysis

Year	$\underline{k}.4i$	$\underline{k}.4i_1$	$\underline{k}.4i_2$
1946	1.35	1.35	1.35
1947	1.42	1.41	1.34
1948	1.43	1.38	1.37
1949	1.38	1.38	1.36
1950	1.51	1.45	1.36
1951	1.46	1.42	1.36
1952	1.37	1.33	1.34
1953	1.37	1.32	1.34
1954	1.35	1.31	1.34
1955	1.43	1.37	1.34
1956	1.40	1.35	1.34
1957	1.37	1.32	1.34
1958	1.33	1.30	1.35
1959	1.38	1.34	1.34
1960	1.34	1.30	1.34
1961	1.34	1.30	1.34
Variation	12.7%	10.9%	2.2%
Largest Change	8.1%	5.1%	2.2%
Mean $\bar{k}$	1.39	1.35	1.35
$\underline{b}$	-.00488	-.00660	-.00119
$\underline{s}$	.0494	.0463	.0106
$\underline{s}_{kt}$	.0444	.0347	.0093
$\underline{v}$	3.6%	3.4%	0.8%
$\underline{vt}$	3.2%	2.6%	0.6%
R^2	-.196	-.436	-.230

Table 3.11. Mark-Up in Manufacturing Industry m, Metals, Metal Products, & misc. together with sub-categories and Percentage of Total Metal Manufacturing Produced by the 4 sub-categories.

Year	Mark-Up			
	4m	4ma	4mb	4mc	4md
1946	1.26				
1947	1.35				
1948	1.39	1.47	1.34	1.28	1.29
1949	1.32	1.42	1.26	1.25	1.24
1950	1.46	1.58	1.37	1.36	1.35
1951	1.46	1.59	1.35	1.39	1.31
1952	1.31	1.40	1.24	1.33	1.24
1953	1.34	1.49	1.21	1.32	1.20
1954	1.31	1.44	1.21	1.33	1.20
1955	1.39	1.57	1.24	1.36	1.25
1956	1.36	1.51	1.23	1.36	1.24
1957	1.33	1.46	1.21	1.31	1.22
1958	1.29	1.38	1.19	1.33	1.22
1959	1.30	1.40	1.20	1.39	1.24
1960	1.26	1.35	1.16	1.35	1.18
1961	1.27	1.33	1.18	1.36	1.23
		Percentage of 4m Produced			
	Check %	4ma	4mb	4mc	4md
1948	100.00	46.53	33.43	7.60	12.44
1949	100.00	45.94	33.17	8.14	12.75
1950	100.01	47.70	32.49	7.83	11.99
1951	100.01	48.75	32.37	8.44	10.45
1952	99.99	44.62	35.20	9.55	10.62
1953	100.00	46.12	34.65	9.14	10.09
1954	100.00	43.91	34.95	10.13	11.01
1955	100.01	48.34	32.27	9.15	10.25
1956	100.00	47.93	31.91	9.69	10.47
1957	100.01	47.36	32.52	9.85	10.28
1958	99.99	43.56	34.34	10.77	11.32
1959	100.00	43.85	34.12	11.17	10.86
1960	100.01	43.27	34.55	11.46	10.73
1961	100.01	40.85	36.10	11.79	11.27

Source: *U. S. Income and Output* 1958, *Survey of Current Business*, July 1962.

Metals Manufacturing & Sub-Categories

4m Metals, metal products, & misc.
4ma Primary metal industries
4mb Fabricated metal products, including ordinance
4mc Instruments
4md Miscellaneous metal manufacturing

Table 3.12. Numerical Values of $\underline{k}$.4m, $\underline{k}$.4m$_1$ and $\underline{k}$.4m$_2$ in the United States with Statistical Analysis

Year	$\underline{k}$.4m	$\underline{k}$.4m$_1$	$\underline{k}$.4m$_2$
1946	1.26		
1947	1.35		
1948	1.39	1.39	1.39
1949	1.32	1.33	1.38
1950	1.46	1.46	1.39
1951	1.46	1.45	1.39
1952	1.31	1.32	1.38
1953	1.34	1.33	1.39
1954	1.31	1.32	1.38
1955	1.39	1.39	1.39
1956	1.36	1.36	1.39
1957	1.33	1.32	1.39
1958	1.29	1.29	1.38
1959	1.30	1.31	1.38
1960	1.26	1.27	1.38
1961	1.27	1.27	1.38
Variation '48-'61	14.7%	14.7%	0.7%
Largest Change	11.0%	9.6%	0.7%
Mean $\overline{k}$	1.34	1.34	1.38
$\underline{s}$	.0632	.0618	.0073
$\underline{v}$	4.7%	4.6%	0.5%

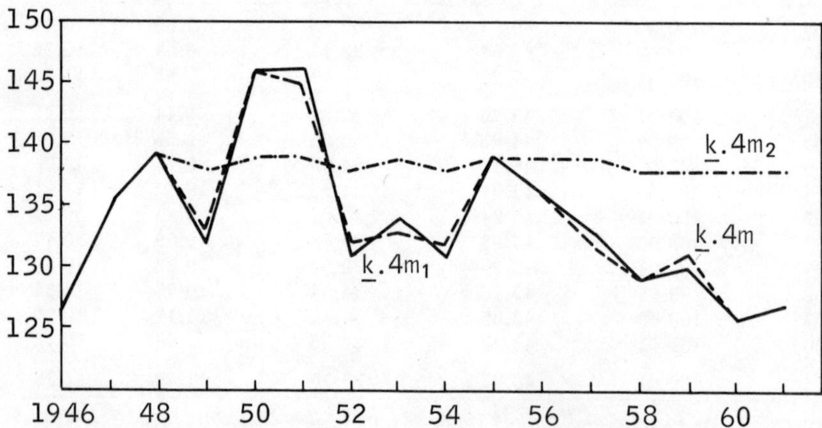

Fig. 3.9. Graph of $\underline{k}$.4m, $\underline{k}$.4m$_1$, and $\underline{k}$.4m$_2$ in the United States.

Electric, and General Motors, partly on the basis of their leadership in their fields and partly on the availability of fairly long series.

Series on Gross Value Added by firms are not available to

divide by their, generally available, payrolls to calculate mark-up. What is available are series on Sales by firms and series which can be manipulated to approximate Gross Value Added. It was decided to calculate both firm mark-up and the ratio (S/W) of Sales to Employee Compensation to see whether S/W is a good standin for k or differs greatly from it in variability.

Table 3.13. gives the derivation of mark-up at U. S. Rubber from 1950 to 1962. Employee Compensation was subtracted from Cost of Sales to derive value Purchased from Others. These purchases were subtracted from Sales to approximate Value Added.

Table 3.13. Derivation of U. S. Rubber Corporation Mark-Up, and Sales/Employee Compensation Ratio together with Rubber Products Manufacturing Mark-Up k.4j. (millions of dollars) Columns: 1. Cost of Sales, 2. Employee Compensation, 3. Purchased from others, 4. Sales, 5. Value added, 6. Mark-Up kUSR, 7. Sales/Employee Compensation S/WUSR, 8. Mark-Up kUSR Index, 9. S/W Index, 10. Rubber Products Manufacturing Mark-Up k.4j Index.

Year	1. -	2. =	3.	4. - 3. =	5.	6.	7.	8.	9.	10.
		W		S		kUSR	S/W			
1946										96
1947										86
1948										88
1949										80
1950	$567.1	$216.6	$350.5	$ 696.5	$346.0	1.60	3.22	100	100	100
1951	656.6	257.5	399.1	838.0	438.9	1.70	3.25	106	101	102
1952	671.6	269.4	402.2	857.1	448.9	1.67	3.16	104	98	91
1953	670.1	302.9	367.2	839.8	472.6	1.56	2.77	98	86	90
1954	627.6	290.1	337.5	782.5	445.0	1.53	2.70	96	84	87
1955	735.0	323.4	411.6	925.5	513.9	1.59	2.86	99	89	92
1956	722.6	331.5	391.1	901.3	510.2	1.54	2.72	96	84	92
1957	703.8	314.1	389.7	873.6	483.9	1.55	2.72	97	86	90
1958	692.4	305.1	387.3	870.6	483.3	1.58	2.85	99	89	91
1959	763.8	330.2	433.6	976.8	543.2	1.65	2.96	103	92	92
1960	762.0	336.3	425.7	966.8	541.1	1.61	2.87	101	89	89
1961	745.6	337.5	408.1	940.4	532.3	1.58	2.79	99	87	87
1962	803.5	358.5	445.0	1,006.8	561.8	1.57	2.81	98	87	

Statistical Analysis	kUSR	S/W	k.4j*
Variation	10.5%	18.4%	14.8%
Largest Change	6.8%	13.1%	11.3%
Mean	1.59	2.90	1.38
s	.0515	1882	.0672
v	3.2%	6.5%	4.9%

Source: *Moody's Industrials* 1958, p. 1751, 1963, p. 2592.

*Analysis is of k.4j in original numbers rather than index. See Table 3.9. 1950-1962.

U. S. Rubber mark-up (kUSR) moved between a high of 1.70 in 1951 and a low of 1.53 in 1954 for a standard deviation of .0515 or relative variability ($v = s/\bar{k}$) of 3.2%. The S/W ratio moved between a high of 3.25 in 1951 and a 1954 low of 2.70; s = .1882, v = 6.5%.

Figure 3.10. shows the indices of kUSR and S/WUSR plotted against the mark-up index of Manufacturing Industry 4j, Rubber

Table 3.14. Derivation of U. S. Steel Corporation Mark-Up, and Sales/Employee Compensation Ratio together with Metals, metal product & misc. Mark-Up k.4m. Columns: 1. Cost of Sales, 2. Wages, salaries, and supplements, 3. Purchased from Others, 4. Sales, 5. Value Added, 6. Mark-Up kUSS, Sales/Employee Compensation S/WUSS, 8. kUSS Index, 9. S/WUSS Index, 10. k.4m. Index. (1947-49 = 100) (millions of dollars.)

Year	1.	- 2. =	3.*	4.	- 3. = 5.*	6.	7.	8.	9.	10.
		W		S		kUSS	S/W			
1941	$1,112	$ 609	$ 503	$1,621	$1,117	1.83	2.66	118	111	101
1942	1,374	771	603	1,863	1,260	1.63	2.42	105	101	
1943	1,512	903	609	1,973	1,363	1.51	2.19	97	91	
1944	1,646	947	698	2,082	1,384	1.46	2.20	94	92	
1945	1,398	816	582	1,741	1,158	1.42	2.13	92	89	
1946	1,207	703	504	1,486	982	1.40	2.11	90	88	93
1947	1,644	901	743	2,117	1,373	1.53	2.35	99	98	100
1948	1,938	1,040	899	2,474	1,575	1.52	2.38	98	99	103
1949	1,722	932	789	2,293	1,504	1.61	2.46	104	103	98
1950	2,074	1,147	927	2,947	2,021	1.76	2.57	114	107	108
1951	2,467	1,342	1,126	3,510	2,384	1.78	2.62	115	109	108
1952	2,404	1,297	1,108	3,132	2.024	1.56	2.42	101	101	97
1953	2,715	1,531	1,184	3,853	2,669	1.74	2.52	112	105	99
1954	2,257	1,343	914	3,241	2,328	1.73	2.41	112	100	97
1955	2,673	1,556	1,117	4,080	2,962	1.90	2.62	123	109	103
1956	2,844	1,603	1,241	4,199	2,958	1.84	2.62	119	109	101
1957	2,835	1,776	1,059	4,378	3,320	1.87	2.47	121	103	99
1958	2,339	1,428	912	3,439	2,527	1.77	2.41	114	100	96
1959	2,530	1,489	1,041	3,598	2,557	1.72	2.42	111	101	96
1960	2,469	1,591	878	3,649	2,771	1.74	2.29	112	95	93
1961	2,328	1,506	821	3,302	2,480	1.65	2.19	106	91	94
1962	2,531	1,459	1,072	3,469	2,397	1.64	2.38	106	99	
			Statistical Analysis							
			Variation			22.2%	17.9%			14.7%
			Largest Change			12.9%	8.7%			11.0%
			Mean			1.71	2.45			1.34
			s			.1159	.1223			.0600
			v			6.8%	5.0%			4.5%

Source: *Moody's Industrials* 1943, p. 2625; 1949, p. 1726; 1958, p. 1364; 1963, p. 1323.

*Figures may not add across because of rounding.

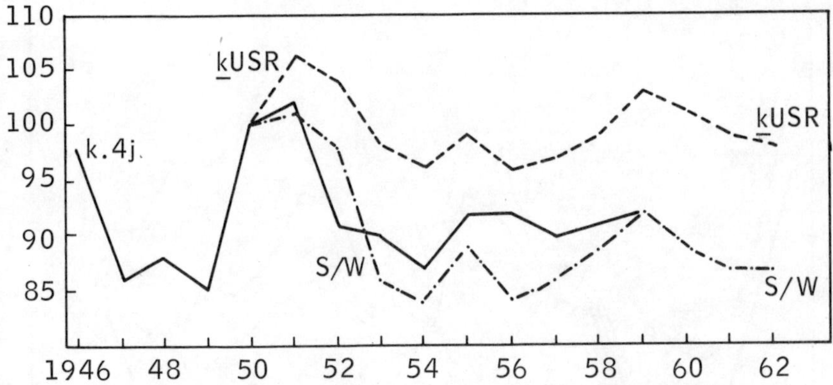

Fig. 3.10. Indices of: *United States Rubber Corporation* Mark-Up kUSR, U. S. Rubber Sales/Employee Compensation Ratio S/WUSR, and Rubber Products Manufacturing Mark-Up k.4j. 1950 = 100

products, from 1946 to 1961. The fluctuation of k.4j is between that of kUSR and S/WUSR in amplitude, with an s of .0672 and v of 4.9%.

Table 3.14. gives the derivation of the mark-up and S/W series at U. S. Steel from 1941 to 1962 together with the index of k.4m, Metals, metal products, & misc., from 1946 to 1961. In contrast to the data just developed for U. S. Rubber, mark-up at U. S. Steel was more variable for the period 1947-1962 than either S/W or k.4m[11] (s being respectively .1159, .1223, and .0600 for relative variability v of 6.8%, 5.0% and 4.5%.)

As Figure 3.11. shows, the indices of kUSS and S/WUSS were close to the same series until the mid 1950s when mark-up rose markedly but the ratio S/W did not. Gardiner Means contends that in the early 1950s the management of U. S. Steel changed their mark-up formula and pricing strategy from that of "profit satisficers" to that of would be maximizers thereby directly causing the "creeping inflation" of the 1950s.[12] If this is true, why would this raise mark-up but not S/W? The apparent answer lies in a growing self sufficiency seen in the relative and even absolute decline in Column 3., "Purchased from Others," of Table 3.14. Throughout

[11] The reconversion year 1946 was omitted because of its unusually low mark-up.

[12] Gardiner C. Means, "Pricing Power and the Public Interest," *Administered Prices: A Compendium on Public Policy*, 88th Congress, Sub-Committee on Anti-Trust and Monopoly of the Committee on the Judiciary, United States Senate; (Washington) GPO 1963 p. 223.

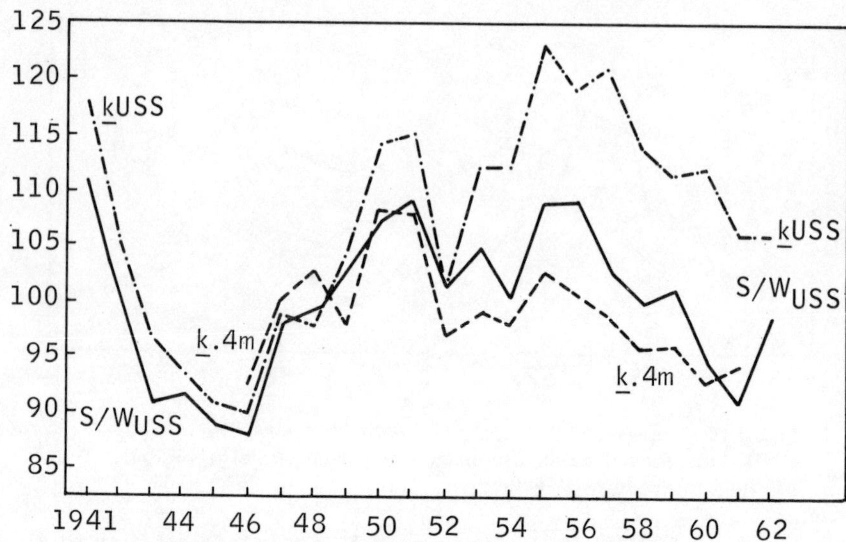

Fig. 3.11. Indices of: *United States Steel Corporation* Mark-Up, kUSS, U. S. Steel Sales/Employee Compensation Ratio, S/WUSS, and Metals, Metal Products & Misc. Mark-Up, k.4m. 1947-49 = 100

the period for which we have data on k.4m it parallels S/WUSS fairly closely.

In Table 3.15. the derivation of mark-up and S/W for General Electric Corporation is given together with the index of k.4o, Electrical machinery manufacturing. In the years between 1947 and 1962[13] kGE and k.4o were close to the same series when reduced to indices, while S/WGE fluctuated considerably more widely.[14] At General Electric the ratio of Sales to Employee Compensation during World War Two was quite high. It fell sharply with peace and shows a generally downward trend, with sharp fluctuations, since. Figure 3.12. presents the three indices visually.

The final corporation for which we have calculated mark-up and S/W is General Motors. *Moody's Industrials* supplies data from which General Motors' mark-up, kGM, can be calculated back to 1934 and compared with S/WGM. Table 3.16. presents the derivation of these ratios together with the index of mark-up in Automobiles and automobile equipment manufacturing, k.4q, from 1946 to 1961. Mark-up at General Motors was somewhat less stable than the ratio of Sales to Employee Compensation, relative vari-

[13] Reconversion year 1946 omitted in statistical analyses.

[14] Relative variabilities, v, are 6.0%, 5.2%, and 11.3% respectively.

ability, v, being 6.2% and 5.2% respectively. However, kGM was considerably more stable than Automobile industry mark-up, k.4q, which had a v of 8.5% from 1947-1961.

The history of General Motors' mark-up is important for any theory which would base aggregate mark-up stability on stable mark-up behavior in the individual firm. As is well known,

Table 3.15. Derivation of General Electric Corporation Mark-Up and Sales/ Employee Compensation Ratio together with Electrical machinery Mark-Up k.4o. Columns: 1. Cost of Sales, 2. Employee Compensation, 3. Purchased from Others, 4. Sales, 5. Value Added, 6. Mark-Up kGE, Sales/Employee Compensation S/WGE, 8. kGE Index, 9. S/WGE Index, 10. k.4o Index. (1947-49 = 100) (millions of dollars)

Year	1. -	2. =	3.*	4. -3. =	5.*	6.	7.	8.	9.	10.
		W		S		kGE	S/W			
1942	$ 832	$ 382	$ 450	$1,171	$ 721	1.89	3.06	115	107	
1943	1,188	472	716	1,534	818	1.73	3.25	105	114	
1944	1,246	464	782	1,534	752	1.62	3.31	99	116	
1945	1,224	400	824	1,467	643	1.61	3.67	98	128	
1946	777	359	418	911	494	1.37	2.54	84	89	83
1947	1,202	560	642	1,525	883	1.58	2.72	96	95	99
1948	1,433	663	770	1,865	1,095	1.65	2.81	101	98	102
1949	1,426	607	819	1,851	1,031	1.70	3.05	104	107	99
1950	1,606	681	925	2,233	1,308	1.92	3.28	117	115	114
1951	1,925	884	1,041	2,619	1,578	1.79	2.96	109	103	108
1952	2,269	949	1,320	2,993	1,674	1.76	3.15	107	110	106
1953	2,695	1,312	1,383	3,511	2,128	1.62	2.68	99	94	102
1954	2,571	1,251	1,321	3,335	2,014	1.61	2.67	98	93	100
1955	2,684	1,372	1,311	3,464	2,152	1.57	2.52	96	88	99
1956	3,155	1,644	1,511	4,090	2,579	1.57	2.49	96	87	98
1957	3,276	1,715	1,561	4,336	2,775	1.62	2.53	99	88	100
1958	3,103	1,640	1,463	4,121	2,658	1.62	2.51	99	88	98
1959	3,219	1,784	1,435	4,350	2,914	1.63	2.44	99	85	99
1960	3,172	1,848	1,324	4,198	2,874	1.55	2.27	95	79	94
1961	3,338	1,904	1,434	4,457	3,023	1.59	2.34	97	82	94
1962	3,577	2,041	1,536	4,793	3,257	1.60	2.35	98	82	
			Statistical Analysis 1947-1962							
			Variation			27.9%	36.4%			19.1%
			Largest Change			27.9%	23.8%			14.0%
			Mean			1.63	2.65			1.32
			s			.0984	.3030			.0680
			v			6.0%	11.3%			5.2%

Source: *Moody's Industrials* 1949, p. 1561; 1952, pp. 1437-38; 1958, p. 2343; 1963, p. 2103.

*Figures may not add across because of rounding.

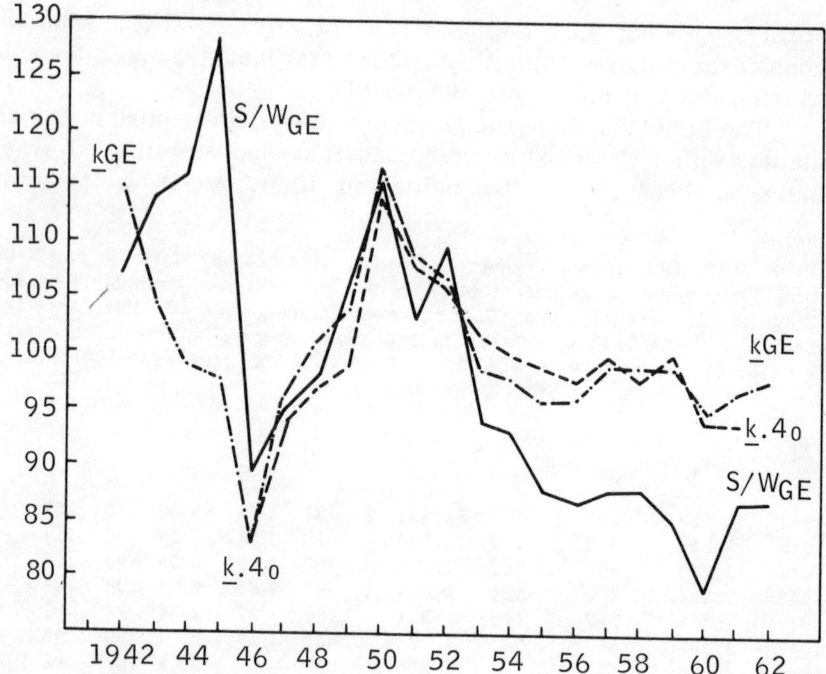

Fig. 3.12. *General Electric Corporation* Mark-Up, kGE, and Sales/Employee Compensation Ratio, S/WGE, together with Electrical Machinery Manufacturing Mark-Up, k.4o. Indices 1947-49 = 100

General Motors sets its prices not on the basis of a stable mark-up over wage costs but to realize a "target" rate of return on stockholders' equity of 20 per cent.[15]

Table 3.17. gives General Motors' net profit as a percentage of its Net Worth (Capital Stock and Surplus) from its establishment in 1917 to 1963. The year 1921 was the only year of loss, but in 1932 the corporation virtually "broke even." The low profits of G.M. during World War II were the result of deliberate policy.

> "The policy as to overall profits of the Corporation on products produced for war purposes is to limit the overall rate of profits from its manufacturing operations, before provision for income and excess profits taxes but after all

[15]Donaldson Brown, "Pricing in Relation to Financial Control," *Manag. and Admin.*, Feb. 1924, 7, 195-198; R. F. Lanzillotti, "Pricing Objectives in Large Companies," *Am. Econ. Rev.*, Dec. 1958, 48, 921-940; General Motors Corp., *General Motors Policies and Practices*, (Detroit) G.M.C., 1955.

Table 3.16. Derivation of General Motors Corporation Mark-Up and Sales/ Employee Compensation Ratio together with Automobiles and Automobile Equipment Mark-Up k.4q. Columns: 1. Cost of Sales, 2. Employee Compensation, 3. Purchased from Others, 4. Sales, 5. Value Added, 6. Mark-Up kGM, 7. Sales/ Employee Compensation S/WGM, 8. kGM Index, 9. S/WGM Index, 10. k.4q Index. (1947-49 = 100) (millions of dollars)

Year	1. -	2. =	3.*	4. -3. =	5.*	6.	7.	8.	9.	10.
		W		S		kGM	S/W			
1934	$ 685	$ 263	$ 422	$ 863	$ 441	1.67	3.28	90	92	
1935	900	328	572	1,156	583	1.80	3.53	97	99	
1936	1,093	403	690	1,439	750	1.86	3.57	100	100	
1937	1,286	484	802	1,607	804	1.66	3.32	89	93	
1938	872	327	546	1,067	522	1.60	3.27	86	92	
1939	1,056	414	642	1,377	735	1.78	3.33	96	93	
1940	1,388	502	886	1,795	909	1.81	3.58	97	100	
1941	1,850	681	1,169	2,437	1,268	1.86	3.58	100	100	
1942	1,882	874	1,008	2,251	1,243	1.42	3.57	76	72	
1943	3,179	1,338	1,841	3,796	1,955	1.46	2.84	78	80	
1944	3,664	1,396	2,268	4,262	1,995	1.43	3.05	77	85	
1945	2,812	1,022	1,790	3,128	1,338	1.31	3.06	70	86	
1946	1,751	887	863	1,963	1,099	1.24	2.21	67	62	66
1947	2,987	1,175	1,812	3,815	2,003	1.70	3.25	91	91	93
1948	3,564	1,306	2,259	4,702	2,443	1.87	3.60	101	101	100
1949	4,199	1,472	2,727	5,701	2,974	2.02	3.87	109	108	107
1950	5,315	1,843	3,471	7,531	4,060	2.20	4.09	118	115	120
1951	5,575	1,906	3,669	7,466	3,796	1.99	3.92	107	110	102
1952	5,656	2,062	3,594	7,549	3,956	1.92	3.66	103	103	101
1953	7,894	2,676	5,218	10,279	5,062	1.89	3.84	102	108	98
1954	7,570	2,610	4,960	9,824	4,864	1.86	3.76	100	105	94
1955	9,129	3,127	6,002	12,443	6,441	2.06	3.98	111	111	113
1956	8,236	2,896	5,340	10,796	5,456	1.88	3.73	101	104	96
1957	8,389	2,955	5,434	10,990	5,555	1.88	3.72	101	104	99
1958	7,476	2,688	4,787	9,522	4,735	1.76	3.55	95	99	82
1959	8,469	3,084	5,385	11,233	5,848	1.90	3.64	102	102	103
1960	9,666	3,487	6,178	12,736	6,588	1.88	3.65	101	102	101
1961	8,593	3.239	5,354	11,396	6,042	1.87	3.52	101	99	99
1962	10,645	3,895	6,750	14,640	7,890	2.03	3.76	109	105	
1963	11,914	4,313	7,601	16,495	8,894	2.06	3.82	111	107	

Statistical Analysis 1947-1963

	6.	7.	10.
Variation	25.6%	22.9%	37.4%
Largest Change	10.8%	8.2%	20.8%
Mean	1.93	3.73	1.68
s	.1205	.1957	.1435
v	6.2%	5.2%	8.5%

Source: *Moody's Industrials* 1940, p. 2014; 1949, p. 2607; 1954, p. 2580; *General Motors Annual Report*, 1943, 1948, 1955, 1959, 1961, 1963.

*Figures may not add across because of rounding.

Table 3.17. General Motors Corporation Net Profits as a Percentage of Net Worth 1917 to 1963 with Index 1947-49 = 100

Year	Profit %	Index	Year	Profit %	Index
1917	13.2	53	1941	18.0	73
1918	6.3	26	1942	13.7	55
1919	18.4	74	1943	11.7	47
1920	8.9	36	1944	13.1	53
1921	-10.5	-43	1945	13.9	56
1922	13.4	54	1946	6.1	25
1923	16.4	66	1947	18.3	74
1924	9.3	38	1948	24.4	99
1925	20.4	83	1949	31.3	127
1926	29.3	119	1950	34.9	141
1927	31.0	126	1951	20.0	81
1928	32.3	131	1952	20.4	83
1929	26.0	105	1953	20.0	81
1930	15.6	63	1954	24.1	98
1931	10.4	42	1955	27.9	113
1932	.2	8	1956	18.4	74
1933	9.5	38	1957	17.2	70
1934	10.9	44	1958	12.6	51
1935	18.0	73	1959	16.2	66
1936	24.5	99	1960	16.4	66
1937	19.8	80	1961	14.8	60
1938	9.9	40	1962	21.9	89
1939	17.4	70	1963	22.3	90
1940	18.0	73			

Source: *Moody's Industrials* 1935, p. 2013; 1941, p. 2587; General Motors *Annual Reports* 1943, 1949, 1955, 1963.

other charges including reserve provisions, to approximately one half the profit margin, expressed as a percentage of sales, realized in the year 1941 largely under the conditions of a competitive market."[16]

From 1917 to 1963 the average rate of profit on stockholders' equity was 17.9%, excluding the war and reconversion years of 1917 to 1919 and 1942 to 1946 profits have averaged 19.2% of stockholders' equity. Thus over the long period G.M.'s managers have come close to their target except when they patriotically lowered their sights in WWII. However, as Table 3.17. indicates, the year-to-year changes in the profit rate have been considerable, varying between -10.5% in 1921 and 32.3% in 1928; post war it has varied between 34.9% in 1950 and 12.6% in 1958.

[16]General Motors Corp., *Annual Report* 1943, p. 23.

Figure 3.13. visually compares the indices of the Mark-Up, Sales/Employee Compensation and Profits/Net Worth ratios from 1934 to 1963 for G.M. with the Automobiles and automobile equipment manufacturing mark-up, k.4q index from 1946 to 1961. While striving for, and not achieving, a stable net profit on stockholders' equity G.M. managers have obtained quite stable gross mark-up on wage cost and sales/wage cost ratios which apparently were not part of their design.

Table 3.18. summarizes our findings regarding relative variability (v = standard deviation/mean) of mark-up at the various levels of aggregation studied in the United States from 1947 to 1961. Several things are notable here. First, there is some increase in variability evident as we disaggregate from aggregate to industry, from manufacturing to the 17 manufacturing industries, from metal manufacturing to its 4 sub-categories, from the 4 manufacturing industries, Rubber products, Metals, Electrical machinery, and Automobiles to 4 major firms supplying these products, U. S. Rubber, U. S. Steel, General Electric, and General Motors. The truest picture is given when we weight v of individual series by the percentage of the relevant total output produced. This much reduces the effect of a few small categories some of them much marred by rounding off of the original data.

Second, mark-up is not clearly more stable than the ratio of sales to wage cost. Indeed, the weighted average relative variability of S/W for our 4 firms was 6.4% while that for mark-up was 7.4%. Lastly, relative variability even at the individual firm level is "fairly small." By way of comparison, the relative variability of Income Velocity (Vy) of the Money Supply from 1947 to 1961 was 14.6% while the v of the ratio of General Motors' Net Profit to Net Worth for these years was 29.7%.

CANADA

The Canadian *National Accounts* give us the breakdown needed to carry the question of k's stability down to the industry level for the entire period 1926-1960, in contrast to the short industry series available for the United States and the United Kingdom. Gross Domestic Product is presented with 15 industrial classifications and corresponding information on employee compensation.[17] Eliminating class number 14--Public Administration & Defense--we

[17] *National Accounts*, 1926-1955, pp. 56-7; 1960, p. 34.

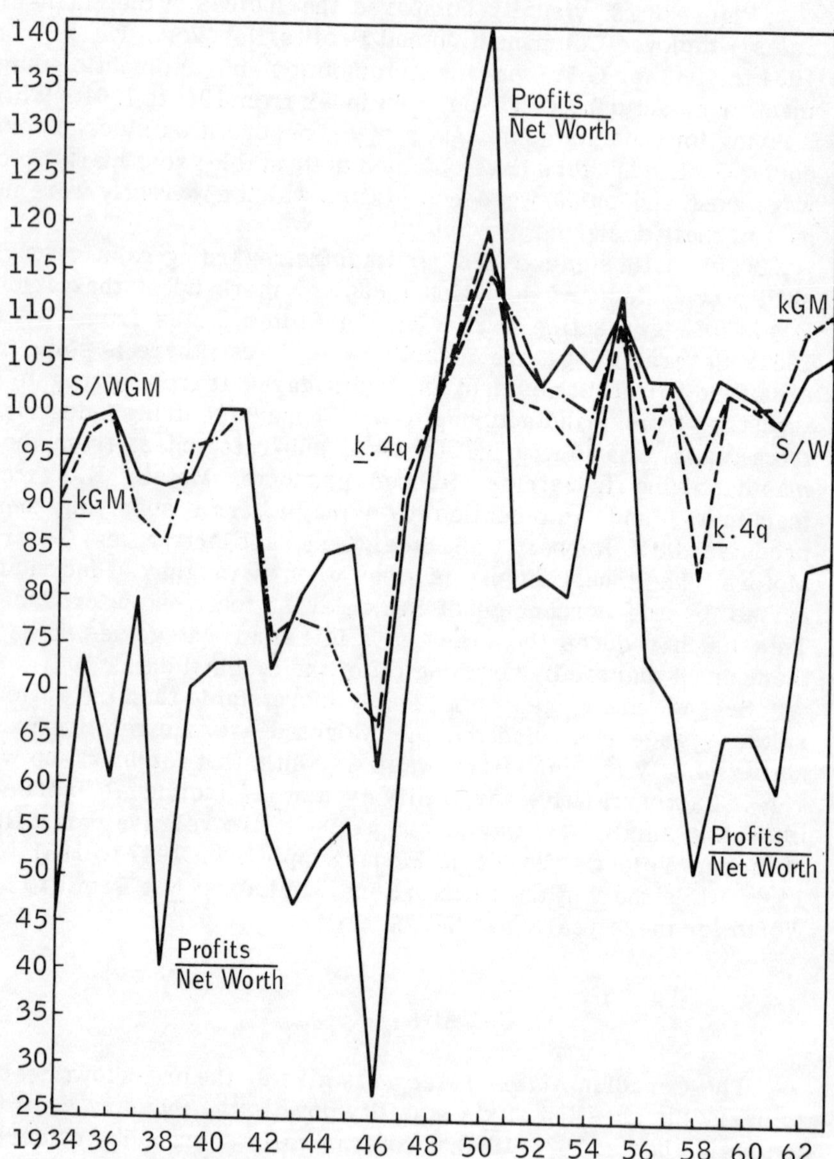

Fig. 3.13. *General Motors Corporation* Ratios: Wage Cost Mark-Up, kGM, Sales/Employee Compensation, S/WGM, Profits/Net Worth, and Automobiles and Automobile Equipment Manufacturing Mark-Up, k.4q. 1947-49 = 100

Table 3.18. Relative Variability (v) of Mark-Up in the Aggregate and at Disaggregate Levels in the United States 1947-1961. (Weighted Averages use Weights of 1953)

	v	Average v	Weighted Average v	Relative Variability (v) of individual series (%)
Aggregate Mark-Up	2.6%			
Disaggregates:				
Industries 1-11		6.1%	4.3%	1. 7.8 2. 7.0 3. 2.4 4. 2.4 5. 4.1 6. 4.0 7. 2.3 8. 7.8 9. 7.1 10. 10.4 11. 10.6*
Sub-Industries 1a - 7b		4.5	4.7	1a 6.8 1b 10.6* 4a 3.8 4b 2.0 6a 4.3 6b 7.7 7a 2.3 7b 3.0
Manufacturing Industry 4.	2.4			
17 Manufacturing Industries a-q		5.4	5.1	a. 2.9 b. 9.0* c. 7.6 d. 2.7 e. 4.4 f. 7.3 g. 2.0 h. 6.3 i. 11.2 j. 5.3 k. 2.8 l. 4.3 m. 4.5 n. 3.5 o. 5.2 p. 4.4 q. 8.5
Manufacturing Industry 4m.	4.5			
4 Metal Mfg.		4.4	5.1	ma. 5.8 mb. 5.3 mc. 2.9 md. 3.7
Sub-categories#				
4 Manufacturing Industries j, m, o, q		5.8	5.5	
4 Manufacturing Firms		6.2	7.4	USR 3.2 USS 6.8 GE 6.0 GM 8.5
Sales/Wage Cost 4 Mfg. Firms		7.4	6.4	USR 6.5 USS 5.0 GE 11.3 GM 5.2

Source: Aggregate Mark-Up, Table 1.1.; Industries 1-11, Tables 3.1. and 3.2.; Sub-Industries 1a. - 7b., Tables 3.4. and 3.5.; Manufacturing Industries a - q, Tables 3.8. and 3.9.; Metal Mfg. Sub-categories, Table 3.11.; Manufacturing Firms, USR Table 3.13.; USS Table 3.14.; GE Table 3.15.; GM Table 3.16.

*Marred by excessive rounding off of data. # 1948-1961.

arrive at Business Domestic Product. This divided by correspondingly reduced employee compensation gives us the aggregate wage cost mark-up and 14 industrial ks. This measure of mark-up, let us dub it kd, is only slightly less stable than k itself as is shown in Table 3.19. and Table 3.21. (Also given in Table 3.19. is kx which will be explained presently.) Numerical values of the 14 industries producing BDP are given in Table 3.20.

The 14 industrial mark-up series vary greatly. Mark-up averages 9.24 (wages 10.8% of gross proceeds) in Agriculture and only 1.17 (85.5%) in Forestry. In nine of the industries mark-up

Table 3.19. Three Canadian Mark-Up Ratios:
k = Business Gross Product ÷ Compensation of Business Employees
kd = Business Domestic Product ÷ Compensation of Business Employees
kx = Non-agricultural Business Domestic Product ÷ Compensation of Nonagricultural Business Employees

Year	k	kd	kx
1926	2.34	2.15	1.84
1927	2.38	2.14	1.85
1928	2.40	2.15	1.87
1929	2.24	2.00	1.82
1930	2.22	2.01	1.84
1931	2.12	1.86	1.77
1932	2.11	1.84	1.72
1933	2.14	1.82	1.71
1934	2.25	1.90	1.75
1935	2.26	1.93	1.77
1936	2.25	1.94	1.80
1937	2.24	1.93	1.78
1938	2.29	2.02	1.84
1939	2.35	2.05	1.87
1940	2.40	2.08	1.88
1941	2.35	2.02	1.87
1942	2.41	2.11	1.87
1943	2.24	1.97	1.79
1944	2.29	2.02	1.77
1945	2.26	2.02	1.80
1946	2.23	1.98	1.76
1947	2.16	1.91	1.71
1948	2.15	1.90	1.69
1949	2.16	1.92	1.73
1950	2.20	1.97	1.78
1951	2.21	1.95	1.72
1952	2.26	1.96	1.75
1953	2.18	1.88	1.72
1954	2.11	1.83	1.72
1955	2.17	1.89	1.77
1956	2.17	1.87	1.75
1957	2.10	1.81	1.73
1958	2.11	1.82	1.72
1959	2.13	1.84	1.75
1960	2.12	1.83	1.73
Variation	2.41 - 2.10	2.15 - 1.81	1.87 - 1.71
Largest	16 points	15 points	8 points
Change	1928-29	1928-29	1942-43
Mean	2.23	1.95	1.78
b	-.00503	-.00574	-.00325
s	.1019	.0976	.0573
s_{kt}	.0814	.0831	.0518
v	4.6%	5.0%	3.2%
vt	3.7%	4.3%	2.9%
R^2	-.251	-.275	-.182

declined from 1926 to 1960, as it did in kd as a whole, but in Agriculture (1), Forestry (2), Mining, quarrying, and oil wells (4), Construction (6), and Storage (8), the trend of mark-up was up.

A glance down column 1. of Table 3.20. makes evident that industry 1. Agriculture is in a class by itself in mark-up variability. Indeed, it is rather a misnomer to speak of a wage cost mark-up in Canadian agriculture where hired labor is relatively so unimportant. Over the period 1926 to 1960 the agricultural "mark-up" varied all the way from 15.17 (wages only 6.6% of gross agricultural proceeds) to 4.40 (22.8%). Agricultural mark-up has a strong up trend from the lows of the great depression, b = +.19272, v = 31.6%. The Canadian agricultural mark-up data strongly confirm the pattern seen in the United States: Agriculture does not have a stable mark-up.

This instability in the agricultural mark-up, together with fluctuations in agriculture's share of Business Domestic Product' accounts for much of kd's movements. If we confine ourselves to the study of mark-up in the non-agricultural economy in Canada the ratio kd becomes kx, a "still more constant constant". This series varies only from 1.88 (wages 53.3% of gross proceeds) to 1.71 (57.5%); b is reduced from -.00574 to -.00325, v from 5.0% to 3.2%. Thus, merely be eliminating agriculture we eliminate much of the downward trend and year-to-year variability of mark-up. See the numerical value of kx in Table 3.19. Table 3.21. presents the statistical analysis of our three Canadian mark-up aggregates; k = BGP/W_b, kd = BDP/W_b, and kx = Nonagricultural Product/Nonagricultural Wages, together with the 14 industries. Like agriculture the minor industry Fishing and trapping (3) has a high unstable mark-up, Mean = 5.17, v = 13.0%.

Industry categories of Transportation, Storage, Communication, and Electric, gas and water utilities (7. - 10.), are presented in the Canadian *National Accounts*, combined from 1926 to 1944. From 1944, when separate k series for industries 7. through 10. first became available, to 1949 mark-up declined greatly in Industry 10., the utilities, and to a somewhat smaller extent in industry 7. Transportation, and 9. Communication. From their 1949 lows mark-up in each of these industries has rebounded strongly recovering much of the ground lost. The combined 7. - 10. mark-up shows a similar pattern with the highest peak occuring in 1942, a slide in mark-up until 1949 and then an upsurge.

As shown in Table 3.21. the relative variability of industry mark-up is considerably more than in aggregate kd. Of the 14

Table 3.20. Wage Cost Mark-Up Factors of the 14 Industries which Produce Business Domestic Product in Canada

Year	1.	2.	3.	4.	5.	6.	7.	8.
1926	7.91	1.12	5.86	1.91	1.65	1.32		
1927	7.88	1.13	5.57	1.91	1.68	1.33		
1928	8.25	1.11	5.86	1.89	1.68	1.29		
1929	6.18	1.13	5.57	2.04	1.67	1.26		
1930	6.28	1.15	5.00	1.88	1.72	1.32		
1931	4.40	1.29	5.00	1.84	1.59	1.32		
1932	5.34	1.17	5.33	1.73	1.49	1.36		
1933	4.68	1.20	5.67	2.11	1.44	1.43		
1934	6.03	1.12	5.25	2.32	1.51	1.53		
1935	6.34	1.10	5.75	2.37	1.52	1.46		
1936	5.58	1.10	6.25	2.52	1.55	1.44		
1937	6.38	1.12	6.25	2.48	1.56	1.43		
1938	7.25	1.20	5.75	2.31	1.60	1.44		
1939	7.31	1.23	6.25	2.41	1.65	1.50		
1940	8.35	1.18	5.80	2.45	1.70	1.44		
1941	7.91	1.16	6.00	2.37	1.69	1.36		
1942	12.21	1.17	5.67	2.30	1.65	1.34		
1943	9.33	1.16	5.36	2.15	1.54	1.34		
1944	12.48	1.10	5.33	1.85	1.50	1.50	1.72	1.37
1945	10.64	1.18	5.50	1.99	1.53	1.65	1.70	1.55
1946	11.09	1.14	5.47	2.03	1.53	1.50	1.56	1.45
1947	10.94	1.13	4.57	2.22	1.50	1.45	1.48	1.45
1948	13.02	1.12	4.44	2.14	1.53	1.43	1.39	1.54
1949	11.94	1.27	4.71	1.96	1.60	1.52	1.34	1.42
1950	11.92	1.31	4.95	2.16	1.64	1.55	1.45	1.48
1951	15.17	1.13	4.90	2.18	1.61	1.41	1.48	1.50
1952	14.94	1.13	4.40	1.86	1.63	1.42	1.44	1.57
1953	13.13	1.19	4.05	1.88	1.47	1.49	1.43	1.69
1954	10.66	1.26	4.24	2.09	1.55	1.49	1.41	1.46
1955	10.98	1.28	4.25	2.34	1.58	1.48	1.53	1.55
1956	11.47	1.19	4.26	2.27	1.60	1.41	1.59	1.61
1957	9.02	1.17	4.19	2.15	1.57	1.44	1.56	1.45
1958	9.77	1.16	4.31	2.05	1.54	1.48	1.50	1.40
1959	9.20	1.18	4.38	2.19	1.55	1.43	1.51	1.51
1960	9.43	1.13	4.41	2.21	1.53	1.40	1.51	1.43

Source: *National Accounts* 1926-1956 pp. 56-7; 1960 p. 34.

Note: Numerical values of BDP produced by each industry and wages paid have been omitted as the source is readily available. Industry 14- Public Administration and Defense- has been omitted as not part of Business Domestic Product. (Here $\underline{k} = 1.00$).

Industries:

1. Agriculture
2. Forestry
3. Fishing and trapping
4. Mining, quarrying, and oil wells
5. Manufacturing
6. Construction
7. Transportation
8. Storage

Table 3.20. (continued)

Year	9.	10.	7.-10.	11.	12.	13.	15.
1926			1.56	1.51	2.19	4.78	1.82
1927			1.53	1.61	2.17	4.71	1.85
1928			1.64	1.58	2.21	4.01	1.99
1929			1.57	1.47	2.11	4.23	1.82
1930			1.50	1.90	2.06	4.09	1.77
1931			1.45	1.52	2.03	4.08	1.74
1932			1.44	1.45	1.88	4.01	1.66
1933			1.46	1.31	1.70	4.06	1.65
1934			1.60	1.31	1.72	3.90	1.64
1935			1.59	1.38	1.85	3.99	1.67
1936			1.64	1.37	1.89	4.00	1.69
1937			1.65	1.34	1.84	3.97	1.72
1938			1.64	1.61	2.00	4.09	1.72
1939			1.73	1.45	1.95	4.45	1.73
1940			1.83	1.52	1.86	4.53	1.75
1941			1.98	1.56	1.90	4.35	1.78
1942			2.09	1.57	2.06	4.62	1.79
1943			2.04	1.51	2.14	4.40	1.81
1944	1.71	4.52	1.92	1.67	2.20	4.37	1.78
1945	1.66	4.09	1.87	1.56	2.24	4.09	1.76
1946	1.52	3.37	1.71	1.61	2.26	3.68	1.71
1947	1.47	3.24	1.66	1.76	2.13	3.19	1.67
1948	1.39	2.75	1.54	1.60	1.95	3.49	1.68
1949	1.33	2.56	1.49	1.64	2.02	3.65	1.67
1950	1.41	2.68	1.60	1.65	1.95	3.94	1.69
1951	1.48	2.66	1.63	1.54	1.73	3.81	1.69
1952	1.52	2.63	1.61	1.70	1.98	3.97	1.66
1953	1.50	2.70	1.61	1.51	1.92	4.05	1.64
1954	1.52	2.82	1.62	1.44	1.84	4.12	1.61
1955	1.56	3.13	1.74	1.46	1.89	4.15	1.62
1956	1.56	3.08	1.78	1.52	1.87	3.78	1.63
1957	1.51	3.05	1.76	1.49	1.81	3.79	1.62
1958	1.50	3.00	1.72	1.45	1.86	3.95	1.59
1959	1.48	3.02	1.74	1.46	1.82	4.03	1.56
1960	1.49	3.10	1.75	1.39	1.73	4.05	1.52

Industries:

9. Communication
10. Electric power, gas, and water utilities
11. Wholesale trade
12. Retail trade
13. Finance, insurance, and real estate
15. Service

industries, only two show a lower v than does aggregate kd (v = 5.0%), but one of them is the very important Manufacturing industry (v = 4.3%). Three of the industries had relative variability of greater than the 11.9% v of Income Velocity in Canada. The simple average of v at the industry level is 9.0%. When the industry vs are weighted by the percentage of total BDP produced by each industry

Table 3.21. Statistical Analysis of kd in the Aggregate and in the 14 Industries Producing Business Domestic Product in Canada 1926-1959.

	kd	1.	2.	3.	4.	5.	6.	7.
Variation*	18.3%	110.1	17.4	42.7	37.2	17.1	26.8	24.8
Largest Change	7.6%	43.9	14.9	17.5	17.9	8.2	11.0	9.2
Mean of k	1.95	9.24	1.17	5.17	2.13	1.59	1.43	1.51
b	-.005740	+.19272	+.00150	-.05102	+.00588	-.00186	+.00398	-.00239
s	.0976	2.9148	.0558	.6725	.2068	.0683	.0814	.0977
s_{kt}	.0831	2.0720	.0527	.3699	.2065	.0629	.0714	.0659
v	5.0%	31.6	4.8	13.0	9.7	4.3	5.7	6.5
vt	4.3%	22.4	4.5	7.2	9.7	4.0	5.0	4.4
R^2	-.275	+.495	+.044	-.697	+.000	-.153	+.230	-.545

	8.	9.	10.	7.-10.	11.	12.	13.	15.
Variation	20.9%	25.0	83.1	36.8	36.8	26.6	40.0	26.8
Largest Change	15.0%	9.2	20.3	8.5	26.8	26.6	17.6	9.7
Mean of k	1.51	1.68	3.08	1.68	1.53	1.97	4.07	1.71
b	+.00332	-.35000	-.04218	-.00534	-.00006	-.00565	-.01322	-.00655
s	.0807	.1943	.5057	.1572	.1237	.1654	.3232	.0907
s_{kt}	.0540	.0886	.1034	.1501	.1237	.1465	.2964	.0637
v	5.4%	11.6	16.4	9.4	8.5	8.4	7.9	5.3
vt	3.6%	5.3	4.4	9.0	8.5	7.4	7.3	3.7
R^2	+.551	-.576	-.800	-.088	-.000	-.216	-.159	-.508

1. Agriculture
2. Forestry
3. Fishing and trapping
4. Mining, quarrying, and oil wells
5. Manufacturing
6. Construction
7. Transportation
8. Storage
9. Communication
10. Utilities
7-10. Combined
11. Wholesale trade
12. Retail trade
13. Finance, insurance, and real estate
15. Service

*Expressed as a percentage of the range of variation. Alternatively variation may be expressed as a percentage of the mean of k. In every case except agriculture the two measures are nearly the same. Variation/mean of agriculture mark-up is 116.5%.

1948 v becomes 9.9%. If 1960 weights are used v becomes 8.1% the reduction being primarily, because of the reduced relative importance of unstable mark-up Agriculture.

WEIGHT COUNTERSHIFTS: k_1 AND k_2

Let us turn to the question of the degree to which weight changes between industries have modified the history of aggregate mark-up in Canada. As a high mark-up industry produces a smaller, or a low mark-up industry produces a larger, percentage of gross product this tends to pull down aggregate mark-up. Moreover, as an industry marked by an unstable mark-up declines in relative importance, kd becomes more stable. Table 3.22. shows that the history of inter-industry shifts in Canada since 1926 has been dominated by just such a movement. While high, unstable mark-up Agriculture has slipped from producing 18.7% in 1926 to a mere 5.9% of BDP in 1960, stable, low mark-up Manufacturing (5) has increased in importance, from 22.4% of BDP to over 28%. Also, industry 6. Construction has increased from 4.3% of BDP in 1926 to over 7% in recent years.

Turning from the secular changes to cyclical changes in the importance of industries we find a more complex pattern. Low, (mean = 1.59) stable ($\underline{v}$ = 4.3%) mark-up Manufacturing is the "perfect" cyclical account. In each of the "trough" years in Real Output (Q); 1933, 1938, 1945,[18] 1954, 1957 the percentage of BDP produced by Manufacturing fell. High, (mean =4.07) less stable ($\underline{v}$ = 7.9%) industry 13. Finance, insurance, and real estate is the "perfect" countercyclical account. Weight shifts between these two industries operate to reduce the fluctuation of aggregate mark-up over the business cycle. In all of the trough years except 1938 and 1945 very high, unstable mark-up Agriculture has behaved in a cyclical manner, that is, falling in relative importance in depression years. The fall in Agricultural prices has been great enough to outweight the rise in percentage of Q produced by Agriculture so that as a percentage of BDP the industry falls. The low, (mean = 1.71), stable ($\underline{v}$ = 5.3%) mark-up Service industry (15.) was a nearly perfect countercyclical account, that is rising in importance in depression years. Weight shifts between these two industries then tend to *increase* the variability of aggregate mark-up over the business cycle. Other accounts behaved inconsistently.

Let us again separate the effects of changes in mark-up *within* industries from the effects of changes in relative importance *between* industries by computing $\underline{k}_1$, with 1926 percentage of output weights and current industry mark-ups, and $\underline{k}_2$, with 1926 industry mark-ups and current weights, from the data contained in Tables 3.20. and 3.22. Table 3.23. gives the numerical values of $\underline{k}_1$ and $\underline{k}_2$ which result from this operation. Figure 3.14. graphs these series together with $\underline{kd}$ and is accompanied by Table 2.22., a statistical analysis of the three series. From these it is evident that nearly all the year-to-year and cyclical variability of $\underline{kd}$ is to be attributed to fluctuation in mark-up *within* industries, shown isolated in $\underline{k}_1$, while nearly all the downward trend in $\underline{kd}$ is attributable to inter-

[18] 1949 was a recession year for the United States and for Canadian Manufacturing. However, total Real Output in Canada rose from an index of 97 in 1948 to 100 in 1949.

Table 3.22. Percentage Distribution of Business Domestic Product at Factor Cost, by Industry, in Canada 1926-1960.

Year	1.	2.	3.	4.	5.	6.	7.	8.
1926..	18.70	1.39	.87	3.27	22.43	4.30		
1927..	17.63	1.38	.78	3.35	22.93	4.19		
1928..	17.11	1.32	.75	3.47	23.04	4.44		
1929..	12.74	1.42	.71	3.98	24.47	5.33		
1930..	12.14	1.18	.58	3.52	24.05	4.89		
1931..	8.40	.98	.49	3.48	23.65	5.02		
1932..	9.95	.82	.49	3.33	22.22	3.45		
1933..	9.39	1.02	.58	4.53	22.05	2.48		
1934..	11.29	1.15	.63	5.52	23.72	2.44		
1935..	11.71	1.21	.63	5.87	24.30	2.73		
1936..	10.21	1.39	.63	6.84	25.01	2.97		
1937..	10.83	1.83	.56	7.32	26.12	3.44		
1938..	12.13	1.17	.50	6.59	25.52	3.35		
1939..	11.74	1.57	.51	6.90	25.95	3.21		
1940..	12.31	1.78	.52	6.45	28.80	3.34		
1941..	10.03	1.68	.62	5.77	32.74	3.88		
1942..	13.82	1.56	.61	4.62	34.42	3.65		
1943..	10.94	1.77	.67	4.12	36.42	3.44		
1944..	14.29	1.78	.69	3.37	33.95	2.64	9.23	.28
1945..	12.49	2.24	.83	3.50	31.86	3.35	9.44	.33
1946..	13.30	2.67	.82	3.64	28.13	4.40	8.64	.29
1947..	12.37	2.47	.57	3.94	29.26	4.92	8.11	.28
1948..	13.05	2.17	.61	4.02	29.91	5.27	7.74	.28
1949..	11.31	1.78	.57	3.87	30.42	5.63	7.20	.26
1950..	10.97	2.26	.63	4.17	30.12	5.59	7.18	.26
1951..	13.14	2.45	.57	4.38	30.19	5.08	7.51	.26
1952..	12.02	1.83	.42	3.86	30.52	5.63	7.21	.29
1953..	9.80	1.77	.39	3.74	30.89	6.49	7.44	.32
1954..	7.14	1.95	.43	4.27	30.34	6.39	7.23	.29
1955..	7.77	1.93	.37	4.71	29.82	6.09	7.56	.30
1956..	7.75	1.82	.39	4.70	29.88	6.88	7.79	.31
1957..	5.84	1.56	.33	4.61	29.80	7.29	6.66	.29
1958..	6.35	1.23	.41	4.23	28.46	7.42	7.08	.28
1959..	5.76	1.25	.36	4.47	28.53	7.40	7.15	.32
1960..	5.92	1.32	.33	4.43	28.17	7.07	6.91	.29

Industries:

1. Agriculture
2. Forestry
3. Fishing and trapping
4. Mining, quarrying, and oil wells
5. Manufacturing
6. Construction
7. Transportation
8. Storage

Source: *National Accounts* 1926-1956 pp. 56-7; 1960 p. 34.

Table 3.22. (continued)

Year	9.	10.	7-10.	11.	12.	13.	15.
1926..			13.34	3.63	8.36	10.38	13.34
1927..			13.24	3.90	8.79	10.54	13.24
1928..			13.58	3.74	9.06	9.41	14.04
1929..			13.37	3.72	9.49	10.97	13.81
1930..			12.99	5.29	9.97	10.98	14.40
1931..			13.93	4.80	10.50	12.58	16.18
1932..			14.49	5.00	9.98	13.95	16.33
1933..			14.87	4.59	9.32	15.04	16.13
1934..			14.76	4.20	9.27	12.38	14.64
1935..			13.99	4.38	9.56	11.65	13.97
1936..			14.01	4.31	9.78	11.45	13.38
1937..			13.26	4.11	9.46	10.27	12.81
1938..			12.93	4.61	9.76	10.50	12.93
1939..			13.32	4.20	9.16	10.91	12.52
1940..			12.84	4.23	8.60	9.64	11.51
1941..			13.30	4.26	8.54	8.47	10.71
1942..			12.76	3.66	7.67	7.92	9.31
1943..			13.83	3.50	8.01	7.72	9.59
1944..	1.50	2.42	13.44	4.03	8.47	7.77	9.58
1945..	1.63	2.38	13.78	4.16	9.44	7.93	10.43
1946..	1.69	2.29	12.91	4.71	10.32	8.05	11.06
1947..	1.65	2.43	12.49	5.32	9.91	7.22	11.34
1948..	1.55	2.33	11.91	4.77	9.35	7.67	11.28
1949..	1.57	2.41	11.45	5.07	10.24	8.09	11.58
1950..	1.65	2.50	11.59	4.95	9.80	8.66	11.27
1951..	1.72	2.43	11.92	4.61	8.52	8.26	10.88
1952..	1.73	2.43	11.66	5.19	9.56	8.56	10.74
1953..	1.79	2.61	12.15	4.75	9.69	9.10	11.22
1954..	2.03	2.86	12.42	4.82	10.01	10.19	12.02
1955..	2.08	2.92	12.86	4.75	9.87	10.11	11.73
1956..	2.09	3.02	13.21	4.95	9.58	9.18	11.67
1957..	2.19	3.31	13.45	5.17	9.70	9.97	12.27
1958..	2.27	3.42	13.05	5.07	10.18	10.67	12.92
1959..	2.20	3.45	13.12	5.17	10.03	10.72	13.21
1960..	2.25	3.58	13.03	5.08	9.75	11.08	13.81

Industries:

9. Communication
10. Electric power, gas, and water utilities
11. Wholesale trade
12. Retail trade
13. Finance, insurance, and real estate
15. Service

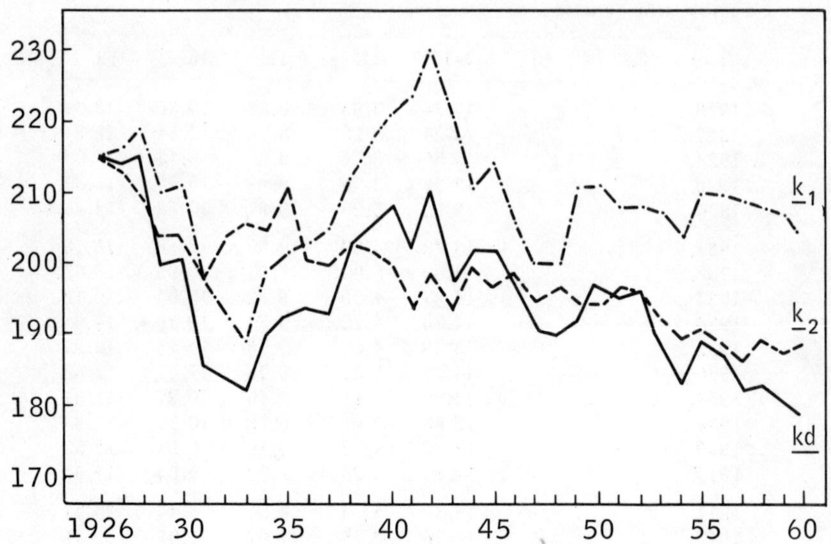

Fig. 3.14. *Canada* kd, $\underline{k}_1$, and $\underline{k}_2$ 1926-1960 with Statistical Analysis.

kd: Variation 1.79 - 2.15, Largest Change 15 points 1928-29, Mean of kd = 1.95, $\underline{b}$ = -.00574, $\underline{s}$ = .0976, $\underline{s}_{kt}$ = .0831, $\underline{v}$ = 5.0%, vt = 4.3%, R^2 = -.275.

$\underline{k}_1$: Variation 1.89-2.30, Largest Change 13 points 1930-31, Mean of $\underline{k}_1$ = 2.10, $\underline{b}$ = -.00019, $\underline{s}$ = .0841, $\underline{s}_{kt}$ = .0841, $\underline{v}$ = 4.0%, vt = 4.0%, R^2 = -.000.

k_2: Variation 1.88-2.15, Largest Change 10 points 1935-36, Mean of k_2 = 1.99, b = -.00637, s = .0708, s_{kt} = .0312, v = 5.6%, vt = 1.6%, R^2 = -.816.

industry shifts. It is notable that industry mark-ups were at their highest point for the 35 year period in mid World War II. This peak in $\underline{k}_1$ is obscured in kd by the structural changes which had occurred. In "cutting off" this peak the weight shifts were stabilizing in their impact. However, kd fell from 1928 to 1931 not only because of the fall in mark-up within industries ($\underline{k}_1$), but also because $\underline{k}_2$ fell, *i. e.* the weight shifts were destabilizing. From 1931 to 1935 weight shifts were such as to raise kd. From 1935 to the present they have acted to reduce kd. In the post-war recessions they have added, slightly, to the cyclical variability of kd. On balance weight shifts were destabilizing and account for the

Table 3.23. Numerical Values of $\underline{k}_1$ and $\underline{k}_2$ in Canada 1926-1960

$$\underline{k}_1 = \frac{1}{\underline{k}_t} \cdot \frac{Z1926}{Z}$$

$$\underline{k}_2 = \frac{1}{\underline{k}1926} \cdot \frac{Zt}{Z}$$

Year	$\underline{k}_1$	$\underline{k}_2$
1926	2.15	2.15
1927	2.16	2.13
1928	2.19	2.10
1929	2.10	2.04
1930	2.11	2.04
1931	1.98	1.98
1932	1.93	2.04
1933	1.89	2.06
1934	1.99	2.05
1935	2.02	2.11
1936	2.03	2.01
1937	2.05	2.00
1938	2.12	2.03
1939	2.17	2.02
1940	2.21	2.00
1941	2.23	1.94
1942	2.30	1.99
1943	2.21	1.94
1944	2.11	2.00
1945	2.14	1.97
1946	2.06	1.99
1947	2.00	1.95
1948	2.00	1.97
1949	2.11	1.95
1950	2.11	1.95
1951	2.08	1.97
1952	2.08	1.96
1953	2.07	1.93
1954	2.04	1.90
1955	2.10	1.91
1956	2.10	1.89
1957	2.09	1.87
1958	2.08	1.90
1959	2.07	1.88
1960	2.04	1.89

Source: Table 3.20. and Table 3.22.

Table 3.24. Wage Cost Mark-Up of the 9 Industries which Produce Business Gross Product in the United Kingdom 1948-1960

Year	Industries								
	1.	2.	3.	4.	5.	6.	7.	8.	9.
1948	2.50	1.12	1.58	1.26	1.74	1.39	2.07	1.34	1.66
1949	2.58	1.15	1.57	1.27	1.70	1.39	2.02	1.31	1.61
1950	2.58	1.15	1.63	1.25	1.73	1.42	2.06	1.34	1.59
1951	2.58	1.12	1.66	1.24	1.70	1.49	2.01	1.36	1.54
1952	2.66	1.10	1.53	1.24	1.75	1.46	1.82	1.29	1.53
1953	2.61	1.14	1.54	1.25	1.79	1.41	1.83	1.28	1.56
1954	2.51	1.13	1.56	1.26	1.84	1.40	1.86	1.38	1.53
1955	2.51	1.11	1.55	1.25	1.82	1.42	1.85	1.35	1.50
1956	2.48	1.18	1.51	1.25	1.86	1.42	1.79	1.36	1.48
1957	2.54	1.14	1.50	1.26	1.87	1.41	1.73	1.31	1.53
1958	2.49	1.14	1.48	1.26	2.00	1.35	1.68	1.31	1.52
1959	2.51	1.15	1.50	1.28	2.05	1.40	1.69	1.31	1.56
1960	2.58	1.18	1.50	1.25	2.05	1.44	1.71	1.29	1.51
1961*	2.82	1.21	1.39	1.29	2.09	1.39	1.68	1.38	1.58
Variation	7.0%	7.0	11.5	3.2	18.7	9.9	20.8	7.5	11.5
Largest Change	3.9%	6.1	8.3	2.4	6.9	4.9	10.1	7.5	3.2
Mean $\underline{k}$	2.55	1.14	1.55	1.26	1.84	1.42	1.85	1.33	1.55
$\underline{b}$	.00045	+.00280	-.01104	-.00088	+.02995	+.00013	-.03028	-.00308	-.00879
$\underline{s}$	.0535	.0230	.0163	.0118	.1200	.0335	.1371	.0306	.0470
$\underline{s_{kt}}$	.0535	.0182	.0102	.0118	.0432	.0327	.0494	.0289	.0334
$\underline{v}$	2.1%	2.0	1.1	.9	6.5	2.4	7.4	2.3	3.0
$\underline{v_t}$	2.1%	1.6	.7	.9	2.3	2.3	2.7	2.2	2.2
R^2	-.000	+.377	-.610	-.000	+.872	+.048	-.632	-.114	-.480

Source: *National Income and Expenditure*, 1961, pp. 11-12.

Industries

1. Agriculture, forestry, & fishing
2. Mining & quarrying
3. Manufacturing
4. Construction
5. Gas, electricity & water
6. Transport & communication
7. Distributive trades
8. Insurance, banking & finance
9. Other services

*Data for 1961 is from *National Income and Expenditure*, 1962, pp. 16-17. It was received after the statistical analysis had been completed, and therefore does not affect the figures. If the 1962 figures are correct, rather large changes occurred in k in several of the industries.

downward trend of kd in Canada (k_2: b = -.00637, R^2 = -.816; k_1: b = -.00019, R^2 . -.000; kd: b = -.00574, R^2 = -.275).

UNITED KINGDOM

Table 3.24. presents mark-up in the 9 industries which produce Business Gross Product ("Gross Output of Total Production and Trade") in the United Kingdom together with a statistical analysis. One industry group, 5. Gas, electricity, and water shows a strong increasing trend (b = +.02995, R^2 = +.872). Industries 3. Manufacturing, and 7. Distributive trades, show considerable downward trend. (Industry 3. b = -.01104, R^2 = -.610 Industry 7. b = -.03028, R^2 = -.632.) The other series show a lesser trend or absence of trend. Only Industry 7. shows a year-to-year change greater than 10 per cent. Mark-up in Industry 1. Agriculture, which in the U. S. and Canada was highly variable, in the United Kingdom displays neither trend (b = -.00045, R^2 = -.00) nor considerable fluctuation (v = 2.1%). A simple average of relative variability of the 9 Industries is a mere 3.6%, when vs are weighted by percentage of total output produced in 1954 its value becomes 2.8%.

Next we wish to separate the impact of fluctuations in k *within* industries from fluctuations in aggregate mark-up caused by changes in importance *between* industries. Table 3.25. sets forth the data on the percentage of the gross output of Total Production and

Table 3.25. Percentage of the Gross Output of Total Production and Trade Produced by the 9 Industries in the United Kingdom

Year	Industries								
	1.	2.	3.	4.	5.	6.	7.	8.	9.
1948	7.08	4.21	38.84	6.26	2.30	9.56	15.76	3.08	12.89
1949	7.14	4.21	38.71	6.33	2.34	9.47	15.73	3.09	12.96
1950	6.56	3.99	40.10	6.14	2.42	9.32	15.89	3.18	12.39
1951	6.22	3.88	40.95	6.03	2.37	9.88	15.57	3.24	11.85
1952	6.47	4.28	40.27	6.38	2.62	10.23	14.63	3.15	11.96
1953	6.23	4.32	41.06	6.63	2.69	9.60	14.63	3.17	11.66
1954	5.69	4.16	41.76	6.64	2.74	9.30	14.82	3.38	11.49
1955	5.36	3.95	41.87	6.62	2.72	9.48	14.76	3.34	11.87
1956	5.15	4.26	41.26	6.95	2.82	9.74	14.60	3.35	11.87
1957	5.19	4.25	41.64	6.81	2.87	9.82	14.68	3.19	11.55
1958	5.14	4.16	41.51	6.92	3.12	9.38	14.78	3.35	11.64
1959	4.92	3.72	41.96	6.93	3.13	9.43	14.82	3.42	11.65
1960	4.69	3.39	42.06	6.83	3.02	9.66	14.85	3.34	12.16

Source: *National Income and Expenditure*, 1959, 1961, pp. 11-12; 1962, 16-17.

Trade produced by each of the 9 industries. Table 3.25. together with the mark-up data of Table 3.24. will enable us to calculate $\underline{k}_1$ and $\underline{k}_2$ for Table 3.26.

Similarly to Canada, interindustry shifts in the United Kingdom have been dominated by the decline of Agriculture and the increased importance of Manufacturing.

The $\underline{k}$ series represents "what would have happened" if within industries mark-ups fluctuated as shown in Table 3.29., but the relative importance of the industries remained what they were in 1948. The $\underline{k}_2$ series holds mark-up within industries constant at their 1948 levels, but allows the relative importance of the industries to change in the manner indicated in Table 3.25. The results of these operations are shown in Table 3.26.

In comparing Table 3.26. with Tables 3.3. and 3.23., it is interesting to note that in the United Kingdom $\underline{k}_2$ shows practically no trend, ($\underline{b}$ = -.002308, R^2 = -.500) and practically no fluctuation,

Table 3.26. Numerical Values of $\underline{k}$, $\underline{k}_1$, and $\underline{k}_2$ with Statistical Analysis.

$$\underline{k}_1 = \frac{1}{\underline{k}it} \cdot \frac{Zi1948}{Z}$$

$$\underline{k}_2 = \frac{1}{\underline{k}i1948} \cdot \frac{Zit}{Z}$$

Year	$\underline{k}$	$\underline{k}_1$	$\underline{k}_2$
1948	1.62	1.62	1.62
1949	1.60	1.61	1.62
1950	1.63	1.63	1.62
1951	1.63	1.63	1.61
1952	1.55	1.56	1.60
1953	1.55	1.56	1.60
1954	1.56	1.57	1.60
1955	1.55	1.56	1.60
1956	1.52	1.54	1.59
1957	1.52	1.53	1.59
1958	1.50	1.51	1.59
1959	1.52	1.53	1.60
1960	1.52	1.54	1.60
Mean of $\underline{k}$	1.56	1.57	1.60
$\underline{b}$	-.008901	-.009286	-.002308
$\underline{s}$	.0422	.0394	.0111
$\underline{s}_{kt}$	.0184	.0180	.0078
$\underline{v}$	2.7%	2.5%	0.7%
$\underline{v}t$	1.2%	1.1%	0.5%
R^2	-.810	-.792	-.500

(variation = 1.9%, v = 0.7%). The $\underline{k}_1$ series has both greater trend, ($\underline{b}$ = -.009286, R^2 = -.792) and greater variability, (variation = 7.7%, $\underline{v}$ = 4.0%, b = -.00637, R = -810) with little variation about this trend, (vt = 1.6%). (See Figure 3.15.)

Weight shifts, which in the United States operated to dampen the swings of $\underline{k}$ slightly so that $\underline{v}$ of $\underline{k}$ was less than $\underline{v}$ of $\underline{k}_1$, do not have this dampening effect in the United Kingdom. Weight shifts had this effect in the U.S. because high mark-up agriculture and finance rose in relative importance during downturns as low mark-up manufacturing fell, and vice-versa during upturns. In the United Kingdom, however, there are not particularly high mark-up industries; even agricultural mark-up averages only 2.55, so this effect has little leverage. Once again Solow's conclusion that weight shifts do not account for aggregate stability is borne out.

MANUFACTURING INDUSTRIES MARK-UP FACTORS

As the figures in Table 3.25. show, over 40 percent of the Gross Output of Total Production and Trade in the U. K. is produced by industry 3., Manufacturing. Further disaggregation of this dominant industry would seem to be useful.

The tables of *National Income and Expenditure*, 1961, and earlier years, together with the *Annual Abstract of the United Kingdom*, 1957 and 1961, can be made to yield such a 14 manufacturing industry disaggregation but not without some difficulties.

First, the Central Statistics Office does not present Business Gross Product (BGP) produced by the 14 manufacturing industries

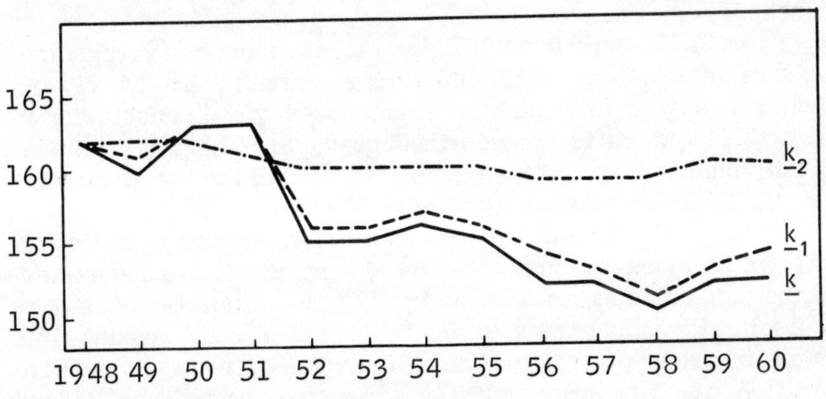

Fig. 3.15. *United Kingdom* $\underline{k}$, $\underline{k}_1$, and $\underline{k}_2$.

for which they present wage and salary (W) data. However, BGP, or Z, figures can be derived by adding to the wage and salary totals the account, "Company Trading Profits by Industry", these profits being defined gross of depreciation and taxes.

Second, the resulting W and Z figures for Manufacturing and its 14 sub-industries will differ from the corresponding data for Manufacturing in Table 3.24. in the following respects.

1. The account "Adjustments" to "Gross Profits of Companies" is not allocated among the sub-classifications. This account has been plus or minus several hundred million pounds for every year.
2. Our Wage and Salary figures for Manufacturing here will differ from those made use of above because: a. Table 3.24. is based on the 1958 Classification of Industries while our data here is based on the 1948 Classification of Industries, modified where possible to conform to the 1958 definitions. b. The 14 Manufacturing industry data is for Wage and Salaries only while the data used previously included employers' contributions to pension funds and other benefits.
3. The Central Statistics Office seems to be everlastingly changing its national income statistics. A user of U. S. statistics becomes used to the fact that data for the latest years are preliminary and will be revised somewhat in the next edition. The British, however, regard all the data as "preliminary" and are still guessing again concerning what *did* happen in 1948 and every year since. Usually the changes are unimportant involving only the last digit, but sometimes they are substantial and they make problems to one trying to piece together series from several editions.

Table 3.27. sets forth the derivation of our disaggregatable measure of mark-up in Manufacturing, which I shall dub k3, and compares it with the mark-up series used for Manufacturing in Table 3.24. which is henceforth dubbed k3i. The final column, k3/k3i, indicates the close correspondence of the two series and that the difficulties listed above have been surmounted.

Table 3.28. presents the numerical value and a statistical analysis of mark-up factors in the 14 manufacturing industries. All the industries except b, c, and k, show declining trends as does k3 itself. Five industries; d, 1, i, m, and n, show considerable downward trend (b greater than -.09). The extremes in relative variation are 13.0% for industry i. Leather, leather goods, and fur; and 1.4% for industry e. Shipbuilding, and marine engineering.

Table 3.27. Derivation of a Disaggregatable Measure of Mark-Up in British Manufacturing (k3); and Comparison with Mark-Up in Industry 3. Manufacturing (k3i). (million pounds)

Year	1. Gross Profits of Companies	2. Wages & Salaries	3. = 1. + 2. Gross Product	4. = 3. ÷ 2. Mark-Up (k3)	5. = Table 3.24. Manufacturing Mark-Up (k3i)	k3/k3i
1948	£ 1,148	£ 2,170	£ 3,318	1.53	1.58	96.8
1949	1,193	2,269	3,462	1.53	1.57	97.5
1950	1,440	2,459	3,899	1.59	1.63	97.5
1951	1,641	2,743	4,384	1.60	1.66	96.4
1952	1,369	2,976	4,345	1.46	1.53	95.4
1953	1,517	3,184	4,711	1.47	1.54	95.5
1954	1,763	3,446	5,209	1.51	1.56	96.8
1955	1,936	3,842	5,778	1.51	1.56	96.8
1956	1,934	4,114	6,048	1.47	1.51	97.4
1957	2,059	4,362	6,421	1.47	1.50	98.0
1958	2,033	4,490	6,523	1.45	1.48	98.0
1959	2,289	4,709	6,998	1.49	1.50	99.3
1960	2,367	5,311	7,678	1.45	1.50	96.7

Source: *National Income and Expenditure*, 1946-1953, p. 22; 1961, p. 13.

When we compare these results with the less disaggregated study in Table 3.24. we see somewhat less stability at this lower level. An unweighted average of relative variability in the 14 Manufacturing Industries is 5.3%, in comparison to 3.6% at the 9 Industry level and 2.7% at the highest level of aggregation. Again using 1954 percentage of output weights we obtain a weighted $\underline{v}$ of 4.4% in comparison with the corresponding value of 2.8% at the 9 Industry level.

Next let us repeat the separation of fluctuations in k3 *within* the 14 manufacturing industries from fluctuation in k3 caused by changes in importance *between* the 14, by the calculation of $k3_1$ and $k3_2$. Table 3.29. presents the relevant data on the percentage of gross product of Manufacturing produced by each of the sub-industries.

Table 3.30. presents the numerical data and statistical analysis of k3i, k3, and our computed "might have beens," $k3_1$ and $k3_2$. In $k3_1$ percentage of total product produced by each sub-industry is held constant at its 1948 value while k3 varies within each sub-industry. In $k3_2$ mark-up is held constant within sub-industries while their relative importance varies. Figure 3.16. charts the 4 series.

Comparing Table 3.30. with Table 3.26. we see that as in the United Kingdom aggregate k_1, $k3_1$ displays both variation and

Table 3.28. Wage Cost Mark-Up in the 14 Manufacturing Industries in the United Kingdom. 1948-1960

Year	Industries													
	a	b	c	d	e	f	g	h	i	j	k	l	m	n
1948	2.10	1.77	1.54	1.45	1.19	1.35	1.45	1.74	1.86	1.32	1.45	1.26	1.59	1.49
1949	2.02	1.75	1.54	1.54	1.21	1.32	1.43	1.75	1.67	1.31	1.43	1.11	1.51	1.55
1950	2.00	1.88	1.62	1.50	1.22	1.43	1.42	1.93	1.70	1.34	1.43	1.23	1.59	1.60
1951	2.06	1.95	1.47	1.54	1.19	1.43	1.53	1.82	1.54	1.28	1.54	1.24	1.78	1.64
1952	1.97	1.70	1.34	1.46	1.19	1.37	1.46	1.53	1.32	1.18	1.45	1.19	1.43	1.37
1953	2.00	1.89	1.28	1.46	1.21	1.38	1.38	1.56	1.42	1.23	1.46	1.18	1.48	1.42
1954	2.06	2.02	1.36	1.49	1.21	1.39	1.40	1.53	1.33	1.25	1.50	1.19	1.56	1.43
1955	2.00	1.95	1.60	1.47	1.21	1.37	1.41	1.45	1.36	1.24	1.50	1.18	1.55	1.41
1956	1.97	1.93	1.55	1.43	1.19	1.27	1.47	1.45	1.29	1.24	1.43	1.16	1.46	1.36
1957	1.93	1.95	1.62	1.44	1.20	1.30	1.44	1.40	1.25	1.23	1.40	1.17	1.41	1.38
1958	1.93	1.87	1.56	1.42	1.18	1.33	1.43	1.33	1.25	1.21	1.41	1.14	1.40	1.34
1959	1.90	1.92	1.62	1.40	1.18	1.33	1.44	1.45	1.43	1.26	1 45	1.16	1.52	1 37
1960	1.85	1.84	1.64	1.36	1.16	1.32	1.38	1.39	1.30	1.25	1.52	1.12	1.38	1.32
Variation	12.7%	14.3	24.7	12.4	5.0	11.9	10.3	36.8	39.2	12.7	9.5	12.7	25.3	21.6
Largest Change	6.6%	13.2	16.4	5.5	3.4	7.4	7.6	17.8	14.1	7.9	7.5	12.7	22.5	18.2
Mean of k	1.98	1.88	1.52	1.46	1.20	1.35	1.43	1.56	1.44	1.26	1.46	1.18	1.51	1.44
b	-.01537	+.00962	+.00811	-.01049	-.00253	-.00621	-.00140	-.04137	-.04039	-.00815	-.00016	-.00584	-.01621	-.02071
s	.0671	.0884	.1142	.0498	.0166	.0461	.0337	.1794	.1870	.0448	.0447	.0409	.0885	.0984
s_{kt}	.0357	.0808	.1104	.0304	.0121	.0388	.0337	.0900	.1102	.0354	.0447	.0353	.0836	.0609
v	3.4%	4.7	7.6	3.4	1.4	3.4	2.3	11.5	13.0	3.6	3.1	3.5	5.9	6.8
vt	1.8%	4.3	7.3	2.1	1.0	2.9	2.3	5.8	7.7	2.8	3.1	3.0	5.5	4.2
$\bar{R}^2$	-.716	+.615	+.065	-.628	-.476	-.290	-.000	-.748	-.653	-.387	+.000	-.254	-.109	-.616

Source: *National Income and Expenditure*, 1959, pp. 13, 28; 1961, pp. 17, 30; 1962, pp. 18, 32.

a. Food, drink, and tobacco
b. Chemical and allied products
c. Metal manufacturing
d. Engineering & electrical goods
e. Shipbuilding & marine engineering
f. Vehicles
g. Metal goods not specified elsewhere
h. Textiles
i. Leather, leather goods. & fur
j. Clothing & footwear
k. Bricks, pottery, glass, etc.
l. Timber, furniture, etc.
m. Paper, printing, & publishing
n. Other manufacturing

trend ($\underline{vt}$ = 2.2%, $\underline{b}$ = -.00879, R^2 = -.519) while $\underline{k3}_2$ shows little trend ($\underline{b}$ = -.00115) and so little variation about this trend ($\underline{vt}$ = .02) that R^2 becomes meaningless. Thus, like the case in the United States (see Table 3.3.), and unlike the case in Canada (see Table 3.23.), the downward trend in mark-up is largely *within* the industries, and changing industrial composition adds but little to it.

We may generalize from these three countries that most of the year-to-year changes in aggregate mark-up come from variation *within* the individual industries. Like Solow we conclude that the

Table 3.29. Percentage of the Gross Product of Manufacturing, ($\underline{Z3}$), Produced by the 14 Manufacturing Industries in the United Kingdom 1948-1960.

	Manufacturing Industries							
Year	a.	b.	c.	d.	e.	f.	g.	h.
1948	12.1%	6.5%	9.0%	17.9%	4.0%	8.9%	5.7%	12.0%
1949	11.8	6.6	9.1	17.6	3.8	9.0	5.6	12.7
1950	10.0	7.0	9.2	19.2	3.3	9.2	5.5	13.8
1951	9.8	7.5	8.1	20.3	3.0	9.1	5.7	13.0
1952	10.7	7.2	8.4	22.5	3.5	10.0	6.0	9.9
1953	10.5	7.7	7.5	21.8	3.5	10.3	5.4	11.3
1954	10.4	8.3	7.5	21.8	3.3	10.6	5.4	10.4
1955	10.2	8.1	9.1	21.9	3.2	10.7	6.6	9.1
1956	10.3	8.4	9.2	22.5	3.4	10.3	5.9	8.9
1957	10.3	8.5	9.6	22.9	3.3	10.3	5.7	8.5
1958	11.0	8.4	9.1	23.1	3.2	10.9	5.7	7.7
1959	10.6	8.7	9.2	22.3	2.9	11.1	5.5	7.9
1960	10.1	8.2	9.7	22.3	2.6	11.1	5.7	7.9

	Manufacturing Industries -						
Year	i.	j.	k.	l.	m.	n.	Check % $\underline{Z3}$
1948	1.2%	5.6%	4.1%	3.2%	6.8%	3.1%	100.0%
1949	1.0	5.7	4.1	3.2	6.8	3.0	100.0
1950	1.0	5.1	3.9	3.0	6.9	2.8	99.9
1951	.8	4.6	4.2	2.9	7.8	3.0	99.8
1952	.8	4.5	4.3	2.9	6.7	2.6	100.0
1953	.8	4.7	4.4	2.9	6.9	2.7	100.4
1954	.7	4.4	4.3	2.8	7.3	2.8	100.0
1955	.7	4.1	4.1	2.6	7.3	2.8	100.5
1956	.6	4.1	4.0	2.5	7.2	2.8	100.1
1957	.5	4.0	3.8	2.5	7.1	2.9	99.9
1958	.5	3.9	3.8	2.5	7.3	2.8	99.9
1959	.6	3.9	3.9	2.5	7.8	2.8	99.7
1960	.6	4.0	4.4	2.6	7.8	3.0	100.0

Source: *National Income and Expenditure*, 1946-1953, p. 22; 1961, pp. 13, 28; 1962, pp. 18, 32.

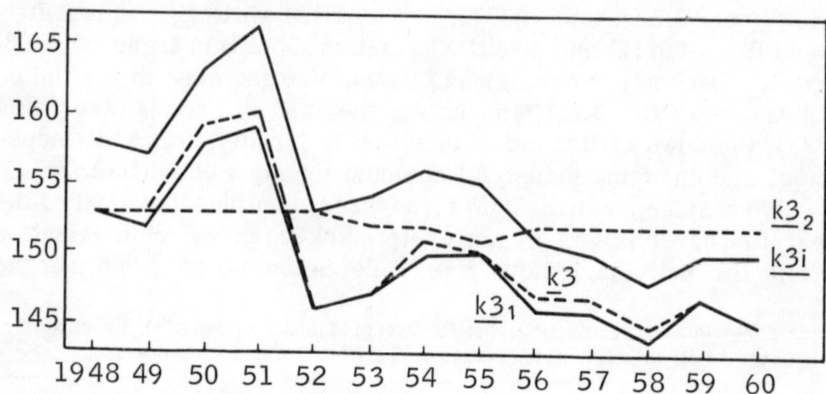

Fig. 3.16. *United Kingdom* k3, k3i, $k3_1$, and $k3_2$.

cyclical shifting of weights between industries does little to offset instability of industrial mark-ups. However, much of the downward trend in mark-up, not discussed by Solow, is attributable to weight shift.

In Canada, the downward trend was almost entirely contained in $\underline{k}_2$, *i.e.* from weight shift. Perhaps if we had been able to disaggregate in the United States and United Kingdom for as many years as in Canada, we should have obtained similar results. Furthermore, in the "young" economy of Canada there is much more room for inter-industry shifts, particularly the agriculture to industry shift, to occur. In 1926, Agriculture, forestry, fishing and trapping contributed almost 21% of BDP, by 1947 this had fallen to less than 16%, and to less than 8% in 1959. In the United States in 1947 Agriculture, forestry and fisheries contributed about 10% of BGP and 5% in 1960. In the "mature" economy of the United Kingdom Agriculture, forestry, and fisheries produced a mere 6.9% of BGP in 1948, which declined to 4.8% in 1961.

PRODUCTIVITY CHANGES IN INDUSTRIES AND SUB-INDUSTRIES IN THE UNITED STATES

For the WCM formulation to be useful for the forecaster or policy maker it is important not only that $\underline{k}$ be constant, or have a constant trend, but that changes in productivity, or A, be predictable as well. In order to study further the trend of A, already discussed at the aggregate level, pp. 18-20. I have constructed price level matrices similar to Table 1.3. for the 11 Industries and

5 of the Sub-Industries in the United States, for the 9 Industries and 6 Manufacturing Industry Groups in the United Kingdom. In the interest of brevity the Productivity(A) series will be presented here rather then the complete matrices.

Table 3.31. presents the aggregate productivity index together with A indices for Industries and Sub-Industries in the United States from 1947 to 1960. Figure 3.17. presents visually the aggregate A index together with the 11 industry A indices. As Figure 3.17.

Table 3.30. Numerical Values and Statistical Analysis of k3i, k3, $k3_1$, and $k3_2$ 1948-1960.

$$\underline{k3i} = \frac{\text{Total Production of Manufacturing}}{\text{Employee Compensation in Mfg.}}$$

$$\underline{k3} = \frac{\text{Gross Profits + Wages \& Salaries in Mfg.}}{\text{Wages \& Salaries in Manufacturing}}$$

$$\underline{k3_1} = \frac{1}{\underline{k3t}} \cdot \frac{Z3\ (1948)}{Z3} \qquad \underline{k3_2} = \frac{1}{\underline{k3}\ (1948)} \cdot \frac{Z3t}{Z3}$$

Year	k3i	k3	$k3_1$	$k3_2$
1948	1.58	1.53	1.53	1.53
1949	1.57	1.53	1.52	1.53
1950	1.63	1.59	1.58	1.53
1951	1.66	1.60	1.59	1.53
1952	1.53	1.46	1.46	1.53
1953	1.54	1.47	1.47	1.52
1954	1.56	1.51	1.50	1.52
1955	1.55	1.50	1.50	1.51
1956	1.51	1.47	1.46	1.52
1957	1.50	1.47	1.46	1.52
1958	1.48	1.45	1.44	1.52
1959	1.50	1.47	1.47	1.52
1960	1.50	1.45	1.45	1.52
Variation	11.5%	9.8%	9.8%	1.3%
Largest Change	8.3%	9.2%	8.6%	.7%
Mean of k	1.55	1.50	1.50	1.52
b	-.01104	-.00868	-.00879	-.00115
s	.0163	.0475	.0464	.0067
s_{kt}	.0102	.0353	.0323	.0003
v	1.1%	3.2%	3.1%	.4%
vt	.7%	2.4%	2.2%	.02%
R^2	-.610	-.449	-.519	*

*Not meaningful with virtual disappearance of s_{kt}

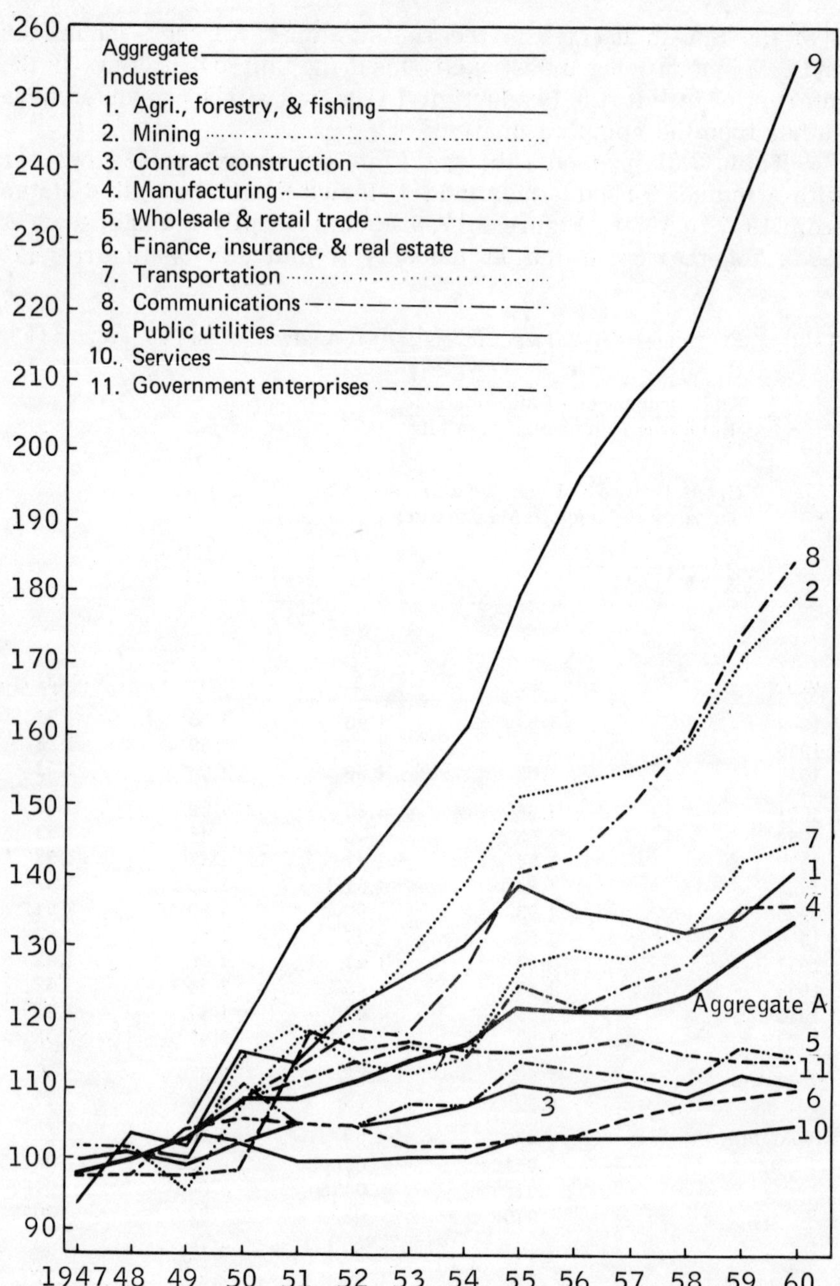

Fig. 3.17. Output per Employee (A) in the Aggregate and 11 Industries Producing BGP in the United States 1947-1960 1947-49 = 100

makes evident the industries have diverged greatly as to their productivity gains, with industry 9. Public utilities increasing output per man two and one half times from 1947 to 1960, while industry 10. Services made practically no productivity gains.

Figure 3.17. also indicates that many of the industry A indices plot as close to straight lines. This near linearity of trend is brought out in the statistical analysis of these A series in Table 3.31. The small variability about trend seen in Figure 3.17. appears in the table as small values of the conditional coefficient of variation of 1% to 5% ($\underline{vt} = \underline{s}_{At}/\text{mean}$).

The aggregate A index has a vt value of 2.6% from 1947 to 1960. If we weight the industry vt values by the percentage of BGP produced by each of the 10 industries in the midyear, 1953, we obtain a weighted average of 2.4%. This indicates that A within industries is, if anything, less variable than in the aggregate.

It would seem therefore that a forecaster or policy maker faced with the task of trying to foresee the inflationary impact of, say, a 4 index point rise in the wages of workers in industry 3., Contract construction, would be on safer ground than economic forecasters usually are if he merely proceeded as follows: assume k either unchanged at its most recent value of 1.40 or reduced to 1.395, since b in this industry is -.00519; subtract the yearly productivity gain of one index point (b of A =+.9736) to reach the estimate that such an increase would raise prices in the industry by 2.5 to 3 index points. He would also be quite safe in estimating the direct impact of this price increase on the aggregate price level, as construction will continue to account for about 5.5 per cent of BGP as is shown in Table 3.2.

To hold that variability about the trend of A gains is so small that it does not seriously inconvenience one concerned with predicting or influencing next year's price level is not to hold that it is "small" in all contexts. Thus a change from 1% to 3% is a dramatic "tripling of the rate of growth" and even smaller changes compounded over time accumulate to very large differences indeed. These long term cumulations are not the problem here, however.

Table 3.21. also gives statistical analysis of A changes in 5 sub-industries for which complete matrices could be developed. The weighted average of the conditional coefficient of variation (vt) of these 5 A series is 4.2% indicating once more somewhat less stability with sub-industries than at the other two levels.

Table 3.31. Output per Employee (A) in the Aggregate, 11 Industries Producing Business Gross Product, and 5 Sub-Industries in the United States 1947-1960, with Statistical Analysis (1947-49 = 100)

Year	Aggregate A = Q/N	Productivity Index A by Industries & Sub-Industries 1.	1a.	2.	3.	4.	5.	6.
1947	98	94	94	102	98	97	100	98
1948	100	104	104	102	98	100	99	98
1949	103	102	102	96	104	103	101	104
1950	109	116	116	108	103	109	111	106
1951	109	114	115	117	105	111	105	106
1952	111	122	123	120	105	114	105	105
1953	114	126	126	129	106	116	108	102
1954	116	130	133	139	108	115	108	102
1955	122	139	142	151	111	125	114	103
1956	121	135	137	153	110	122	113	103
1957	121	134	136	155	111	125	112	106
1958	123	132	134	158	109	128	111	108
1959	129	134	137	171	112	136	116	109
1960	134	141	145	180	109	136	115	110
Statistical Anaysis:								
b	+2.5275	+3.2901	+3.5780	+6.4681	+ .9736	+2.9165	+1.2000	+ .6418
s	10.32	14.34	15.50	26.12	4.37	11.94	5.48	3.59
s_{At}	3.03	5.45	5.59	5.18	1.89	2.00	2.67	2.49
v	9.0%	11.7%	12.4%	19.5%	4.1%	10.2%	5.1%	3.5%
vt	2.6%	4.4%	4.5%	3.9%	1.8%	1.7%	2.5%	2.4%
R^2	+.914	+.856	+.870	+.961	+.813	+.972	+.762	+.494

Year	Productivity Index A by Industries & Sub-Industries 6a.	6b.	7.	7a.	7b.	8.	9.	10.	11.
1947	98	95	100	105	95	97	96	100	104
1948	100	107	101	103	98	100	100	100	98
1949	103	105	99	91	107	103	104	100	98
1950	106	110	113	104	121	109	119	103	99
1951	107	112	119	111	128	113	133	100	119
1952	105	117	114	109	118	118	140	100	116
1953	102	116	113	108	119	117	150	101	117
1954	106	116	115	112	119	127	160	101	115
1955	112	114	128	128	128	140	180	103	115
1956	113	116	130	136	126	143	196	103	116
1957	110	130	129	136	126	150	207	103	117
1958	110	135	132	145	124	159	215	103	115
1959	114	135	143	154	136	175	236	104	114
1960	114	140	145	162	136	185	255	105	114
b	+1.1165	+3.1055	+3.4571	+4.8308	+2.5473	+6.5626	+12.3582	+.35165	+1.2418
s	5.03	13.27	14.41	20.88	11.99	27.09	50.21	1.69	7.48
s_{At}	2.35	4.19	4.30	7.54	6.25	6.02	6.18	.85	5.57
v	4.7%	11.3%	12.0%	17.1%	10.0%	20.7%	30.6%	1.7%	6.7%
vt	.2%	3.6%	3.6%	6.2%	5.2%	4.6%	3.8%	.8%	5.0%
R^2	+.782	+.900	+.911	+.869	+.728	+.951	+.985	+.750	+.446

Source: *Survey of Current Business*, October 1962, pp. 13-14, 16. *U. S. Income and Output* 1958, p. 211.

Table 3.32. Output per Employee (A) in the Aggregate, 9 Industries Producing Business Gross Product, and in 5 Manufacturing Groups in the *United Kingdom* 1948-1960, with Statistical Analysis (1954 = 100)

Year	Aggregate $A = Q/N$	Productivity Index A by Industries and Mfg. Groups 1.	2.	4.	5.	6.	7.	8.
1948	87	74	90	88	80	83	95	99
1949	89	80	93	93	83	86	98	92
1950	92	83	96	93	84	88	101	97
1951	94	88	99	90	88	93	98	96
1952	93	93	98	92	88	93	94	94
1953	98	97	98	97	92	97	97	96
1954	100	100	100	100	100	100	100	100
1955	101	102	100	99	104	104	101	102
1956	103	113	100	101	109	103	100	97
1957	104	116	99	102	112	104	99	98
1958	104	118	95	102	118	103	101	101
1959	107	124	96	105	122	109	107	109
1960	109	133	100	109	133	115	111	114
Statistical Analysis:								
$\underline{b}$	+1.7747	+4.6319	+.4231	+1.5275	+4.2582	+2.3463	+.4615	+1.1421
$\underline{s}$	6.736	17.436	4.29	5.99	16.39	10.45	3.06	5.77
$\underline{s}_{At}$	1.074	1.963	2.59	1.80	3.01	2.11	2.47	3.89
$\underline{v}$	6.8%	17.2%	4.4%	6.1%	16.2%	11.2%	3.1%	5.8%
$\underline{vt}$	1.1%	1.9%	2.7%	1.8%	3.0%	2.3%	2 5%	3.9%
R^2	+.975	+.987	+.636	+.910	+.966	+.959	+.353	+.544

Year	9.	3.	a.	Manufacturing and manufacturing groups b. c.	& g./d. e.	& f/h. i.	& j/k. l.	m. n.
1948	97	85	102	76	83	86	93	78
1949	97	88	102	77	85	89	96	84
1950	97	93	98	85	88	93	99	90
1951	98	95	98	88	92	98	95	93
1952	101	91	99	82	94	93	89	85
1953	101	96	101	91	95	96	99	92
1954	100	100	100	100	100	100	100	100
1955	102	103	101	103	104	105	102	103
1956	103	103	102	106	105	101	103	100
1957	104	105	104	107	106	104	103	102
1958	107	104	104	106	97	104	100	102
1959	107	112	107	119	102	110	110	109
1960	111	116	110	127	111	112	116	115
$\underline{b}$	+1.0165	+2.4231	+.7846	+4.0528	+1.7319	+1.8637	+1.5341	+2.5385
$\underline{s}$	4.03	9.55	3.94	16.77	8.05	7.83	7.26	11.76
$\underline{s}_{At}$	1.39	2.80	2.36	3.92	3.96	3.42	3.80	3.29
$\underline{v}$	3.9%	9.6%	3.8%	16.8%	8.3%	7.8%	7.2%	12.0%
$\underline{vt}$	1.4%	2.8%	2.3%	3.9%	4.1%	3.4%	3.7%	3.4%
R^2	+.882	+.914	+.641	+.945	+.758	+.809	+.726	+.906

Source: *National Inçome and Expenditure*, 1961, pp. 6, 11-12
Annual Abstract of Statistics, 1959, 1961, pp. 243, 247-249.

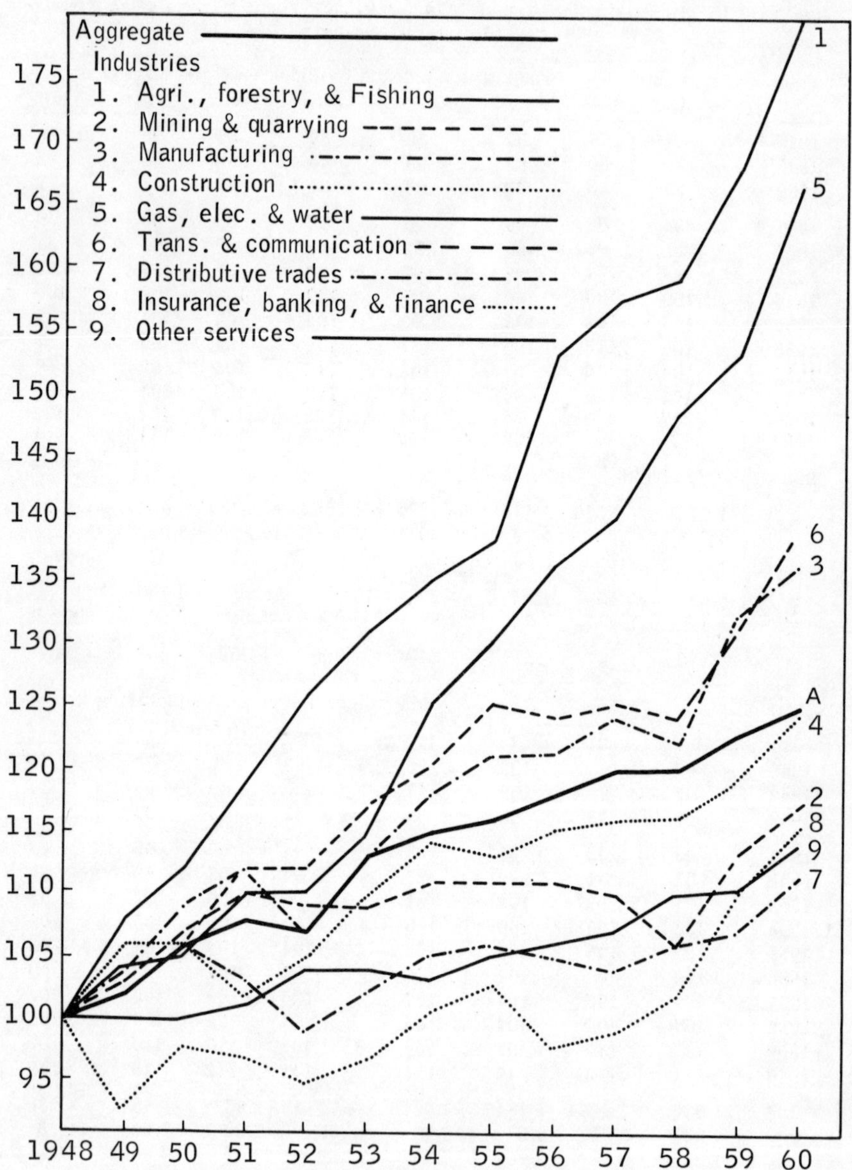

Fig. 3.18. Average Output per Employee (A), in the United Kingdom in the Aggregate and in the 9 Industries. 1948 = 100

PRODUCTIVITY CHANGES IN INDUSTRIES AND MANUFACTURING GROUPS IN THE UNITED KINGDOM

Table 3.32. presents productivity series in the aggregate, in 9 British Industries, and in 6 Manufacturing Industry groups for the years 1948-1960 with statistical analyses. Again, productivity gains vary greatly between industries and groups but in most cases have near linear trends. The British Agriculture, and Gas, electricity, and water, Industries show gains of more than 4 index points *per annum* while Mining and quarrying, and Distributive trades, have averaged increases only one tenth as large. The Manufacturing group, Chemicals and allied trades, also show annual gains of more than 4 index points. Figure 3.18. is a graph of the productivity indices of the 9 Industries.

Again we see some increase in relative variability about trend as we disaggregate. For aggregate A vt is 1.1%, an average of vt of A of the 9 Industries weighted by 1954 output percentages is 2.5%. In the Manufacturing aggregate vt of A is 2.8%. In the 6 Manufacturing groups the weighted vt average is 3.5%. Manufacturing productivity is increasing at a somewhat greater rate than in the British economy as a whole (b3 = +2.42308 versus a b of +1.77473 for the entire economy).

Chapter 4

THE FREQUENCY DISTRIBUTION OF MARK-UP

It is standard operating procedure in econometrics to treat an economic variable in which we are interested, such as k or V, as a linear function of several other variables plus the stochastic element "u" or "error".[1] If one wished to use this approach to "explain" the variation and trend of mark-up, the more important determinants would appear to be such things as: the percentage of BGP produced by agriculture, the percentage of the population in employee status, the absolute level of k, the capital-output ratio and capital per head, the rate of change in real output per head, and, if we could hit on a good representation of it, the degree of competition. Perhaps the percentage of industry output produced by the 3 or 4 largest firms could serve here.

I shall not, however, now demonstrate my painfully acquired knowledge of Doolittle solutions, Von Neumann ratios, and success in getting time on a computer. Weintraub wishes us to accept k as constant, or constant ±e, a "drift item".[2] Let us see how well this formulation will serve us.

The econometrician, having developed as his explanatory variables the influences which economic theory or observation show to have strong and systematic effects on the determinate, consigns all other influences to a normally distributed error term with an expected value of zero. Normal distributions occur when the causal forces are: numerous, of approximately equal weight, homogeneous over the universe from which observations are drawn, independent of one another, and symmetrical in their effect on the variable. If it can be shown that the variation in k is close to normally distributed, the case for our simple procedure will be strengthened and our confidence in use of the properties of the

[1] Good examples would be the works of Friedman, Selden, and Macesich already cited on the "determinants" of monetary velocity. Such variables as cost of holding money, cost of money substitutes, rate of change of prices, and real per capita disposable income, are ground through simple and multiple regression analysis and some significant coefficients are obtained along with much autocorrelation.

[2] Weintraub, *General Theory*, p. 59.

normal curve in predicting the future values of k, "*t* testing" etc. will be much enhanced. On the other hand, a large departure from normality would indicate the presence of one or more non-random determinants of mark-up which we should ignore to our hurt. Furthermore, it is important to the usefulness of the WCM that the standard deviation of the frequency distribution of k be "small", for if changes are too large exceptions to the Law of the Price Level will become embarrassing.[3]

THE FREQUENCY DISTRIBUTION OF MARK-UP IN THE UNITED STATES

The first matter to resolve is whether we are to study the frequency distribution of absolute year-to-year changes or relative changes. The decision is for relative changes because of their comparability between time periods, levels of aggregation and countries. There are two methods of obtaining such relative functions: the first is to divide the absolute changes by the mean of the relevant k series, the other is to use the index numbers already developed. Index series are biased and account must be taken of the base over which the index number change occurs.[4] Since k is close to constant at an index of 100 rather than climbing sharply as P and R, the degree of bias is small and the index numbers will distort the actual frequency function but little.

Table 4.1. sets forth the frequency distribution of absolute changes in mark-up in the U. S. since 1899; these changes reduced to relative changes by dividing them by the mean of k (2.1167)[5]; and the changes in the mark-up index. These changes were debiased by dividing each change by its base. Figure 4.1. sets forth these distributions visually, together with a statistical analysis of all the relative mark-up distributions. All of our varient frequency distributions of aggregate k in the United States are single humped

[3]As pointed out above, large changes in k do not necessarily cause an exception to the Law of the Price Level. For example, k might rise 10 points, P rise 11 points, and R rise 1 point. Such movements occurred in the U. S. during and immediately after World War I and at the beginning of the depression. (See Figure 1.2. and Table 1.6.). On the other hand, small exceptions to the Law can occur in response to very small movements in k if P and R do not have a strong upward or downward trend. (See mid 1920s Figure 1.2.) However, large exceptions cannot occur without relatively large changes in k.

[4]Thus a 1 index point change from 49 to 50 is twice as large as a change from 99 to 100.

[5]Mark-up data for years 1899-1929 multiplied by 1.069. See Table 1.3.

Table 4.1. Frequency Distributions of Various Measures of Mark-Up Changes ($\Delta \underline{k}$) in the United States 1899-1961.

	Frequency			
			Measures of Relative Change	
Size of Change	Absolute $\Delta \underline{k}$	$\frac{\text{Absolute } \Delta k}{\text{Mean of } \underline{k}}$	Index $\Delta \underline{k}$	Debiased Index Δk $2(\underline{k}_t - \underline{k}_{t+1}) / \underline{k}_t + \underline{k}_{t+1}$
-24	1			
.				
-14	2			
.				
-12	2		1	
-11		1		
-10				1
-9	2			
-8	2		2	
-7	3	2		
-6	2	2	1	3
-5	3		1	2
-4	1	4	4	4
-3	1	5	6	7
-2	3	4	2	2
-1	3	4	2	2
0	6	17	14	14
+1	8	11	9	9
+2	5	4	8	10
+3	6	3	3	4
+4	1	2	3	1
+5	3	1	2	1
+6	1		2	1
+7	2	1	1	
+8	2			
..				
+10	1			1
+11		1		
+12			1	
.				
+15	1			
.				
+24	1			
Check Number	62	62	62	62

Source: Absolute $\Delta \underline{k}$ from Table 1.1. and Table 1.2. with adjustment factor 1.069 for years 1899-1929.
Index $\Delta \underline{k}$ from Table 1.3.

with zero mean (in all cases $\bar{k}$ lies well within one standard error of zero) and close to symmetrical. The standard deviation or ($\underline{s}$) is somewhat greater than 3, and in every case but one the measure χ indicates a slight negative skewness, *i.e.* the long tail of the distribution is to the left, large negative changes in $\underline{k}$ being more fre-

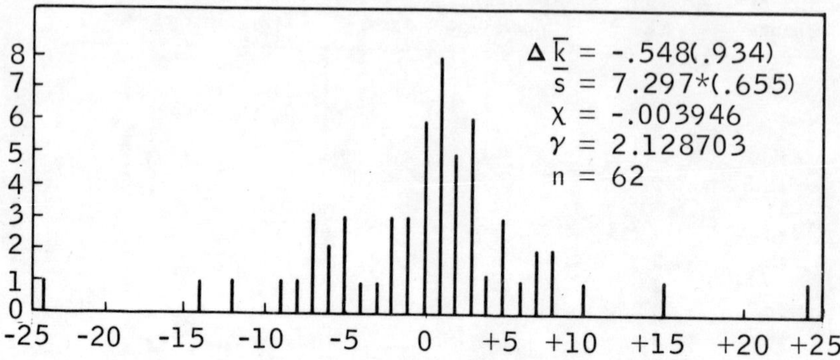

Fig. 4.1a. Frequency Distribution of Absolute Changes in Mark-Up ($\Delta \underline{k}$), in the United States 1899-1961 62 Observations

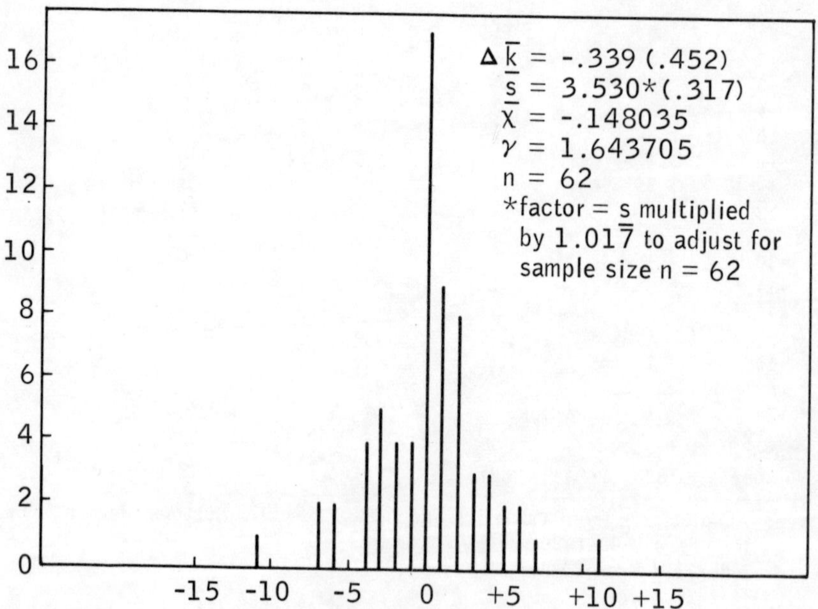

Fig. 4.1b. Frequency Distribution of Relative Changes in Mark-Up ($\Delta \underline{k}/\bar{k}$), in the United States 1899-1961 62 Observations

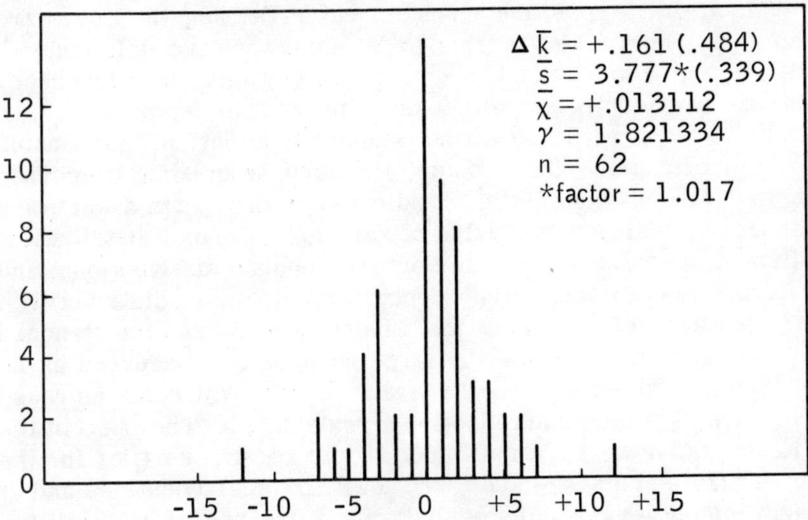

Fig. 4.1c. Frequency Distribution of k Index in the United States 1899-1961 62 Observations

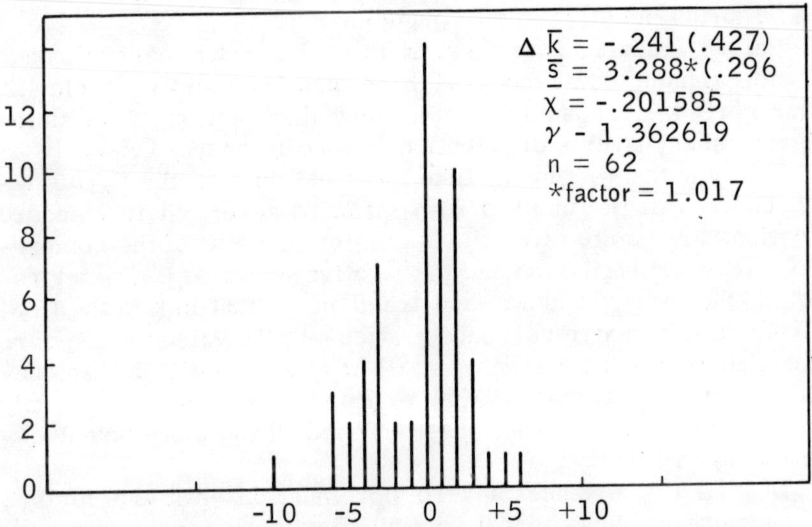

Fig. 4.1d. Frequency Distribution of Debiased k Index in the United States 1899-1961 62 Observations

quent then large positive changes and reflecting the downward trend in k. There also seems to be somewhat of a deficiency of small, 1 and 2 index point, negative changes in k. The frequency functions of Δ k are somewhat more peaked, or leptokurtic, than normal curves with the same standard deviation, a valuable characteristic given the economist's purpose in being concerned with k. This characteristic is indicated by the fourth descriptive measure, γ, which has a value of zero for a normal distribution, positive values for more than normally peaked distributions, and negative values for more flat-topped, or platokurtic, distributions.

The effect of debiasing the k index is to reduce the standard deviation somewhat, since the large changes in k occurred in the pre-1929 period when k was somewhat larger, with some increase in negative skewness and reduction in peakedness. The effect of the operation is, however, small, and would be still smaller for the shorter time series we have to work with in other countries and at disaggregated levels and we shall therefore henceforth omit the operation. Nor is the relative distribution resulting from division of absolute changes by the mean enough different from the distribution resulting from division by an arbitrary base year so that we need use the former measure. We shall therefore adopt the simplest procedure, and from now on develop merely the frequency distributions of the k index at various aggregation levels in the U. S., Canada, and the United Kingdom.

Before studying k further, it is of interest to carry through with the running comparison we have made of k and V. Table 4.2. and Figure 4.2. presents the frequency distribution of V_y in the original numbers, this distribution divided by the mean of V_y ($\overline{V}_y$ = 137.524), and the V_y index. Like the k distribution, the V_y distributions are single humped with mean of zero. Their standard deviations are two to three times greater than that of the comparable mark-up distribution and the negative skewness is greater reflecting the stronger downward trend in V_y that in k in the U. S. In view of the extreme concentration of Δ k values at the zero point, that is, for k not to move at all or at any rate less than one-half an index point, the fact that V_y failed to change in value only *once* in the 62 periods under observation is all the more noteable--some constant!

Despite the absence of zero movement observations for V_y, the measure γ shows that its distribution is also more than normally peaked. We may perhaps take these concentrations around zero as systematic elements reflective of behavior, *i.e.* large

Table 4.2. Frequency Distributions of Three Measures of Income Velocity Changes (ΔV_y) in the United States 1899-1961.

	Frequency		
		Measures of Relative Change	
Size of Change	Absolute ΔV_y	ΔV_y /Mean of V_y	Index ΔV_y
-34	1		
.			
-30			1
.			
-25		1	
-24	1		
.			
-22	1		
-21	1		2
.			
-19	1		1
.			
-17	1	1	1
-16		1	
-15		1	1
-14	1	1	
-13			1
-12		1	
-11	1		
-10	1	1	1
-9			2
-8	1	1	
-7	2	1	1
-6	5	1	3
-5	3	2	2
-4	1	8	3
-3		1	1
-2	6		4
-1	6	12	7
0	1	1	1
+1	2	6	4
+2	4	2	3
+3	2		1
+4		5	1
+5	3	2	5
+6	2	1	1
+7	2	3	2
+8	1	1	2
+9	1	3	1
+10	2	1	2
+11	1	1	2
+12	2	2	3
+13	1		
+14	1		1
+15	1	1	1
+16	1		
+17	1		
+18			1
.			
+21	1		
	62	62	62

Source: Table 1.4.

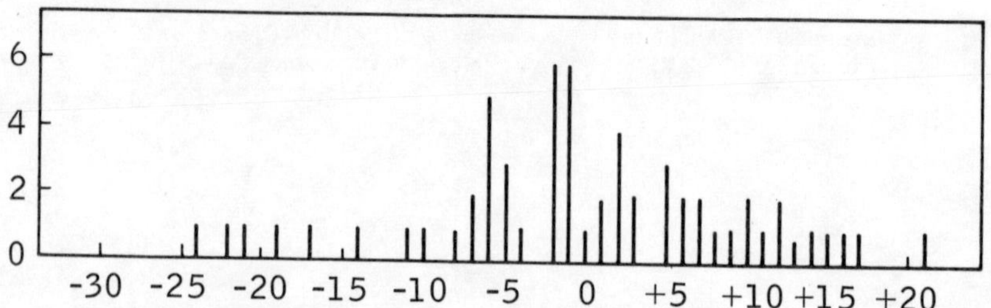

Fig. 4.2a. Frequency Distribution of Absolute Changes in Income Velocity (ΔV_y), in the United States 1899-1961 62 Observations

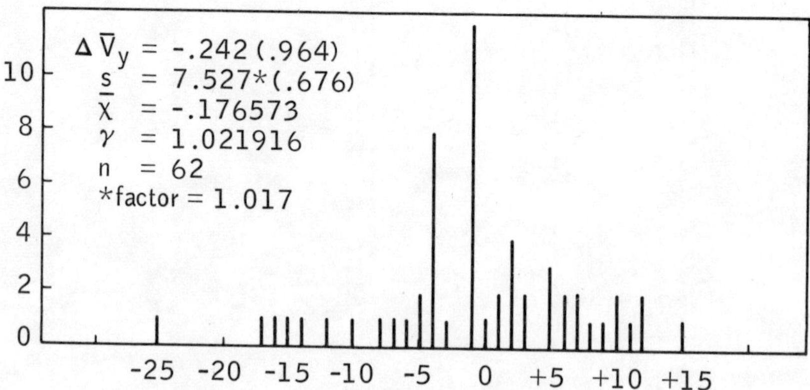

Fig. 4.2b. Frequency Distribution of Relative Changes in Income Velocity ($\Delta V_y / \bar{V}_y$), in the United States 1899-1961 62 Observations

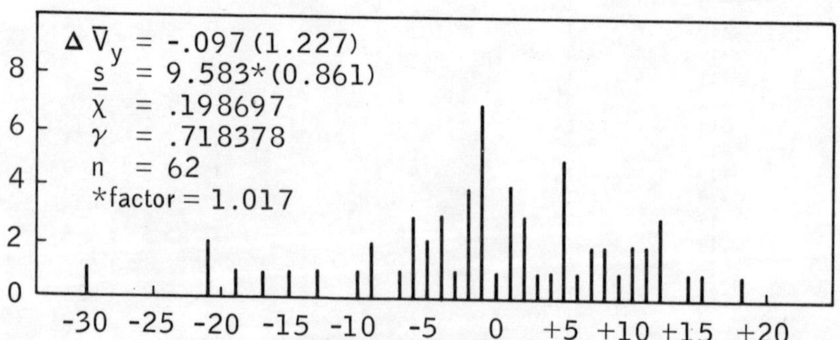

Fig. 4.2c. Frequency Distribution of V_y Index in the United States 1899-1961 62 Observations

firms rigid mark-up policies, or persistence of transactions motives for holding money.

As we saw in Chapter One, the Income Velocity of Circulation has been as variable in recent years as in any period for which we have record. On the other hand, year-to-year changes in mark-up appear to have become smaller, so much so that one hesitates to accept the view that they are "random samples" from a mark-up universe which has remained homogeneous since 1899. Figure 4.3. explores this reduction in the variability of the k index since 1929 in comparison with the earlier period. As can be seen in Figure 4.3a., in the earlier period the year-to-year changes in k varied all the way from -12 to +12 with a standard deviation (s) of 5.139. There is a moderate positive skewness and negligible leptokurtosis. The distribution of the k index changes since 1929, however, is much less variable, s = 1.852, and the skewness is negative, χ =-.3340. Despite the fact that in 12 out of the 32 changes since 1929, k did not change in value, the distribution is not leptokurtic, γ = -.6712, because of the near absence of small negative changes. Figure 4.3c. shows how the complete k distribution combines these two quite different periods.

Intuitively it seems clear that the variability of k had decreased since the turn of the century. Furthermore, we can account for a great deal of this reduced variability by the decline in the relative importance of agriculture as was seen in Chapter Three in the section on Canada. It is, I think, nevertheless startling how confident statistical theory enables us to be of this conclusion. A t test of the significance of the difference of these standard deviations (s) (5.139 - 1.852 = 3.287) yields a value of 4.8239. This may be interpreted as meaning that if the normal mark-up "universe" had actually remained homogeneous throughout, the probability of obtaining the result we have, two standard deviations varying as these do, is less than one is several thousand. We may therefore take it as demonstrated that mark-up has become significantly less variable over time.

THE FREQUENCY DISTRIBUTION OF THE DISAGGREGATED k INDEX IN THE UNITED STATES

Let us now make use of the industrial mark-up data we developed in Chapter Three, to study further the frequency distribution of k. Table 4.3. presents: the frequency distribution of the aggregate k index from 1947 to 1961, the sum of 10 Industry disag-

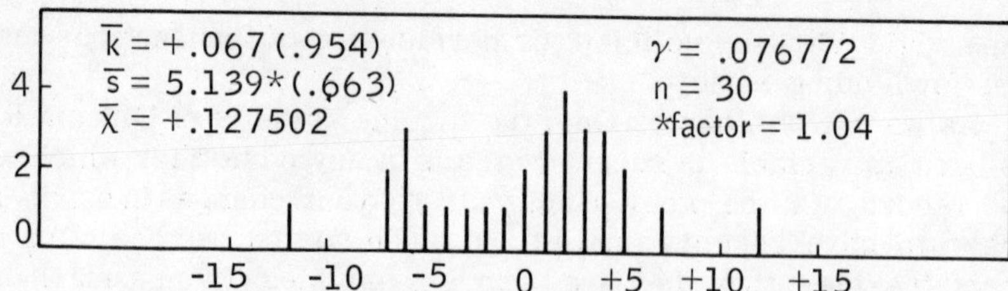

Fig. 4.3a. Frequency Distribution of k Index in the United States
1899-1929 30 Observations

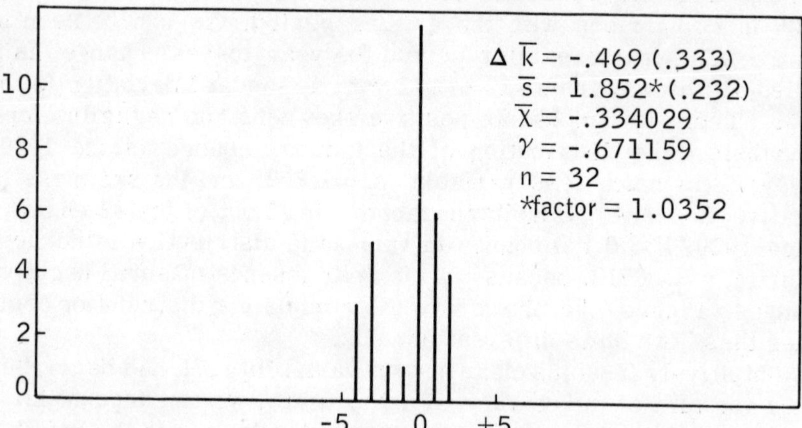

Fig. 4.3b. Frequency Distribution of k Index in the United States
1929-1961 32 Observations

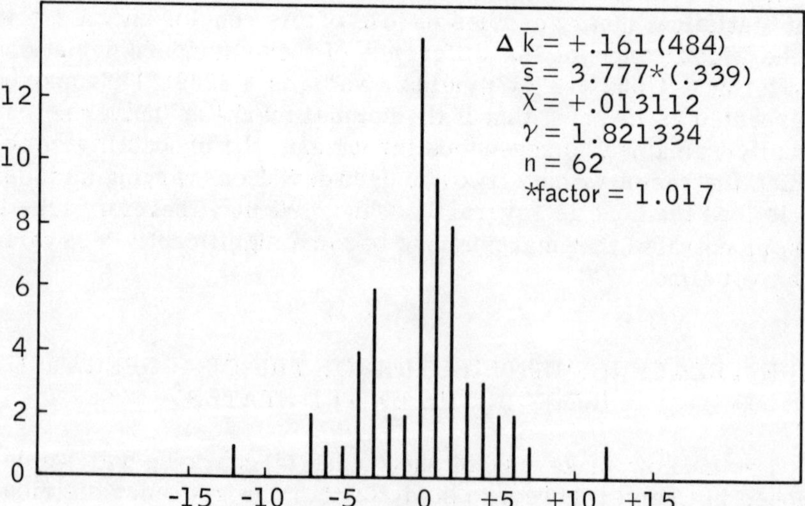

Fig. 4.3c. Frequency Distribution of k Index in the United States
1899-1961 62 Observations

Table 4.3. Frequency Distribution of: Aggregate k Index 1947-1961, the Sum of the 10 Industry Disaggregation, the Sum of the k Index in Industries 1. 4. 6. and 7, the Sum of the k Index in 7 Disaggregated Sub-Industries. Manufacturing k.4 Index, and the Sum of the k Index in 21 Manufacturing Industries & Sub-Categories.

	Frequency					
Size of Change	Aggregate k	10 Industries	Industries 1, 4, 6, 7	7 Sub-Industries	Mfg. Industry	21 Mfg. Sub-Inds. & Cat.
-21						1
-20						1
-18						1
-17						2
-16				1		
-15		1	1			2
-14						1
-13						3
-12						1
-11						1
-10						1
-9		1	1	2		3
-8		1	1	2		4
-7				1	1	2
-6		1		2		13
-5		2		3		12
-4		4	3	5		22
-3	2	12	7	4	4	25
-2	1	16	8	16	2	28
-1		21	8	10	1	34
0	8	20	8	9	3	33
+1	3	11	1	7		22
+2		16	5	7		27
+3		4	1	4		12
+4		4	2	3	1	12
+5		6	1	2	2	4
+6		4	2	2	1	3
+7		2	1	2		7
+8		1	1			6
+9				2		6
+10		1				2
+11		1		2		2
+12				1		2
+13		1	1			3
+14						1
+15						2
+16						1
*						
+18						1
+19						1
+20						1
+21						1
*						
+27						1
Check n	14	130	52	87	15	307

Source: Aggregate from Table 1.3., others, Tables 3.1, 3.4, 3.8, 3.11.

gregation,[6] the sum of the k index in the disaggregatable industries 1, 4, 6, and 7, the sum of the k index in the seven disaggregated subindustries,[7] industry 4, Manufacturing, and the sum of 21 Manufacturing Industries and Sub-Categories k index.[8] Figure 4.4. graphs each of these distributions together with their statistical description. As Figure 4.4a. indicates, in eight of the last 14 changes the value of the aggregate k index has not changed, twice k fell 3 index points, once it fell 2 points, three times it rose a point. A negative skewness is evident with χ=-.2473 and negligible platokurtosis.

Figure 4.4b. depicts the sum of the changes in k in the 10 profit motivated U. S. industries. Except for fairly marked leptokurtosis the frequency distribution is normal, the positive skewness (χ = +.0302) being negligible. Admittedly we have ignored an important aggregation problem in giving equal importance to a 2 index point change in manufacturing, which produces over 30% of BGP, and a 2 point change in mining, which produces 3%. However, in nearly every industry there is a strong central tendency toward a mean close to zero and the variability is the least in industries 4. 5. 6. and 10, which together account for 70% of the output, therefore weighting the changes would decrease the variability.

Figure 4.4c. is the graph of the summed k indices in the four disaggregatable industries. The standard deviation is greater here than in 10 industries, (4.295 - 3.706 = .589). However, this is attributable almost entirely to industry 1. Agriculture, of which more presently. Figure 4.4d. is the distribution of k in the 7 subindustries and shows again the familiar "all but" normal curve. The standard deviation is again somewhat larger than at the next highest level (4.527 - 4.295 = .232).

Figure 4.4e. is the distribution of k in the Manufacturing Industry aggregate and 4.4f is the graph of the summed k indices in the 21 Manufacturing Industries and Sub-Categories into which we have disaggregated manufacturing. Again s is larger at the lower level of aggregation (6.195 - 4.293 = 1.902).

Let us assess, by means of the "*t*" test, the significance of these differences in s at various aggregation levels and time periods. The standard deviation of k at the 10 industry level of

[6] Government enterprises omitted as not profit motivated.

[7] Sub-industry 7a. omitted as marred by rounding.

[8] Sub-categories 4ma-4md used instead of 4m. Metals and metal products and 2 sub-categories of 4e, Lumber and furniture products, used instead of 4e increasing series from 17 to 21.

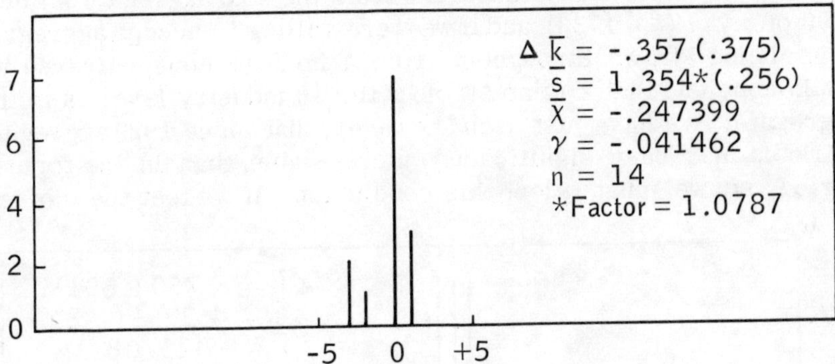

Fig. 4.4a. Frequency Distribution of k Index in the U. S. 1947-1961
14 Observations

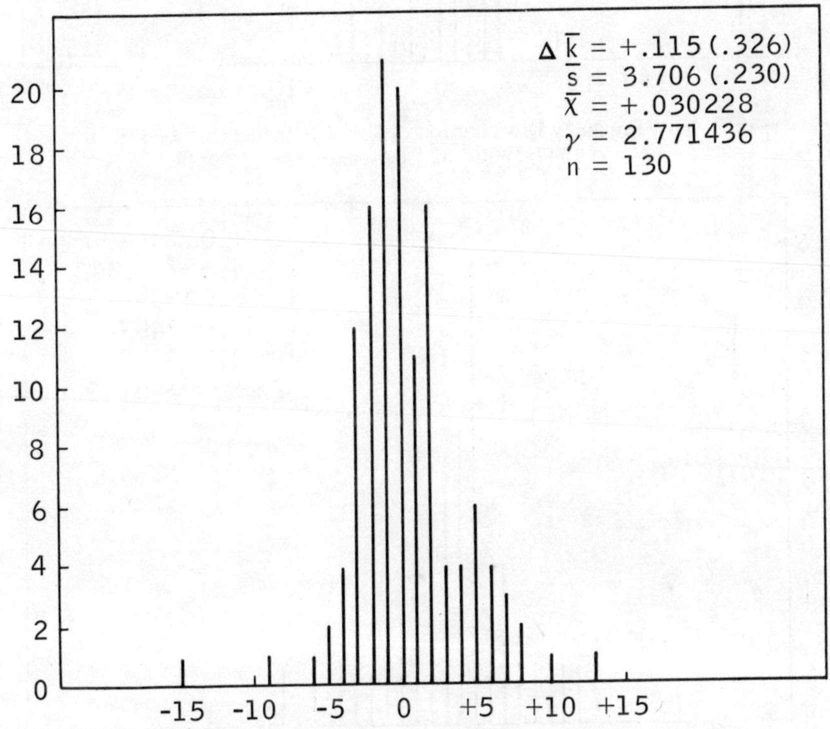

Fig. 4.4b. Frequency Distribution of k in U. S. Industries 1 - 10
1947-1960 130 Observations

3.706 is not significantly different from the s of aggregate k since 1899 of 3.777 (t =.1733), and if we were willing to accept aggregate k as being drawn throughout from a homogeneous universe we would conclude that k is as stable at the 10 industry level as in the aggregate. We have just seen, however, that since 1929 aggregate mark-up has been significantly more stable than in the former period, so we must reject this conclusion. If we test the s of the

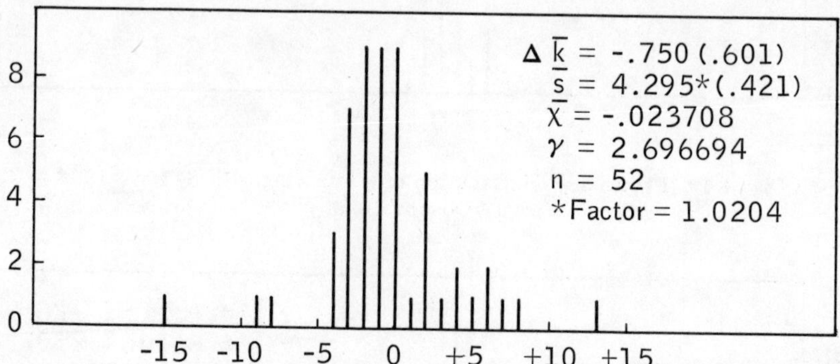

Fig. 4.4c. Frequency Distribution of k in U.S. Industries 1, 4, 6, & 7; 1947-1960 52 Observations

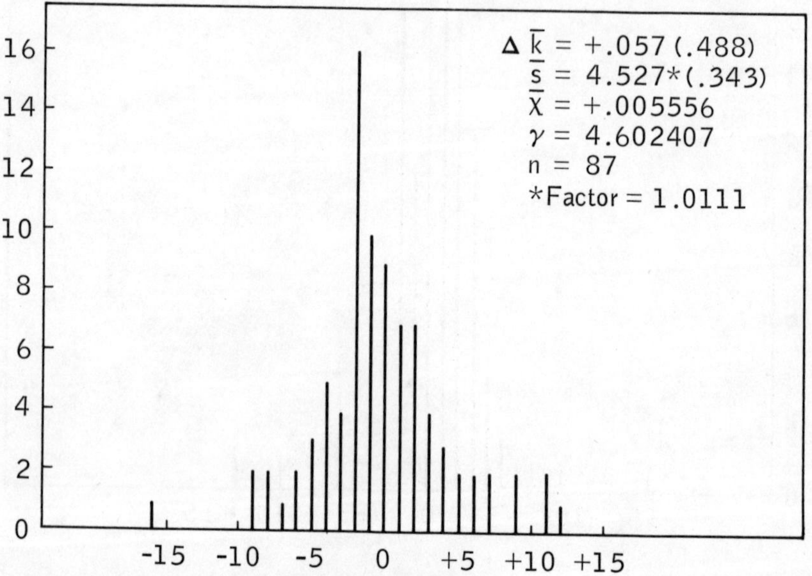

Fig. 4.4d. Frequency Distribution of k in U. S. Sub-Industries 1a, 4a, 4b, 6a, 6b, 7a, & 7b. 1947-1960 87 Observations

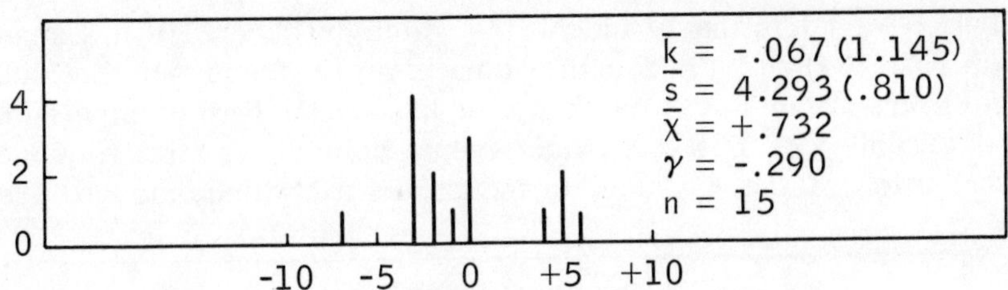

Fig. 4.4e. Frequency Distribution of k.4 Manufacturing
15 Observations

10 industries from 1947 to 1960 against the s of aggregate mark-up from 1947 to 1961 (3.706 - 1.354 = 2.352) we obtain the highly significant t value of 6.2387, compelling us to the conclusion that there is virtually no possibility that mark-up is as stable within industries as it is in the aggregate.

Next we test the difference in s in the 10 industries and in the 4 disaggregatable industries and get a nonsignificant t of .8777. The difference in variability between the 4 industries and their 7 sub-industries is likewise nonsignificant (t = .4273). However, when we compare the 10 industries to the 7 sub-industries the difference does become significant with a t value of 4.527. When we test the difference in s in industry 4. Manufacturing and the 21 series Manufacturing disaggregate we obtain a t of 2.246 which is significant at .05 but not at .01. These tests are summarized in Table 4.8.

Next, let us compare the frequency distribution of mark-up indices in the leading manufacturing firms and the industries of which they are a part. Table 4.4. gives the 8 distributions. Table 4.7. has their statistical description (χ and γ being omitted here). When we test $\bar{s}$ of firm and industry we find no significant differences, in fact $\bar{s}$ of $\bar{k}$ GE and $\bar{k}$ 4j are practically identical (6.707 and 6.736 respectively). Table 4.8. summarizes these tests as tests number 8-11.

THE FREQUENCY DISTRIBUTION OF k IN CANADA

Table 4.5. presents our Canadian data on the frequency distribution of $\bar{k}$ from 1926 to 1961. The first column is for the $\bar{k}$ index. The second is that of $\bar{kd}$ (=Business Domestic Product/Compensation of Business Employees). The third column given the frequency distribution which results from summing the frequency distribution of kd in the 14 industries which produce BDP in Canada from 1926 to 1959. The fourth column gives the frequency distribution of non-agricultural mark-up, or kx, and the fifth column sums disaggregate kx. The sixth and seventh columns are the frequency distribution of the 4 Canadian industries for which data are pre-

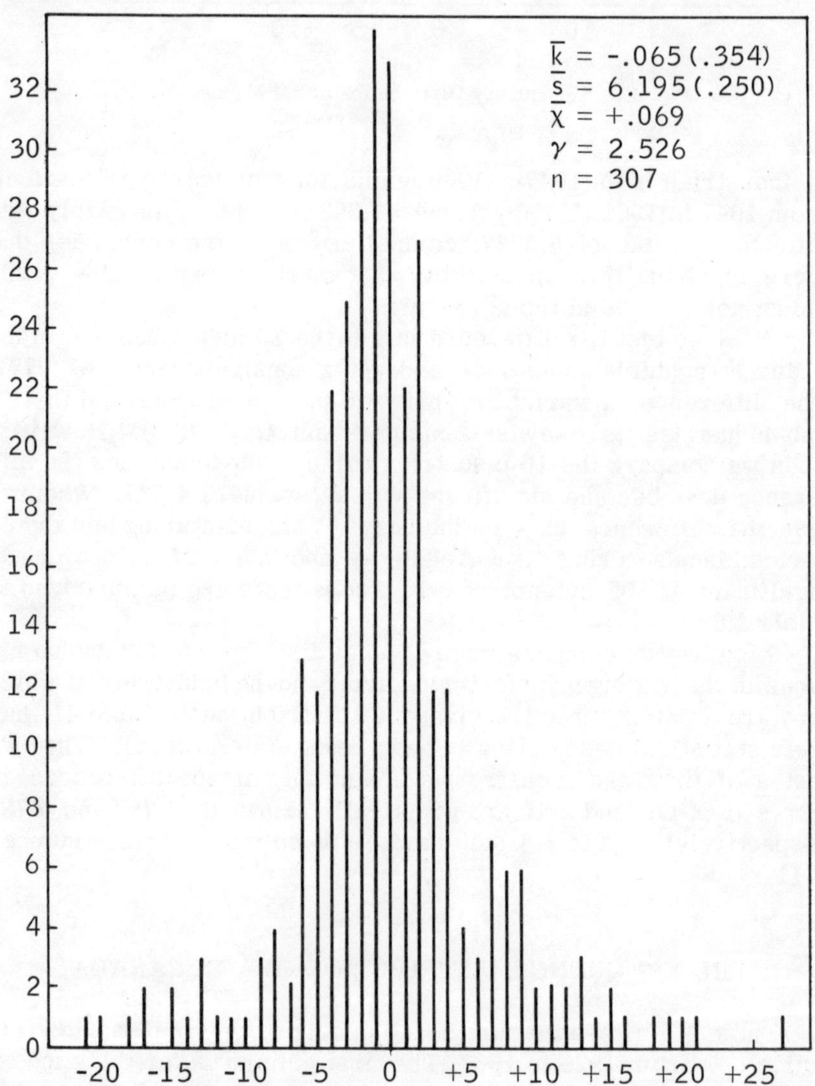

Fig. 4.4f. Frequency Distribution of 21 Manufacturing Sub-Industries and Categories. U. S. 1947-1961 307 Observations

Table 4.4. Frequency Distribution of: Rubber Goods Industry, k.4j; U.S. Rubber Corporation, kUSR; Metals, Metal Products & Misc., k.4m; U. S. Steel Corporation, kUSS; Electrical Machinery, k.4o; General Electric Corporation, kGE; Automobiles & Automobile Equipment, k.4q; General Motors Corporation, kGM.

Size of Change	Frequency							
	k.4j 1950-1961	kUSR 1950-1962	k.4m 1946-1961	kUSS 1946-1962	k.4o 1946-1961	kGE 1947-1962	k.4q 1947-1961	kGM 1947-1961
-18							1	
-17							2	
-16								1
*								
-14				1				
-13	1							
*								
-11			1					
-10								1
*								
-8						1		
-7				1				
-6		1		1	1			1
-5			1		1			
-4	1			1	1	1	1	1
-3	2	1	2	1	1		1	
-2	1	4	3		4	1	2	1
-1	1	1		1	1	1	1	2
0	1		2	2	1	3		2
+1	1	1	1	2	1	1		
+2	2	1	1	1	1	1		
+3		1	1		1	2	1	
+4		1						
+5						1		
+6	1	1	1	1				
+7			1				2	1
+8								1
+9				1				1
+10			1	1				1
+11				2				1
+12						1		
+13						1	1	
*								
+15					1			
+16					1			
*								
+19						1	1	
*								
+21							1	
*								
+24								1
*								
+27							1	
Check n	11	12	15	16	15	16	15	15

Table 4.5. Frequency Distribution of: Aggregate k Index, Aggregate kd Index 1926-1961, the Sum of the kd Index in the 14 Industry Disaggregation, Aggregate Non-Agricultural Mark-Up kx, Sum of the kx Index in 13 Industries, Grouped kd Industries 7-10, and the Sum of the kd Index in Industries 7 to 10 from 1944 to 1959 in *Canada*.

Size of Change	Frequency						
	Aggregate k	Aggregate kd	14 Industry	Aggregate kx	13 Industry	Grouped kd 7-10	Summed kd 7-10
-28							1
*							
-24			1				
-23			1		1		
*							
-21			2		1		
-20							1
*							
-18						1	1
-17			1				1
-16			4		2		1
-15			1				
-14			2		1		
*							
-12			2		2		
-11			4		4		1
-10			7		7	1	1
-9			8		7		
-8	1	1	6		6		
-7	1	1	9		9		2
-6			11		10		4
-5	1		10		8		3
-4	1	2	20	1	19	2	3
-3	3	2	18	2	18	1	4
-2	3	4	29	3	28	1	4
-1	3	4	28	2	27	1	4
0	8	8	35	8	33	2	3
+1	4	4	33	4	31	1	1
+2	6	4	31	6	30	2	3
+3	3	1	15	6	13		6
+4		3	17	3	15	1	2
+5	1	1	10		9		6
+6			9		8		3
+7			8		8	1	
+8			11		9	1	2
+9			5		4		1
+10			8		8		
+11			6		6		
+12			4		3		1
+13							1
+14			1		1		
*							
+17			1				
*							
+20			1		1		
*							
+26			1		1		
+27			2				
*							
+36			1				
n	35	35	363	35	330	15	60

Table 4.6. The Frequency Distribution of: The Aggregate k Index 1948-1961, The Sum of the 9 Industries k Index, Manufacturing k.3 Index, The Sum of the 6 Manufacturing Groups k3g Index, The Sum of the 14 Manufacturing Industries k3i Index, in the *United Kingdom*.

Size of Change	Frequency				
	Aggregate k	9 Industries	Manufacturing k3	6 Mfg. Groups	14 Mfg. Industries
-22					1
*					
-19					2
*					
-17					1
*					
-15				1	
-14					1
-13				1	1
-12				1	1
-11					1
-10		1			1
-9		1	1		2
-8					3
-7				2	3
*					
-5	1	2		1	12
-4		2		10	13
-3	1	12	1	5	8
-2	1	13		5	15
-1	3	12	2	12	20
0	4	21	3	4	17
+1	3	12	3	5	14
+2		14	1	9	16
+3		12	1	4	8
+4		1		5	8
+5		2		1	3
+6		3		2	5
+7				1	2
+8				1	4
+9				1	
+10				1	2
*					
+12					2
+14					1
*					
+18					1
	13	108	12	72	168

sented grouped until 1944. Column six is the distribution of industries 7-10 grouped from 1944 to 1959, while column seven is the sum of individual distributions.

Table 4.7. summarizes the statistical analysis of these seven Canadian distributions as series 19 through 25. The three aggregate series k, kd, and kx are 19, 20, and 21, respectively. All three have means slightly less than zero and some negative skewness reflecting the downward trend of mark-up since 1926. The skewness is greatest in kx ($\chi = -.341$) because of the removal of the agricultural industry within which the trend of mark-up has been up. The standard deviation of k is 2.866 while s of kd is 2.924. Removing Agriculture reduces s of kx to 2.154. Aggregate k and kd are slightly leptokurtic, while kx is slightly platokurtic.

Next let us compare the distributions of disaggregate kd and kx (Table 4.7., series 12 and 14). The mean of both distributions is well within its own sampling error ($s_{\bar{k}}$) of zero. The standard deviation of kd is 6.705 which is reduced to 5.655 in kx.[9] Skewness is negligible so that except for marked leptokurtosis (γs of 3.699 and 1.652 respectively) the two distributions are close to normal.

The last comparison is between the industries 7-10 grouped and disaggregated (Series 26 and 27). As regards mark-up stability, these industries have been "bad actors", Industries 7., Transportation, 9. Communication, and 10. Utilities, plunging in mark-up during the post World War II inflation and then climbing fairly steadily. Of the group, only 8. Storage shows small fluctuations with little trend. The standard deviation of kd 7-10 is 5.469, while that for the sum of the four separate industries' kd s is equal to 7.314. Is this difference significant? Again turning to the familiar *t* test we obtain a value of 1.919 which is significant at the .05 level.

As for the other differences in mark-up variability which we have observed in Canada, the situation is as follows: the difference between aggregate and disaggregate kd and kx are highly significant and virtually dispose of any lingering idea that mark-up is as stable at the industry level as in the aggregate. In the case of the test of aggregate and disaggregate kd the *t* value is 8.959. For the same test of aggregate and disaggregate kx the value obtained is 7.365. These tests are so conclusive because so many years data for the industries are available in comparison with the weaker tests possible in the United States and the United Kingdom.

[9] Similarly in the U. S. removing Agriculture from disaggregate k reduces s from 3.706 to 2.972 for kx. However, s of aggregate kx in the U. S. is larger than that for k; s = 1.840 and 1.352 respectively.

Table 4.7. Summary of Statistical Analysis of Frequency Distributions of Mark-Up in the United States, Canada, and the United Kingdom

No. of Series	Series	n	$\bar{k}$	$s_{\bar{k}}$	s	s_s	χ	γ
	United States							
1.	Absolute k 1899-1961	62	-.548	(.934)	7.297	(.655)	-.004	2.129
1a	Relative k 1899-1961	62	-.339	(.452)	3.530	(.452)	-.148	1.644
2.	k Index 1899-1961	62	+.161	(.484)	3.777	(.339)	+.013	1.821
2a	k Index 1899-1929	30	-.067	(.954)	5.139	(.663)	+.128	0.128
2b	k Index 1929-1961	32	-.469	(.333)	1.852	(.232)	-.334	-.671
2c	k Index 1947-1961	14	-.357	(.375)	1.354	(.256)	-.274	-.042
3.	Debiased k 1899-1961	62	-.241	(.421)	3.288	(.296)	-.202	1.363
4.	Dis* k 1-10 1947-60	130	+.115	(.326)	3.706	(.230)	+.030	2.771
5.	Dis k 1, 4, 6, 7 '47-60	52	-.750	(.601)	4.295	(.421)	-.172	2.697
6.	Dis k 1a, —7b '47-60	87	+.057	(.448)	4.527	(.343)	+.006	4.602
7.	kx 1947-1960	13	-.154	(.531)	1.840	(.361)	-.001	-1.479
8.	Dis kx 1947-1960	117	+.436	(.271)	2.972	(.271)	+.331	1.165
9.	k.4 1947-1963	15	-.067	(1.145)	4.293	(.810)	+.732	-.290
10.	Dis k.4 1947-1961	307	-.065	(.354)	6.195	(.250)	+.069	2.526
11.	k4.j 1950-1961	11	-1.363	(1.546)	4.887	(1.042)		
12.	kUS Rubber '50-62	12	-.166	(1.074)	3.560	(.726)		
13.	k4.m 1947-1961	15	.067	(1.431)	5.356	(.978)		
14.	kUS Steel 1946-1962	16	1.000	(1.892)	7.328	(1.295)		
15.	k4.o 1947-61	15	.667	(1.800)	6.736	(1.229)		
16.	kGE 1947-1962	16	2.188	(1.623)	6.707	(1.186)		
17.	k4.q 1947-1961	15	2.200	(3.828)	14.326	(2.616)		
18.	kGM 1947-1961	15	1.933	(2.721)	10.181	(1.859)		
	Canada							
19.	k 1926-1961	35	-.343	(.492)	2.866	(.343)	-.542	0.615
20.	kd 1926-1961	35	-.257	(.501)	2.924	(.341)	-.217	0.595
21.	Dis kd 1926-1959	363	-.069	(.352)	6.705	(.249)	-.021	3.699
22.	kx 1926-1961	35	-.200	(.369)	2.151	(.257)	-.341	-.612
23.	Dis kx 1926-1959	330	+.152	(.312)	5.655	(.220)	+.008	1.652
24.	kd 7-10 1944-1959	15	-.333	(1.462)	5.469	(.999)	-.023	-.405
25.	Dis kd 7-10 1944-'59	60	-.083	(.952)	7.824	(.668)	-.205	1.169
	United Kingdom							
26.	k 1948-1960	12	-.769	(.514)	1.782	(.349)	-.386	0.777
27.	Dis k 1948-1960	108	.000	(.266)	2.754	(.187)	-.118	0.667
28.	k3 1948-1960	12	-.417	(1.000)	3.349	(.684)	-.131	2.656
29.	Grouped k3 1948-1960	72	-.417	(.536)	4.516	(.370)	-.196	1.663
30.	Dis k3 1948-1960	168	-.661	(.430)	5.559	(.303)	-.741	1.153

*Disaggregate

Explanation of Statistical Symbols

$\underline{n}$ = Number of observations of year-to-year change in mark-up ($\Delta\underline{k}$).

$\bar{k}$ = Mean of $\underline{k}$ deviations from zero = $\frac{\Sigma f(\Delta k - 0)}{n}$

$s_{\bar{k}}$ = Standard Error of the mean $\frac{s}{\sqrt{n-1}}$

$\underline{s}$ = Standard Deviation = $\sqrt{\frac{\Sigma f(\Delta k - 0)2}{n}}$

s_s = Standard Error of the Standard Deviation = $\frac{s}{\sqrt{2n}}$

χ = Skewness = $\frac{\sqrt{\beta 1}(\beta 2 + 3)}{2(5\beta 2 - 6\beta 1 - 9)}$

γ = Kurtosis (peakedness) = $\beta 2 - 3$

Where $\beta 1 = \frac{\left(\frac{\Sigma f(\Delta k - 0)^3}{n}\right)^2}{\left(\frac{\Sigma f(\Delta k - 0)^2}{n}\right)^3}$ $\qquad \beta 2 = \frac{\frac{\Sigma f(\Delta k - 0)^4}{n}}{\left(\frac{\Sigma f(\Delta k - 0)^2}{n}\right)^2}$

Table 4.8. Tests of Significance of Differences between Standard Deviations in the United States, Canada, & the United Kingdom

Test	Mark-Up Series		s	t	Significances
					Significant at .05 = 1.645* " " .01 = 2.326**
	United States				
1.	2a. k 1899-1929		5.139		
	2b. k 1929-1961		1.852		
		Dif	3.287	4.6823	Very significant
2.	2. k 1899-1961		3.777		
	4. Dis* k 1-10 '47-60		3.706		
		Dif	0.071	0.1733	Non-significant
3.	2c. k 1947-1961		1.354		
	4. Dis k 1947-1960		3.706		
		Dif	2.352	6.2387	Very significant
4.	4. Dis k 1-10 '47-60		3.706		
	5. Dis k 1, 4, 6, 7 '47-60		4.295		
		Dif	0.587	0.8777	Non-significant
5.	5. Dis k 1, 4, 6, 7 '47-60		4.295		
	6. Dis k 1a, —7b '47-60		4.527		
		Dif	0.232	0.4273	Non-significant
6.	4. Dis k 1-10 '47-60		3.706		
	6. Dis k 1a, —7b '47-60		4.527		
		Dif	0.821	1.5120	Non-significant
7.	9. k4 1947-1963		4.293		
	10. Dis k4 1947-1961		6.195		
		Dif	1.902	2.246	Significant at .05
8.	11. k4.j 1950-1961		4.887		
	12. U.S. Rubber '50-62		3.560		
		Dif	1.326	1.044	Non-significant
9.	13. k4.m 1947-1961		5.356		
	14. k U.S. Steel '47-62		7.328		
		Dif	1.972	1.215	Non-significant
10.	15. k4.o 1947-1961		6.736		
	16. k G.E. 1947-1962		6.707		
		Dif	.029	.006	Non-significant
11.	17. k4.q 1947-1961		14.326		
	18. k G.M. 1947-1961		10.181		
		Dif	4.145	1.292	Non-significant
	Canada				
12.	20. kd 1926-1961		2.924		
	21. Dis kd 1926-1959		6.705		
		Dif	3.781	8.959	Very Significant
13.	22. kx 1926-1961		2.151		
	23. Dis kx 1926-1959		5.655		
		Dif	3.504	7.365	Very Significant
14.	24. kd 7-10 1944-59		5.469		
	25. Dis kd 7-10 '44-59		7.824		
		Dif	2.355	1.919	Significant at .05

*Disaggregate

**For a "one tailed test." If this is considered to be a "two tailed test" significance levels are 1.959 and 2.576.

*Difference

Table 4.8. continued

Test	Mark-Up Series		s	t	Significance
	United Kingdom				
15.	26. k 1948-1960		1.782		
	27. Dis k 1948-1960		2.754		
		Dif	0.972	2.455	Significant at .01
16.	28. k3 1948-1960		3.349		
	29. Grouped k3 '48-60		4.516		
		Dif	1.167	1.496	High non-significant
17.	28. k3 1948-1960		3.349		
	30. Dis k3 1948-1960		5.559		
		Dif	2.210	2.955	Significant at .01
	International Comparisons				
18.	2. U.S. k 1899-1961		3.777		
	20. Can. kd 1926-1961		2.924		
		Dif	0.853	1.773	Significant at .05
19.	2b. U.S. k 1929-1961		1.852		
	20. Can. kd 1926-1961		2.924		
		Dif	1.072	2.247	Significant at .05
20.	2c. U.S. k 1947-1961		1.354		
	26. U.K. k 1948-1961		1.780		
		Dif	0.426	0.591	Non-significant
21.	4. U.S. dis k 1-10 '47-60		3.706		
	21. Can. dis k 1926-1959		6.705		
		Dif	2.999	8.847	Very significant
22.	4. U.S. dis k 1-10 '47-60		3.706		
	27. U.K. dis k 1-9 '48-60		2.754		
		Dif	0.952	3.216	Significant at .01

The "*t*" Test of the Significance of a Difference between Standard Deviations

The test is designed to assess whether the two standard deviations could have been drawn from the same parent universe. The *t* test consists of dividing the observed difference between standard deviations by the standard error of the difference which is computed by the formula:

$$s_{s1} - s_{s2} = \sqrt{s_{s1}^2 + s_{s2}^2} \quad \text{where } s_s^2 = \frac{s^2}{2n}$$

A *t* value of 1.645 represents a difference so great that it would occur between two sample standard deviations drawn from the same normally distributed parent population only 1 time in 20, i.e. 19 times out of 20 such a difference between samples would signify that the larger standard deviation is "significantly" larger than the other at the .05 level.

THE FREQUENCY DISTRIBUTION OF MARK-UP IN THE UNITED KINGDOM

Finally, we turn our attention to the British data we have developed in Chapter Three for light on the problem of the frequency distribution of k. Table 4.6. presents the frequency distributions of: 1. aggregate k, 2. the sum of the 9 Industry k distributions, 3. the distribution of the Manufacturing Industry k3, 4. the sum of the 6 Manufacturing Groups k3g distribution, and finally, 5. the sum of the 14 Manufacturing Industries k3. distributions.

Again the statistical analysis of these distributions is given in Table 4.7. (Series 28-32). The aggregate k in Britain is highly skewed; χ = -.386, $\bar{k}$ of -.769 is more than its sampling error from zero, and mildly leptokurtic, γ = 0.777. Disaggregate k with its zero mean, small skewness, χ = -.118 and moderate leptokurtosis γ = 0.677 is again close to a normal curve. The standard deviation of aggregate k is 1.780, for disaggregate ks is 2.754. The difference is just significant at the .01 level (t = 2.455).

The standard deviation of the Manufacturing aggregate, k3, is a large 3.349 because of the 9 index point fall between 1951 and 1952. If this one change were excluded s would fall to about 1.400. The distribution has mild negative skewness, χ = -.131 and marked peakedness γ = 2.656. The standard deviation of the sum of the 6 Manufacturing groups is 4.516 with usual negative skewness, χ = -.196 and peakedness γ = 1.663. When we sum the distributions of the 14 Manufacturing industries s becomes 5.559 and negative skewness becomes marked; the mean of -.661 is more than its sampling error from zero, χ = -.741 and γ becomes 1.153. The difference in s of k3 and grouped k3 is just short of significance at .05 (t =1.496) while the difference between s of k3 and disaggregated k3 is significant at .01 (t =2.955.) We may conclude that the British data are consisted with the evidence developed in the United States and Canada that mark-up becomes less stable as we disaggregate.

COMPARISON OF STANDARD DEVIATIONS IN THE THREE COUNTRIES AT THE SAME LEVEL OF AGGREGATION

As a final use of the "t" test let us compare the standard deviations of our mark-up measures in all three countries at the same level of aggregation. The first comparison is of s of k in the U. S. from 1899 to 1961 and in Canada from 1926 to 1961. The relevant figures are 3.777 - 2.924 = .853 yielding a t of 1.773 which is significant at .05. Still greater significance is seen if we compare mark-up in the U. S. from 1929 to the Canadian data from 1926. The figures are 1.852 =2.924 =1.072 yielding t = 2.558 which may be interpreted as meaning that mark-up in Canada fluctuated significantly more than in the United States.

Next let us compare aggregate mark-up in the U. S. and the

U.K. The standard deviation of k from 1947 to 1961 was 1.354 in the U. S. and from 1948-1961 was 1.780. The difference of .426 yields a t of only 0.591 which is nonsignificant.

Turning to disaggregated mark-up measures, we have data for Canada from 1926, but for the U. S. and U. K. from only 1947 and 1948 respectively. Therefore, it is not too surprising that over the entire period 1926-1959 Canadian industry mark-ups have fluctuated very significantly more than have U. S. industry mark-ups from 1947-1960. The figures are 6.705 - 3.706 = 2.999, t = 8.847. However, the U. S. and U. K. data are for substantially the same period and the significant difference obtained may be taken as good evidence of greater industrial mark-up stability in the U. K. than in the U. S. The figures are 3.706 - 2.754 = .952, t = 3.216.

Table 4.7. summarizes the statistical analyses of the frequency distributions of mark-up at the levels of aggregation for which we have data in the United States, Canada, and the United Kingdom. In all we have a total of 34 distributions, however, several are merely the same series treated slightly differently, or cut into shorter time periods. Table 4.8. brings together the 22 significance tests made of differences in s of these frequency distributions.

Chapter 5

CONCLUSIONS AND RECOMMENDATIONS

At the end of Chapter One we posed four questions concerning the near constancy of mark-up which had been observed in the United States since 1899. Let us now bring together the data we have gathered and analyzed in order to attempt some answers to these questions.

Question One: Is this greater constancy of Mark-Up than Velocity to be found in other national economies?

Yes. In every one of the confrontations developed between k or kg and V or Vg indices in 16 countries, with the possible exception of Japan, mark-up was more stable than velocity. In 10 of these 16 countries the superiority of mark-up in this respect was marked to overwhelming. (United States, see Figures 1.2 and 1.3; Australia, Figure 2.1; Canada, 2.2; Finland, 2.3; India, 2.4; Netherlands, 2.6; Norway, 2.7; United Kingdom, 2.9; New Zealand, 2.17; and Peru, 2.18.) In 5 countries mark-up's superiority was less marked (Ireland, 2.5; Sweden, 2.8; Brazil, 2.13; France, 2.14; and Greece, 2.15) leaving only Japan where kg and Vg were about equally unstable.

Defeat in war, (Japan, France) or in some cases mere participation in war seems to effect k's stability more than depression, boom, or inflation, (U. S. in WW I, Australia in Korean War, New Zealand in WW II) not only at the time of the war but in a tendency for mark-up to fall and remain at a lower level subsequent to the war. (U. S. after WW I and WW II, Canada after WW II, Australia after Korea, Norway, France, Japan, and New Zealand after WW II.) However, Sweden, which did not fight, had lower mark-up after World War II than before it, while the Netherlands had a higher post war mark-up.

In Chapter One we stated the "Law of the Price Level" as the proposition that Price (P) varies as does Unit Wage Cost (R) because k is (almost) constant. We found that few exceptions occurred (8 out of 65 year-to-year changes in the U. S. from 1899 to 1964 or 12%) and all were small (less than 3 index point difference). This Wage Cost Mark-Up law was then contrasted with an Equation of Exchange "Law" that Price varies as does the Ratio of Money to Real Output (r) because V is (almost) constant. This law was contradicted in 36 of the 65 one year changes observed, or 55% of the time and 19 of the exceptions were more than 3 index points, the largest being 37 index points!

Our international comparisons of mark-up and velocity indicate that similar results will obtain in nearly every country and time period.

The long run trend of mark-up is down, pp. 61-64, to treat of the "constancy" of mark-up is to treat of its small year-to-year variability about this small downward trend.

Question Two: Is this near constancy merely the net resultant of offsetting shifts within and between industries, shifts which may or may not occur in the future, or is k also stable at lower levels of aggregation?

Considerable effort was expended in an attempt at a definite answer to this question. Mark-up in the United States was disaggregated into 11 industries and 8 sub-industries, one industry, Manufacturing was further disaggregated into 17 Manufacturing industries. Lastly, mark-up figures were developed for 4 leading manufacturing corporations. These studies were supplemented by disaggregation of Canadian mark-up into 14 Industries from 1926 and disaggregation of British mark-up into 9 Industries and Manufacturing into 14 Manufacturing industries from 1948.

Notice was taken of Robert Solow's test of the degree to which fortuitous shifts in the relative importance of industries has smoothed out aggregate shares. Solow, working with 1/ky data, concluded that the weight shifts deserved practically no credit for the aggregate stability observed. In fact there were slightly destabilizing on balance, see pp. 71-72.

Solow's results were checked both by comparing the observed and theoretical variance, s^2, of aggregate k and by calculating fixed weight k_1, and fixed mark-up k_2 values at all levels of industrial disaggregation developed. Our data are strongly confirmatory of Solow's that, "the aggregate share varied just about as much as it would vary if the individual sector shares fluctuated independently with positive and negative intercorrelations approximately offsetting each other".[1]

[1]Solow, "A Skeptical Note", p. 624.

In Canada, it was found that nearly all the year-to-year variability of mark-up is attributable to fluctuations in mark-up *within* constituant industries, while nearly all of the downward trend of k was attributable to interindustry shifts, notably the relative decline of agriculture and increase of manufacturing.

The variability of mark-up definitely increases as we disaggregate, however. This can be most readily seen in the increase in relative variability (v = standard deviation/ mean) of mark-up seen in Table 3.18. Aggregate mark-up in the U. S. from 1947 to 1961 had a v of 2.6%. Over the same period the 11 industry disaggregation had weighted v of 4.7%. Similarly, v of the Manufacturing industry was 2.4%, while a weighted average of v of the 17 manufacturing industry disaggregation was 5.1%. Finally when we compare 4 manufacturing industries with 4 leading manufacturing firms weighted relative variability increases from 5.5% to 7.4%.

In order to assess the statistical significance of this increasing variability frequency distributions were developed and analyzed for all our mark-up indices. The various mark-up distributions took on most of the properties of the Normal Curve of Error except for frequent leptokurtosis, or "peakedness", which is helpful given the economist's reasons for being interested, and negative skewness which comes from mark-up's characteristic downward trend. Normal curves occur where the forces causing variation are numerous, of approximately equal weight, homogeneous over the universe from which observations are drawn, independent of one another, and symetrical in their effect on the variable. Mark-up distributions near normality, indeed "super normality" in that there is a greater than normal tendency for variations to cluster close to the zero mean, is important to the econometric forecaster or policy maker concerned with price level and "guidelines" phenomena. These facts justify the simple procedure of treating k as either constant, or a constant linear function of time, consigning all other influences to the error term. This is in distinct contrast with Income Velocity where the other influences are so important that those who study V feel constrained to bring in many variables to account for its girations. Having established, rather than merely assumed, the normality of mark-up distributions we turned to "*t*" tests of the significance of the increasing standard deviations (s) observed as we disaggregated. In all three countries studied the standard deviation of the industrial disaggregations was significantly larger than that for aggregate mark-up. Significantly larger s was also observed when manufacturing was disaggregated in the U. S. and U. K. than in the manufacturing aggregate. However, the differences in s between the mark-up distributions of 4 leading manufacturing firms and their corresponding industries were all non-significant.

It was also found that mark-ups in the United Kingdom, both aggregate and disaggregate are significantly less variable than the corresponding distribution in the United States while Canadian mark-ups were significantly more variable. It was also established that variability of aggregate mark-up in the U. S. has decreased significantly over time.

Even at the lowest levels of aggregation studied mark-up was characteristically more stable than aggregate monetary velocity. The relative variability of Income Velocity in the U. S. from 1947 to 1961 was 14.6%. No U. S. industry, sub-industry, manufacturing industry disaggregate or firm had a v for thi eriod exceeding 10.6% and most had vs half to one third as large as this. Similar results were obtained in the U. K. Only in Canada do we find mark-up series with greater variability than aggregate velocity. Relative variability of Canadian agriculture was 31.6%, v of Fishing and Trapping was 13.0% and v of the Utilities was 16.4% while velocity had a v of 11.9% from 1926 to 1964.

Question Three: Is the trend in Output per Employee (A) stable at disaggregated as well as aggregated levels in various countries?

The statistical measures of the linearity of the trend of productivity gains and variability about that trend are R^2 = "explained variation", s_{At} = "conditional coefficient of variation" and vt = "relative conditional variation" = s_{At} / mean of A. The last measure is the easiest to understand and compare.

In studies made of productivity gains in U. S. and U. K. disaggregate it was found that each industry, sub-industry and manufacturing disaggregate was a case unto itself as to the rapidity with which productivity gains were made. However, small variability[2] about these approximately linear trends[3] were seen in small values of vt. In the U. S. the aggregate A series for 1947-1960 had a vt value of 2.6%. The weighted average of vt values of U. S. Industries for the same period was 2.4%. For 5 sub-industries the weighted vt of A was 4.2%. Similarly in the U. K., for

[2]As noted above, p. 121 a productivity change from 2% to 3% is a 50% change and thus from some points of focus "large" rather than "small".

[3]As is shown on pages 18-20, over the period 1913-1961 in the U. S., the trend of aggregate A was not linear, but log linear. However, for short periods the linear trend is accurate enough.

aggregate A vt was for 1948-1960 1.1%, for the 9 Industries it was 2.5%. In the manufacturing aggregate vt of A was 2.8%, for the 6 manufacturing groups weighted vt was 3.5%. The small degree of variability of A increases the usefulness of the WCM equation for the forecaster and policy maker. (See pp.118-125 for this discussion.)

Question Four: Can we account theoretically for the varying degrees of fluctuation in different countries, time periods and levels of aggregation?

There is a simple way to deal with the problem of explaining the near constancy of mark-up we have so often observed in aggregate and disaggregate series: we can deny that the constancy is there and accuse the statisticians of fudging the figures. This is the tack taken by Messrs. Macesich and Colberg in their review of Weintraub's *General Theory*. Concerning the work of the U. S. Department of Commerce, they write:

> "While the agency probably does a good job with the information and other resources at its command, statisticians working on the extremely complicated national income estimates would probably be the first to admit that many components are very rough. Statistics for the important construction industry, for example, are known to be extremely poor. It is entirely possible that a good deal of the relative stability of k actually arises from the use of such a factor in making the national income estimates in some sectors".[4]

But why stop here in calling into question the accuracy of Commerce's figures? Why not maintain that velocity actually *is* a constant, but that Commerce's factors so distort the figures that it doesn't show up? We have seen that this use of "factors" which make the ratio Z/W stable and Z/M unstable appears in virtually every country studied in this paper!

If we dismiss the idea that mark-up stability is a mere optical illusion foisted on us by the world's statisticians, we are left with a difficult task. As Weintraub has written, "The near-constancy of the wage share is one of the best established and poorest explained facts in our science".[5]

[4] George Macesich and Marshall Colberg, "Professor Weintraub's General Theory," *Southern Economic Review*, Vol. XXVII No. 1, July 1960, p. 58.

[5] Sidney Weintraub, "A Keynesian Model of the Price Level and the Constant Wage Share," *Kyklos* Vol. XV 1962 Fasc. p. 714.

MACRO EXPLANATIONS OF MARK-UP STABILITY

Kalecki, who as much as anyone may be credited with commencing the discussion, explained the mark-up rigidity he observed in the U. K. and U. S. by growing monopoly power balancing productivity gains.[6] Weintraub offers an explanation of why mark-up tends to "get stuck":

$$\frac{d}{dN}\left(\frac{wN}{Z}\right) = \frac{w}{Z}\left(1 + \frac{N}{w}\cdot\frac{dw}{dN}\right) = \frac{W}{Z}\quad(1 = E_w - E_z) \quad (4.3)$$

Examining (4.3), the E_w and E_z in the parenthesis denote the elasticity of money wages and the elasticity of aggregate proceeds respectively. Suppose money wage changes are nil as employment expands, so the $E_w = 0$. Reflecting on E_z, this refers to the relative employment advance; with constant returns it is equal to 1 and with diminishing returns $E_z < 1$. Manifestly, therefore, if $E_w = 0$, and $E_z < 1$, the wage share must fall in an employment advance.

Consider, however, the possible magnitude of the fall in the wage share. The entire parenthesis in (4.3) is multiplied by w/Z; in the United States today, this "multiplier" is of the order of $4,500/$450,000,000,000. Small wonder, therefore, that the wage share will at best change in trifling amounts... It should be noted that in empirical work, where discrete changes are observed, the parenthesis of (4.3) would be multiplied by $w\Delta N/Z$ rather than by w/Z. Thus:

$$\frac{W\Delta N}{Z}\quad(1 + E_w - E_z) \quad (4.3b)$$

Still, even for an employment advance of 1,000,000 men the parenthesis-multiplier of (4.3b) becomes about ($4,500,000,000/$450,000,000,000), or about 1/100. A change in the wage share of one per cent or so per annum is thus not to be ruled out in a large employment movement."[7]

Additional macro theories which could account for macro share stability include variants of the aggregate production function con-

[6] Michal Kalecki, "The Distribution of the National Income", *Essays in the Theory of Economic Fluctuations*, (New York: Blakiston 1939) pp. 197-217.

[7] Weintraub, "A Keynesian Model of the Price Level," pp. 716-717.

cept. Schumpeter, somewhat dubiously, referred to this concept as a possible stable shares explanation as follows:[8]

> "Now, *if there were any sense in speaking of a national production function at all*, first-order homogeneity of this function would supply a very simple explanation of a remarkable fact, namely, the relative constancy of the main relative shares of 'factors' in the national dividend."

A very considerable literature exists concerning a particular production function, the Cobb-Douglas, which is often fitted to the historical data.[9] The form of the Cobb-Douglas *imposes* constant relative shares on the two factors regardless of their quantities, and since, as we have seen, the shares are in fact close to constant, the fit is generally "good". Unfortunately, this tells us little as to causation in the real world.

MICRO EXPLANATIONS OF MARK-UP STABILITY

Solow, however, maintains that we have no need of a special macro theory to explain this aggregate stability since "whatever exceptional stability" there has been is attributable to the components. Weintraub likewise holds that the WCM focuses on "behavioral or structural relationships"[10] and the EOE does not.[11] Let us explore micro explanations of micro and macro stability and unstability.

The behavioral relationships on which the WCM focuses are accounting, engineering and managerial conventions in individual firms and industries which result in "formula," "full-cost" or "mark-up," pricing. Deprived of such a base in behavior the WCM

[8] Joseph A. Schumpeter, *History of Economic Analysis*, (New York: Oxford 1954) p. 1042.

[9] The more important journal articles would include: C. S. Cobb and P. H. Douglas, "A Theory of Production," *AER/S* 18: 139-65 March 1928. M. Broufenbrenner, "The Cobb-Douglas Function and Trade Union Policy," *AER* 29: 793-96 Dec. 1939. P. N. Douglas, "Are There Laws of Production," *AER* 38: 1-41, Nov. 1948. M. S. Reder, "An Alternative Interpretation of the Cobb-Douglas Function," *Econometrica* 11: 259-64 July-Oct. 1943. E. H. P. Brown, "The Meaning of the Fitted Cobb-Douglas Function," *QJE* 71: 546-60 Nov. 1957.

[10] Weintraub, *General Theory*, p. 5.

[11] Many would not concede this, of course, holding that velocity or cash balance phenomena do reflect liquidity preference behavioı, response to interest changes, price changes and price expectations and so on.

would also, "only indicate the movement in components and not the causal factors."[12]

Such fixed gross mark-up over Unit Wage Cost behavior of firms would also account for the phenomenon which was well documented in Chapter 2,[13] that k has far greater cyclical stability than does k_y or "net mark-up," (k_y = National Income/Employee Compensation). The cyclical behavior of the depreciation, and indirect business taxes, which make up the difference between BGP and National Income produced by Business, explain the smaller cyclical variability of gross mark-up (k) than net mark-up (k_{yb} = NI_b/W_b).

Indirect business taxes and capital consumption allowances are very stable in dollar amount over the business cycle, as are the interest and rent accounts, and consequently vary greatly as a percentage of the total.[14] A simple numerical example will make evident that if *via* "full cost" pricing businessmen succeed in holding their k ratio constant while their gross proceeds fluctuate, the nearly constant depreciation and tax accounts will cause k_y to fluctuate much as it is observed to do. In the example in Table 5.1., if, in succeeding years BGP is equal to $100, $80, and $110, the k ratio is fixed at 2.00, and interest, rents, depreciation and taxes are constant, k_{yb} assumes successive values of 1.60, 1.50, and 1.64.

There is no conflict between this and Weintraub's macro explanation above: complete fixity of mark-up within the firm means that $E_w = E_z$. Ability to maintain this fixed mark-up implies a certain insolation from market forces imposing competitive, rapidly changing prices. However, we must consider that ours is an economy where the 50 largest manufacturing corporations

[12] *Ibid.*

[13] pp. 44-51

[14]

(All dollar figures in billions of dollars)

Year	Capital Consumption Allowances	Indirect Business Taxes	Total	BGP	Per Cent of BGP
1929	$8.6	$7.0	$15.6	$94.8	16.4
1931	8.2	6.9	15.0	68.0	22.1
1933	7.1	7.1	14.2	48.7	29.2
1937	7.5	9.2	16.7	80.5	20.7

Source: U. S. Department of Commerce, *National Income* 1954, p. 164.

Table 5.1.[15] Constant Gross Mark-Up ($\underline{k}$), and Fluctuating Net Mark-Up($\underline{k}_{yb}$).

Year	1	2	3
Business Gross Product	100	80	110
less:			
Depreciation	10	10	10
Indirect taxes	10	10	10
National Income produced by Business	80	60	90
Wages and salaries	50	40	55
Interest and rents	10	10	10
Profits	20	10	25
$k^a = BGP/W_b$	2.00	2.00	2.00
$k_{yb}^b = NI_b/W_b$	1.60	1.50	1.64

a Constant Gross Mark-Up
b Fluctuating Net Mark-Up

account for 23 percent of the value added by manufacturing, while the 150 largest manufacturing corporations account for a total of 35 per cent.[16] Even in industries such as construction, where concentration is not great, accepted cost-plus a fixed percentage formulae are widely used. As we have seen in the U. S. p. 68, Canada p. 106, and the U. K. p. 110, the variability of mark-up in construction is very small.

"Full cost" price setters faced with a change in total proceeds with interest, rent, depreciation and indirect taxes all fixed, vary the volume of output and employment while leaving mark-up unchanged. With a fall in proceeds total profits fall and wages as a percentage of total *income* rises ($\underline{k}_{yb}$ declines) while wages as a percentage of gross *proceeds* remains all but constant ($\underline{k}$ unchanged). Putting this relationship in terms of the law of the price level; $P = \underline{k}R$, or $P = \underline{k}\overline{w}/\overline{A}$, we see that such behavior means that price makers will only vary unit price as unit cost varies, and this varies as the ratio of the average wage to output per man varies. This behavior was found to be characteristic of manufacturing firms in the U. S., whether in oligopolistic or unconcentrated industries, by Yordon who states:

[15] This table and accompanying discussion also appears in my article, "The Constancy of the Wage Share: The Canadian Experience," *Rev. of Econ. & Stat.* Vol XLV, No. 1, February 1963 pp. 84-94.

[16] *Concentration Ratios in Manufacturing Industry* 1958, Senate Sub-Committee on Antitrust and Monopoly, 87th Cong. 2d sess.(Washington 1964) p. 8.

> "...insensitivity of prices to demand change is not confined to highly oligopolistic industries, but is characteristic of most manufacturing industries. On the whole, inflationary pressures seemed to be transmitted through the two groups of industries in a similar manner; prices were insensitive to demand changes, but were rapidly and fully responsive to cost increases."[17]

Lanzillotti, who carried out extensive interviews with the executives of 20 very large corporations, found that the "principal and collateral" pricing goals cited were:

> "...(1) pricing to achieve a target return on investment; (2) stabilization of price and margin; (3) pricing to realize a target market share; and (4) pricing to meet or prevent competition."[18]

He notes that those companies who cited goal (1) as their principal goal actually did somewhat better than their target rate in the prosperous years 1947-1955 covered by his survey, because they were able to operate at somewhat above their "standard volume." Goals number (1) and (2) are fully compatable, in fact, as Lanzilotti states, the distinction between target return and cost-plus as pricing philosopies is "hard to define."

> "The difference...lies in the extent to which the company is willing to push beyond the limits of a pricing method to some average-return philosophy. According to a General Motors executive, the target plays a prominent role in the formulation of the cost-plus method. But in the case of International Harvester, U. S. Steel, A & P, Johns-Manville, Alcoa, or Union Carbide, it seems fair to say that the pricing executive set the prices of many products on a cost-plus basis (except where competition precludes such action) *without questioning the appropriateness of the traditional mark-up.*"[19]

Lanzillotti states that General Motors officials cited Donaldson Brown's, "Pricing in Relation to Financial Control," an article which first appeared in 1924, "so frequently as an accurate repre-

[17] W. J. Yordon, Jr., "Industrial Concentration and Price Flexibility in Inflation: Price Response Rates in Fourteen Industries 1947-1958," *RES*, Aug. 1961, p. 287.

[18] R. F. Lanzillotti, "Pricing Objectives in Large Companies," *AER* 58: Dec. 1958, pp. 922-23.

[19] R. F. Lanzillotti, p. 932.

sentation of their present pricing that it warrants emphasis,"[20] an indication of the continuity of the target set and the mark-up methods used to achieve it.

Goals (1) and (2) are fully compatable with stable shares in gross output. With a low level of output the fixed mark-up is absorbed by overhead, depreciation, and interest so that profits may be negative, at higher output levels the "break even" point is reached and net profits appear, and at still higher levels profits become handsome. Thus the relative variability of General Motors Corporation mark-up from 1947 to 1963 was 6.2% while the v of their Net Profits to Net Worth ratio target (of 20% return on investment) was 29.7%. See pp. 92-97 for this discussion. This mark-up stability is obscured by our traditional focus on National Income shares generated in the firm and industry, and only becomes clear as we shift our focus to shares in Business Gross Product.

Goals (3) and (4) are less conducive to stable mark-up as the competitive situation of the firms change over time. Let us pause to consider what competitive and oligopoly theory would lead us to expect concerning mark-up stability and the extent to which these clues from theory are confirmed by our data.

1. We should expect the stability of mark-up to vary with the nature of competition in industries. In an industry such as agriculture, where conditions approach those of perfect competition and it is impossible neatly to control supply, sellers become "price takers" rather than "price makers" and we should not expect to see a stable industry mark-up. On the other hand, where there is oligopoly or monopoly, trade association or resale price maintenance agreements, together with continuously controlable production, we have the ingredients for administered prices and stable gross mark-up.
2. We should not expect wage cost mark-up formulae to be in use in an industry where wage cost is only a small fraction of total cost. Examples of this would be financial institutions, real estate, and agriculture.
3. The effect of public regulation of certain utilities on the industry's mark-up stability is difficult to foresee. If the regulating board uses wage or total cost formulae in rate making and changes rates without undue delay as costs change, we should see very stable shares. On the other hand, we can well conceive of situations where administra-

[20] *Ibid.*

tive delay and political decision making would give the opposite result.

4. Where industry mark-ups are changing, their trend should be correlated with the relative expansion or contraction of the industry. That is, we should expect an industry with rising mark-up over time to be producing an increasing fraction, and an industry with a falling $\underline{k}$ to be producing a falling fraction of BGP. This expectation comes from the familiar proposition of micro-analysis that capital and labor flow into an industry where greater than normal returns are realized and leave industries which cannot maintain a normal return. This expectation is subject to qualification if there are special circumstances such as very rapid productivity gains and a relatively fixed demand for industry output. Here rising $\underline{k}$ would be compatible with constant or falling industry fraction of BGP and falling industry employment.

Turning to our data we see much confirmation of these expectations and some unresolved puzzles. Our series for the U. S. and Canada indicate that a high, unstable, wage cost mark-up is characteristic of agriculture. The height of the mark-up is the consequence of the small size of agricultural firms and the large fraction of the total labor supplied by the enterpriser. The instability of the mark-up reflects the inability of millions of farmers to adjust continuously supply to inelastic and shifting demand. In agriculture "windfall" gains and losses from fluctuating prices cause large fluctuations in distribution. Mark-up is therefore less stable in a country with a large agricultural sector than in one where agriculture is a minor industry; in Australia than in England.[21]

In Canada, we accounted for most of the downward trend of aggregate mark-up as caused solely by the dwindling importance of agriculture. Also, its decline accounted for much of the increased stability of Canadian mark-up in the more recent period:

[21] The United Kingdom since 1948 has had a very stable agricultural mark-up; ($\underline{v}$ = 2.1%), see pg. 110. It would seem that the British system of "fore pricing" in domestic agriculture must account for much of this stability. As the government's guaranteed prices for the 12 basic agricultural products are described by Loucks, "The *actual* prices for *crops* are announced at least 18 months before harvest time and the *actual* prices for *livestock* products for the next 12 months, while for *livestock* products *minimum* prices also are announced for from two to four years ahead." William N. Loucks, *Comparative Economic Systems* (6th ed; New York: Harper 1961) p. 368.

see pp. 99-104 for this discussion. It is probable that mark-up was less stable in the U. S. for the period 1899-1929 covered by Arthur Grant's data than in the post 1929 period, largely because of the greater percentage of output produced by agriculture in the earlier years. It is also probable that the greater stability of U. S. mark-up than Canadian mark-up, and U. K. than U. S., can be largely accounted for by the varying importance of agriculture in the three countries: as agriculture continues to "lose weight" in developing countries we may expect increasing mark-up stability.

Turning to proposition number 2 and the financial institutions and real estate industries given as examples we do indeed see rather unstable mark-ups in these industries in the U. S. and Canada, where wages are a small fraction of total costs, and a stable industry mark-up in the U. K. where wages are the major cost. U. S. Industry 6. Finance, insurance and real estate combines low, fairly stable, mark-up Finance and insurance ($\underline{\bar{k}6a}$ = 1.52, v = 4.3%) and very high, less stable, mark-up Real estate ($\underline{\bar{k}6b}$ = 20.03, $\underline{v}$ = 7.7%) for an all over mark-up average of 4.47 and $\underline{v}$ of 4.0%. The corresponding Canadian industry, 13, has a $\underline{\bar{k}}$ of 4.07 and $\underline{v}$ of 7.9%. In the U. K. $\underline{\bar{k}8}$ = 1.33, $\underline{v}$ = 2.3%. See Tables 3.1., 3.4., 3.20., and 3.26.

Our data do not give a clear picture of the effect of regulation on mark-up stability. If we take the Gas, electricity and water utilities, Transportation, and Communication as the particularly regulated industries we see diverging results. In Canada the mark-up of regulated industries 7-10 from 1926 to 1959 had a high $\underline{v}$ of 9.4%. Since 1944 when data on the individual industries have been available, each of the industries' mark-ups have fluctuated widely. See Tables 3.20. and 3.21. Generally, mark-ups in these industries nose dived during the rapid inflation immediately after WW II, then climbed from about 1950 to regain much of their 1944 value. Score one for the law's delay.

In the U. S. since 1947 mark-up in Transportation has had very little trend or variation ($\underline{v}$ =2.3%) while mark-up of Communication has steadily risen ($\underline{b}$ =+.0328, $\underline{v}$ = 7.8%, $\underline{vt}$ = 3.3%) as have Public Utilities ($\underline{b}$ =+.0476, $\underline{v}$ = 7.1%, $\underline{vt}$ = 1.9). See Table 3.1.

In the U. K. since 1948 the Utilities have also had rising mark-ups ($\underline{b}$ = +.0300, $\underline{v}$ = 6.5%, $\underline{vt}$ = 2.3%) while Transportation and Communication displays virtually no trend ($\underline{b}$ =+.00013) and little fluctuation ($\underline{v}$ = 2.9%). Perhaps U. S. and U. K. regulated industry mark-ups fell immediatly after the war as in Canada before rising, but we lack the data. Perhaps too, other influences are important here as rising importance of gas, or the extraordinarily high productivity gains these industries have been making. See Figures 3.17. and 3.18.

Proposition 4 that k have a rising trend in expanding industries and fall in relatively declining industries, is confirmed more often than it is contradicted. On a quick count I find that out of the 78 disaggregate mark-up series developed in Chapter 3, 42 confirm the proposition, 29 refute it, and 7 neither confirm nor refute (as when neither percentage produced nor mark-up have discernible trend, or when k moves but percentage produced has no trend). Many of the exceptions are rather glaring ones, however. For example, in all three countries Agriculture's weight in the economy is declining, but in Canada and the United Kingdom agricultural mark-up is rising strongly. In all three countries Manufacturing is increasing in importance, but Manufacturing mark-up is falling.

Within the Manufacturing industries disaggregate both interesting confirmations and refutations occur. The "sick" British and American Textile, and Apparel industries confirm by losing mark-up and percentage of total output, but the U. S. Metals, Electrical machinery, and Automobile categories all show rising importance with some fall in mark-up. The generally downward trend of mark-ups after the Korean War account for many of the refutations, *i.e.* k falls, often less than the average, while the industry expands in relative importance. Obviously the "other things" which theory holds "equal" for us have been having important effects here.

Many examples of the short run changes in the industry output percentage and mark-up changes being positively correlated are evident, but exceptions are also numerous. As seen in Chapter 3 and 4, variability of sub-aggregate mark-ups remained moderate and so it was not considered necessary to develop and test multiple regression equations to explain their behavior.

RECOMMENDATIONS FOR FURTHER MARK-UP STUDIES

The results of this study suggests strongly that further disaggregations of mark-up in the United States be carried out to the level of the individual firm. Such studies should settle the question of k's grounding, or lack of grounding, in micro stability. Unfortunately, the Department of Commerce has only recently put its industry series in the form which enables us to calculate fine disaggregations of k rather than ky. Recent issues of the July number of *Survey of Current Business* have included all the information necessary to develop very fine disaggregations of k, but only from 1956 to the present. However, the disaggregated National Income by Industry series, taken back to 1929 in *National Income* 1954 needs only the addition of the missing Depreciation Charges and Indirect Business Taxes series to enable this valuable information to be obtained. It would seem probable that the Department has this data and could make it available.

Should fine disaggregations be stymied by lack of data it would be worthwhile to work up from the income statements of firms, as was done for U. S. Rubber, U. S. Steel, General Electric and General Motors, for all the firms in an industry. These studies will also establish whether or not the Sales/Wages ratio can stand-in for firm mark-up.

It would also be useful if the United Nations Statistical Office modified its national accounts reporting system to allow the separation of the government and household sector so that k could be calculated rather than kg. For many of the less developed nations the data remain highly inadequate.

It is possible to disaggregate k in Australia, Netherlands, and Norway. When these studies have been made the similarities and differences to those in industry mark-ups in the U. S., Canada and the U. K. could be developed. Perhaps some light could be shed on the question of what effect these country's differing attempts to regulate wages has had on industry mark-up factors.

FINAL COMMENTS AND CONCLUSIONS

Before concluding let us state three, perhaps obvious, but none-the-less-powerful, reasons why mark-up will continue in the future to fluctuate less than velocity so that the WCM "Law of the Price Level" will be valid.

Firstly, k is a constrained variable and V is not. By this is meant that the wage share can hardly be more than 100 per cent or less than zero per cent of gross income. Furthermore, with some 75-85 per cent of the population in employee status most of the lower range of the wage share, *i.e.* upper range of mark-up, is ruled out as literally impossible without a revolution. On the other hand, mark-up can scarcely approach 1.00 where wages become equal to Business Gross Product, and production go forward.

We can define no such absolute limits to the possible swings of velocity. There is no compelling reason why it cannot triple or quintuple, or be cut to one tenth of its former value should money stocks or payment habits change drastically.

Secondly, monetary theorists are doubtless right that the Money/Goods ratio has "something to do" with the price level, but it is only common sense that the *cost level has "much more* to do" with the price level. Indeed, as we have demonstrated, the Unit Wage Cost Index(R) (practically) *is* the Price Index (P) because its link (k) is (practically) constant.

Thirdly, the reflection that some of the larger swings in V, particularly the post World War II climb in velocity, have been caused by central bank attempts to influence P by manipulating M, leads to a final wry supposition. It may be that mark-up has been so much more stable than velocity because no "control" agency has attempted to use its stability to gain its policy ends, and that political contests and decisions as to how high mark-up should be might destroy its rigidity! At the moment, however, this possibility remains remote and an increasing mark-up stability seems assured.

The final conclusion of this study is this: the work of economists and policy makers coping with price level problems becomes more fruitful as their thinking shifts from the demand determinant focus on money to the cost determinant focus on wages. It seems clear that we cannot have full employment *and* stable prices without some agreed on formula to keep wage hikes within overall productivity gains, with price cuts in those industries enjoying more than average gains balancing the rising costs of services where productivity gains lag.

INDEX